T0148607

THE
BECKONING LIGHT AND
HOME TO THE LIGHT

Ellen Wallace Douglas

Order this book online at www.trafford.com
or email orders@trafford.com

Most Trafford titles are also available at major online book retailers.

A Course in Miracles excerpts from Viking Penguin 1996 edition.

Bible excerpts from King James Version.

This book contains many quotations from *A Course in Miracles* by Foundation for Inner Peace, published
by Viking Penguin. However this book is neither authorized nor endorsed by the Foundation for Inner
Peace nor Viking Penguin. Readers are encouraged to read *A Course in Miracles*.

Archangel Gabriel Lessons printed with permission

Printed in the United States of America.

ISBN: 978-1-4669-5730-5 (sc)
ISBN: 978-1-4669-5731-2 (e)

Trafford rev. 09/06/2012

 www.trafford.com

North America & international
toll-free: 1 888 232 4444 (USA & Canada)
phone: 250 383 6864 ♦ fax: 812 355 4082

THE BECKONING LIGHT

CONTENTS 1

Dedicated to all my angels, masters, teachers and guides, who, though unseen, assiduously and constantly protect and guide me.

The sight of Christ is all there is to see. The song of Christ is all there is to hear. The hand of Christ is all there is to hold. There is no journey but to walk with Him. ACIM 24: V: 7: 7-10

FOREWORD

n In *A Course in Miracles*, the Workbook for Students ends by stating: "You do not walk alone. God's angels hover near and all about. His Love surrounds you, and of this be sure; that I will never leave you comfortless." What more could we need? If only we would remember this, how effortless our lives would be.

This book portrays a message of hope. In it we are again reminded that God has given us everything we could ever need to live life joyously. We are reminded of our own power to create, and we are shown how to use that power for our highest good. We are reminded of how much God loves us and that we remain as perfect as we were when He created us.

Ellen's books never disappoint. When I had the privilege and pleasure of assisting Ellen as she wrote her first book, *The Laughing Christ*, I witnessed the extensive research and attention to detail that Ellen brings to her writing. This book is a wonderful interpretation of the lessons that were brought forth by the Archangel Gabriel. For those of us who heard Gabriel's lessons in truth, It brings back the memory and joy of being in the presence of one of God's messengers. And for anyone who missed the opportunity—what a treat is in store for you! The Light beckons. Enjoy your journey.

Joan Waters

PREFACE

When the idea of writing this book first came into my consciousness, I thought "What a bold idea to think that I could produce a writing that would explain the answers that humanity has sought since time immemorial. For centuries humans have asked "Why am I here?" "How did I get here?" and "Where am I going?"

When I decided that the title for my first book would be *The Laughing Christ* (publ. 2002), I told a friend. She said, "Isn't that too bold?" I answered her that the contents were bold. As I prepared to write this book I referred to Webster's definition of bold: showing or requiring a fearless daring spirit. impudent, presumptuous. Assured, confident.

This writer was truly blessed to be in the company of several other spiritual seekers to hear the wisdom of the ages presented by Archangel Gabriel through a dedicated minister and natural medium. It is because of this blessing and the knowledge of the wisdom that I was impelled to write this book.

Archangel Gabriel visited the Earth from 1987 to 1999. He told us eleven other master teachers came to this planet about the same time also, to centers of light where they would be welcomed. All these heavenly teachers taught but one lesson: Wake up, humanity, to the fact that you are all children of God, and live your life from the Lord God of your Being.

After writing seven other books, I turned to the idea of passing on Gabriel's teachings regarding our journey from Heaven to Earth (in consciousness, not reality), and what is entailed in returning unto the Father in Heaven. I believe that I have the fearless and daring spirit to do so. The basis of this attitude is the fact that for twelve years I listened to Gabriel, took notes, asked questions, and adapted the lessons to my life to the best of my ability.

My words may seem impudent and presumptuous, yet I know that Archangel Gabriel brought us only truth. Thus I am assured and confident that in relating our journey away from God (in our consciousness only), and back home to Him, this writing will assist those who are ready to understand, accept and put into daily practice the lessons Gabriel taught.

The previous books of this author made constant reference to Gabriel's seminars which consisted of one day presentations about one subject. Gabriel also gave many lectures of 20-30 minutes each. This book will focus mostly on these evening lectures. These brief talks were directed to the general public, represented by the few listeners who came to learn from an archangel. The day-long seminars expounded on these brief lessons, to those who sincerely sought a deeper understanding. Therefore, the reader is encouraged to listen to the cassettes/CDs available of Gabriel's seminars, as well as to read the shorter presentations which are available in print. See Bibliography.

When this book speaks of earth life and 'the other side,' the author is not suggesting there are only two realms of existence. We have all heard the term 'seventh Heaven,' and there are many more realms beyond the Heaven we have heard about. The Heaven we speak of often is a realm called the astral plane. It is the next plane up from earthly life. There is no death; there is no hell. There is only life because God created all there is.

It is interesting to hear a person say that "If God is in charge why is there so much chaos in the world?" When God created us he gave us free choice. The chaos we see around us is not God's creation but rather of our own making. It has all been brought about by humankind. We, the human family, are the only begotten Son of God. We have simply lost an awareness of that divine connection. Each of us is an individualized portion of God. There is no place that God is not, and He abides in us as our very Essence. That is what Jesus the Christ meant when he said the Kingdom of God is within. Jesus the man came to demonstrate the Christ love that resides in us all, regardless of any dogma or belief system we espouse. Jesus came to bring the Christ Light to Earth, to ground that light for all humanity for all time to come. It was the early Christian leaders who fashioned a hierarchy for a formal church, with levels of power and expressions of pomp.

The author refers to a variety of books and many of the teachings of Archangel Gabriel. All the students who were privileged to hear Gabriel and all those who read and hear his teachings are instructed to pass on the lessons Gabriel taught. This is the wisdom of the ages. This is the truth to live by. This is the way back home to God in our consciousness.

I feel assured and confident in this undertaking, for I have prayed that only truth come through me to the printed page. Statements which seem bold but are not referenced came from Gabriel, yet in some cases I cannot recall the day or the seminar at which he spoke them. The words are emblazoned in my memory. One such statement is, "Walk you in the light. You *are* the light."

When one is guided, inspired to write, there must be a trigger that puts one on such a dedicated path. For me the trigger was a letter from an angel. My beloved teacher, Rev. Penny A. Donovan, gave me a laminated page with the image of a scroll. It was February 2, 1998. She told me that a few days earlier an angel interrupted her supper to produce this letter for me:

Dear Ellen,

You have within you now the knowledge and ability to fulfill your every desire. As co-creator with God you have

Power beyond measure,

Truth beyond evidence,

Love beyond circumstance.

Before you is the empty page of each hour for you to write your contribution to the Divine Scheme of Life. God does not tell you what to write; He only tells you Write! According to your belief so shall it be demonstrated. You can draw to you at will the manifestation of your assignment in Perfect Joy and Peace.

The pen is in your hand.

With love always,
Your Guardian Angel

A few weeks later, that same year, I began research for my first book *The Laughing Christ*. Throughout the years of my writing career I have been divinely guided. When I tune into spirit as I sit at the computer keyboard, words flow until the topic is finished. Whenever I seem to be on a plateau and guidance does not come, suddenly I receive a thought of what direction I should take and then I am off and running again, guided assuredly by many unseen helpers: teachers, masters, and guides.

As I reviewed this book in February of 2010 I decided to ask a dear friend about the title. We discussed several. She reminded me that 'with thought and meditation' the correct title would come to me. All through its writing I thought the title would be *Journey to Awakening*, but as I proceeded with the final edit this new title came to me. There are many references to light in the Bible. Some are:

God is Light (Is. 2:5).
God sent John to bear witness of the Light (John 1:8).
Jesus told us that he was the light of the world (John 8:12, 9:5).
We are children of light (Luke 16:8, John 12:36, I Th. 5:5).

In *A Course in Miracles* we find: *When I said, 'I am come as a light into the world,' I meant that I came to share the light with you"* (*T*—5: VI: 11: 1).

The Course (T—11: III: 6:1-2):
The children of light cannot abide in darkness, for darkness is not in them. Do not be deceived by the dark comforters.

Also, (W pt II: 333: 2: 1):
Father, forgiveness is the light You chose to shine away all conflict and all doubt, and light the way for our return to You.

In the text, ACIM and *The Course* refer to the book *A Course in Miracles.*

INTRODUCTION

For verily I say unto you, that many prophets and righteous men have desired to see those things which ye see, and have not seen them; and to hear those things which ye hear, and have not heard them. Matthew 13:17

It would be presumptuous of this writer, indeed, to even think that I could bring to the printed page the answers to questions asked by humankind since time began. Presumptuous, that is, unless I was blessed with the privilege of hearing the answers from an archangel. Archangel Gabriel, to be exact. He is the announcer of the ages, by his own definition.

At the beginning of the Age of Pisces, Archangel Gabriel appeared to Mary. In the Gospel according to Luke (1:31) we find: *Fear not, Mary, for you have found favour with God. And, behold, thou shalt conceive in thy womb, and bring forth a son, and shalt call him JESUS.* It would be centuries before Isaiah's prophesy came true, but it did, with the next turning of the ages.

From the Old Testament, we find that twice Jesus' birth had been prophesied by Isaiah (9:6): *For unto us a child is born, unto us a son is given: and the government shall be upon his shoulder: and his name shall be called Wonderful, Counsellor, The mighty God, The everlasting Father, The Prince of Peace.*

Isaiah 7:14: *Therefore the Lord himself shall give you a sign; Behold, a virgin shall conceive, and bear a son, and shall call his name Immanuel.*

Gabriel went to Joseph to be sure that he would accept Mary's conception, and said, *Joseph, thou son of David, fear not to take unto thee Mary thy wife: for that which is conceived in her is of the Holy Ghost. And she shall bring forth a son, and thou shalt call his name JESUS: for he shall save his people from their sins.* Matthew 1:20-21

I boldly state here that Archangel Gabriel came to us to teach us—not something new, not to become a "Gabriel follower", or to bring a new religion. He came to wake us up. Gabriel said he came to *remind us of what we already know, but have forgotten.* He reminded us that we need awakening because we have slept for thousands of years. He told us that the Garden of Eden is an allegory, not an actual story. He reminded us that as *Adam slept* (Gen. 2:21) he never, throughout the remainder of the Bible, woke up.

Humanity, in effect, fell asleep to its own divinity. Gabriel came to awaken us to our holy selves, for we are made as part of God, *not merely in His Image.* We are as much a part of God as the clay is part of the ceramic bowl.

The reader may choose to discount Gabriel's teachings, and you may be correct, if I told you that I alone heard his words, or if I told you I saw the archangel in a night vision or a trance. If I told you that I was high on drugs, such as alcohol, you would probably question their validity. However, I was awake, sober, and alert, with all senses functioning, and of a sound mind. I was sitting in a large room with dozens of other people—seekers, like myself. Also, it was not a singular event. Gabriel came many times over a period of twelve years. He was the only archangel to come to earth to teach, but he told us that eleven other master teachers also came, to various places on Earth, about the same time—the turning of the ages from Pisces to Aquarius—with the same message. One of the master teachers was Ramtha, who came through J.Z. Knight, in California.

Many, many topics were taught to us by Archangel Gabriel. The focus of this book is the process of devolution and evolution, for we have devolved away from God (in our consciousness) to this alien world we call Earth. In thus explaining our devolution and what we must do to evolve back to God, consciously, Gabriel, in effect, discounted Darwin's theory.

Of course it is easy to accept Darwin's theory when we see that the human form and the organs of the apes are so similar to our own. Darwin himself said there was a missing link. There is no link to be missed, for Darwin's theory remains a theory. If we accept the idea that we are physical beings only, Darwin makes much sense. However, Gabriel made it clear that we are children of God and God created us from Himself, and God is Love. Therefore we are love, loved and loveable.

In the beginning, we did, in fact, live in an Eden. It was the Spirit World of God, without beginning or end. We lived in spirit form there. We had no physical form, we communicated by thought instead of words. We loved one another and we all loved God, our Creator. Heaven was, and still is, our natural habitat. God gave us free choice across the board (angels have free choice only in the realm of good). God gave us imagination. We used our free choice and imagination to begin a journey downward, away from God's sweet Realm of peace, love, joy and abundance. The vibration of spirit is the highest vibration in existence.

We decided, at some point, to create something *other than* the perfection in which we existed, and began a journey through several planes of existence, slowing constantly the vibrational rate, until we came to the lowest plane of vibration, physical form. The other planes of existence through which we devolved include the mental plane and the astral plane. Physical form is the lowest possible vibration. We are at the nadir point of vibration. We have no place to go but UP! Is this so difficult to accept, given the negativity that prevails on earth at this time? All negative thoughts come from the ego of humankind, not the Mind of God. Love is not negative. Lusts may lead to negative behavior, but love that is eternal is not negative in any way. It is the unconditional love; the agape love described by Paul, in his first letter to the Corinthians, Chapter 13.

This book begins with the origin of the spirit of us, not the body of us. God is the Creator of our spirit selves. The physical body is birthed by our physical parents. However, we choose the shape and design of it before we come to earth. Our subtle bodies—mental and astral—are of our own design, also. Spirit permeates all the bodies. The ego and the personality are our very own. The soul of us is the memory bank of every experience we ever had on earth—throughout all our lifetimes here.

The astral plane is the plane we live on, in our astral body, between incarnations on earth. While on the astral plane we review the life just lived and plan our lives on our next 'visit' to Earth. From our perspective on the astral plane we know the lessons we need to learn. We often say and firmly believe; that 'we can't choose our parents, but we can choose our friends.' This is untrue. We choose all those who will interact with us on earth, whatever their relationship to us. Each is in our experience to teach us a lesson. We may learn it or we may not learn it. We have free choice. The next time on the astral plane we will see which lessons we learned and which ones we did not learn. Then we design another lifetime. Part of our form while on earth is the energy centers, or chakras, which are consonant with the endocrine glands and learning about them we can learn more about ourselves.

Earth is the only planet where the beliefs in sickness and death still prevail. As long as we see ourselves as only a physical form we will accept the idea that the body has a mind of its own and we suffer physical and emotional pain seemingly without reason or cause. We plan our own lives and make for ourselves a heaven or hell on earth, by choosing the illness, the "accident", the circumstance that will present a lesson to us. We are totally responsible for our lives, those people with whom we interact and all experiences we have. Would a God of Love bring us pain, suffering, and injury?

Throughout the ages humans have sought to know the future.
Divination is as old as humans. From Genesis to Revelation Scripture mentions several kinds of divination. *A Course in Miracles* was given to us by Jesus the Christ through a dedicated channel. Disbelief in channeling bars communication with the spirit world. That is another choice we have. Time and space are figments of our imagination. In the spirit world there is no need for either.

In the Bible, Jesus told us: *He that believeth on me, the works that I do shall he do also; and greater works than these shall he do; because I go unto my Father* (John 14:12) Before Jesus was born he experienced many lifetimes. Current authors write of them. Gabriel explained in detail some of them. Jesus was not Adam, as this writer thought. Adam was a fictitious person. Gabriel told us that Jesus had many previous incarnations, as we have, but he described only the lives of Jesus in which a significant shift in consciousness was made. Just prior to his incarnation as Jesus, he was Buddha. When one reads the teachings of Buddha, the similarity is clear. He had also lived as Hermes and others. Jesus the Christ came as an example for us. He was the way-shower for his spiritual siblings, all humanity. He proclaimed it often in the Bible.

The *Going Home* section contains information we can apply to our lives as we seek to return unto God, our Source. This is the dawning of the Age of Aquarius. More significantly, it is the Age of Spirituality. The word 'spirituality' comes from 'spirit,' which means 'breath of life.' God gives us the breath of life. This is the age in which humanity is ready for the symbolic meanings in Scripture. The Bible is symbolic from first to last. In Jesus' time the symbolism was not understood. But Jesus knew one day we would be capable of comprehending the deeper meaning of his words. Today we find *A Course in Miracles* requires our deeper thought. It is not an easy read. But Gabriel pointed out that it will stand beside the Bible in importance, in centuries to come. Why would it not, when it was brought to us by our elder brother, the Master Teacher himself? In *The Course* he often quotes his own words from Scripture and explains them.

Prayer is talking to God and Meditation is listening to God. They are examples of communication. There are people on earth now who have communicated with animals, plants, and even water. There is an oneness to all life. Finally, from recent books, there is a description of the other side—the astral plane—to where we will adjourn upon our 'death' on Earth. The environment has been described as well as the houses, and the activities available to us on that lovely plane.

It is the author's hope that the reader will see the needless cycle of the karmic ride and how we can get off it and return to God and Heaven, our natural habitat; our one true home.

Gabriel's farewell message, December 2, 1999, included:

"Beloveds, in my twelve years of your time upon the earth, the one true lesson that I desire greatly for you to know is how beautiful you are and how meaningful your life is . . . the greatest heroes of the world are the simple, everyday people who live their lives trusting God and knowing the goodness that is in them."

CHAPTER 1

Happenings in Summerland

"Who knows but life be that which men call death, And death what men call life?"[1]

When studying the Bible I found that one of the most perplexing phrases was Jesus' comment to one of his disciples, who told Jesus that he had to go bury his father. Jesus answered, *Follow me; and let the dead bury their dead.* Matt. 8:22

Later, when I was forty-nine years of age, I sought a psychic message from a medium named Millie. My father came to me and said he was waiting for me, to show me around, "the light is different here; the colors are different". Then my mother came to me through Millie and said, with her typical pedantic air, "You are the ones that are dead, you know." A few years later Archangel Gabriel explained that we earthlings are dead to the knowledge that we are spiritual beings, breathed forth from God, and forever His beloved children. Gabriel came, with eleven other celestial beings, to awaken all humanity to its own divinity.

The world we live in is the world we believe in, because everything we perceive with our senses confirms the idea that physical form is all there really is, and when we stop breathing we are no longer present on earth. Yet, somehow, through the centuries people have had a persistent belief that there is something beyond this life. After reading several books about communication from the other side to earthlings, I realized how important it is to inform the general reader about such things. I was encouraged to do so when I read in Boss' book: "YOU SHOULD HELP OTHERS TO UNDERSTAND WHAT IT IS LIKE HERE". [2] Many authors have written about the other side to help believers know the truth and assist questioners to understand.

"The belief that death is the end of the personality is, in the context of human history, a novel one. Almost all people since the beginning of the human race have believed in some form of life after death. Only in recent times, and only in Western countries, have a large number of people maintained that death is oblivion. It may be this disbelief in the afterlife that provoked the growth of Spiritualism in the West." [3]

Life after death is not only accepted by many, but it is not unusual to hear people mention 'the other side' referring to life after death. For example, when the nineteenth century naturalist, John Muir, saw the Grand Canyon for the first time, his comments went something like this: If you saw all other canyons on earth you would marvel at this one as though you were on the 'other side.' A recent movie entitled *What Dreams May Come* provided some interesting graphic visuals in a human effort to show the imagery of the other side.

Terms applied to entities on the other side, such as ghosts, discarnate spirits, manes, shades, apparitions etc. bring to mind fears of unexplained threats and uncontrollable dangers. There is no such thing as ghosts. Webster defines ghost: 'the seat of life or intelligence.' There is a fascinating book entitled *Don't Call Them Ghosts* (2004) by Kathleen McConnnell in which she states:

"Please don't call them ghosts. Ghosts are something people tell stories about at Halloween. People think ghosts have to be spooky or frightening. We have the spirits of three young children living in our attic, and my heart aches for each one of them." She relates this story about children who remained in a home to which they were "earth bound", and with the help of Mrs. McConnell came to the point where they could leave for the other side, and they did, as described at the end of the book.

In 1932 A Roman Catholic priest in Germany, Johannes Greber, wrote of his interaction with the spirit world. The book is entitled *Communication with the Spirit World of God*. An English translation was published in 1974. His opinion about the unwillingness to accept the idea of communication between the worlds:

> "If there is a Beyond, peopled by a world of spirits, conclusive proof is forth coming only if those spirits will visit and enlighten us, for they alone are able to tell us the truth about the great questions relating to an after-life. So long as this gap

between the spirit world and our own remains unbridged, so long shall we remain in the darkness of uncertainty and endure the pangs of gnawing doubt . . ."[4]

Many books have been written from the other side, through a scribe, including: *A World Beyond, The Unobstructed Universe, Return From Tomorrow, In Silence They Return, Life After Life, The Dead are Alive, The Life Beyond Death, A World Beyond,* and *Life in the World Unseen. Intra Muros,* published in 1898, is a book written by Rebecca Ruter Springer, describing experiences on the other side that she recalled after reviving from a three-year coma. It was republished in 1994 under the title *Into The Light.* One can almost feel Springer's frustration in reading her words more than one hundred years ago:

"I can only dimly show the close linking of the two lives—the mortal with the divine—as they then appeared to me, I may be able to partly tear the veil from the death we so dread, and show it to be only an open door into a new and beautiful phase of the life we now live." [5]

Lest one think that Springer's decision to recall her experiences were spurious, we note that she had a deep and abiding faith in God and a reverence for the Bible. Springer refers to Scripture throughout her book, indicating her Christian background: "I have aimed principally to give such incidents as would . . . make apparent the reverence and love all hearts feel toward the blessed Trinity for every good and perfect gift, and to show forth the marvelous power of the Christ-love even in the life beyond the grave." [6]

It is likely that many clergy believe in spirit communication because they often attend a dying person, and when people are near death they frequently see loved ones. One clergyman tells us, "Shall we stop at that poor line, the grave, which all our Christianity is always trying to wipe out and make nothing of, and which we always insist on widening into a great gulf? Shall we not stretch our thought beyond, and feel the lifeblood of this holy church, this living body of Christ, pulsing out into the saints who are living there, and coming back throbbing with tidings of their glorious and sympathetic life?" [7]

'The other side' refers to that realm we enter after our earthly demise, so called 'death.' There are many planes of existence (*In my Father's house are many mansion* John 14:2*)*. We all have heard the term 'seventh Heaven,' indicating a series of realms beyond Earth. On earth we exist in physical form. Upon our transition to the next realm—the astral plane—we exist in an astral body. It is exciting to read the descriptions of the other side, because it gives credence to its existence and it enables us to visualize the actual place instead of accepting the vague notion that a nebulous holiness may prevail there.

The Other Side

The Environment
The terrain, it is reported, is similar to that of the Earth. It consists of roads, forests, buildings, and waterways.

Landscape

> There are no roads as we know them on earth, but rather broad, extensive thoroughfares in the cities and elsewhere. Thick, green grass covers these roadways. In place of pavement is an alabaster-like material in delicate pastel shades. The buildings are also of this material. Grass grows only to a well-trimmed state. There are many splendid trees to be seen, none of which is malformed as on earth, due to wind and insects. As with the flowers, so with the trees. They live incorruptible, clothed always in their full array of leaves of every shade of green . . . and forever pouring out life to all those who approach near them. Fruit trees are constantly full of fruit at prime ripeness. When the fruit is picked, more fruit takes its place. The flowers had an astonishing feature I noticed when I drew near to them, and that was the sound of music that enveloped them, making such soft harmonies as corresponded exactly and perfectly with the gorgeous colors of the flowers themselves.[8]

Another author tells us about the vehicles seen on the other side, while visiting a school for children: "There I saw a wagon move out and come toward us . . . driven by a young boy, who handled the vehicle with ease. I could hear a low purr, similar to an electrically-charged battery-driven car . . . suspended on axles. 'We do not use wheels; instead we equip all vehicles with what we call shoes: they look like your earthly ice skates and sleighs'." *Journey into the Spirit World* by Bertha Harris

Being a devout Christian, Mrs. Springer noticed that there were no churches in Heaven and reports, "At first this somewhat confused me, until I remembered that there are no creeds in heaven, but that all worship together in harmony and love—the children of one and the same loving Father." [9] However, there is a temple there and we have the benefit of its description by two separate authors:

The Temple
"Upon the summit of this gentle slope a Temple stood, whose vast dome, massive pillars and solid walls were of unsullied pearl, and through whose great mullioned windows shone a white radiance that swallowed up the golden glow of the twilight and made it its own." [10]

Mr. Borgia also reported a trip to the temple: "As we drew close to the temple we could already feel ourselves being, as it were, charged with spiritual force . . . Great gardens surrounded the temple, heavenly music sounded and delicate perfumes filled the air. The service included a visitor from the higher realms." [11]

The sea

The sea is described as saltless, tideless, and calm. Of the sea Borgia says, The most glorious panorama of ocean spread out before us . . . Its colouring was the most perfect reflection of the blue sky above, but in addition it reflected a myriad of rainbow tints in every little wavelet . . . From where we were, I could see islands of some considerable size in the distance—islands that looked most attractive and must certainly be visited! And floating upon this superb sea, some close at hand—others standing a little way out, were the most beautiful boats—though I think I am not doing them justice by calling them mere boats. Ships would be more apposite. I wondered who could own these fine vessels, and was told . . . that we could own one ourselves if we so wished.[12]

There is such a similarity between the earth plane and the other side and yet the quality and content of the various aspects differ greatly.

The River
" . . . flowers blooming placidly down in the depths, among the many-colored pebbles with which the entire bed of the river was lined."[13]

Time
'There was no measurement of time as we measure it here, although many still spoke in the old-time language of "months" and "days" and "years". I have no way of describing it as it seemed to me then. There were periods, and allotted times; there were hours for happy duties, hours for joyful pleasures, and hours for holy praise. I only know it was all harmony, all joy, all peace, at all times and in all conditions.' [14]

Gabriel explained to us that on the earth plane time is an illusion.[15] He posed the question: If we are speeding on a train and bounce a ball, how far does the ball travel? We quickly think 'about six feet.' But this does not take into consideration the speed of the train, the rotation of the earth on its axis, or the revolution of the earth around the sun.

Absence of night
What . . . we may call "day" was full of a glorious radiance, a roseate golden light, which was everywhere. There is no language known to mortals that can describe this marvelous glory. It flooded the sky; it was caught up and reflected in the waters; it filled all heaven with joy and all hearts with song. After a period much longer than our longest earthly day, this glory mellowed and softened until it became a glowing twilight full of peace. The children ceased their playing beneath the trees, the little birds nestled among the vines,

and all who had been busy in various ways throughout the day sought rest and quiet. But there was no darkness, no dusky shadows even—only a restful softening of the glory.[16]

Upon reading this, one is reminded of *The Revelation of St. John the Divine*: *And the gates of it shall not be shut at all by day: for there shall be no night there.* Rev. 21:25. We wonder at all aspects of the spirit world, when we are willing to consider even its existence. Borgia mentions the light on the other side:

"Here there is no night and day by the alternation of which time can be measured. It is perpetual day. The great celestial sun for ever shines . . . we have no recurrent seasons of spring, autumn, and winter. Instead we enjoy the glory of perpetual summer—and we never tire of it." [17] Regarding 'the great celestial sun', the reader is directed to a book entitled *The Aquarian Gospel of Jesus the Christ*. In the Introduction of that book the Central Sun is described, and that is the celestial sun of which Borgia speaks.

The absence of night is also mentioned in *A Course in Miracles:* "It is not lit with artificial light, and night comes not upon it. There is no day that brightens and grows dim . . . Nothing is there but shines, and shines forever." [18]

Geographic location of the spirit world
Borgia devotes six pages to this topic. Here is one paragraph:
"The spheres of the spirit world are ranged in a series of bands forming a number of concentric circles around the earth. These circles reach out into the infinity of space, and they are invisibly linked with the earth world in its lesser revolution upon its axis, and, of course, in its greater revolution round the sun. The sun [of Earth] has no influence whatever upon the spirit world. We have no consciousness of it at all since it is purely material." [19]

It must be noted here that the following description of the spirit world by Archangel Gabriel was given to us on March 8, 1997 in his seminar entitled *Ring of Fire*:

"The spirit world has no geographic delineations. It is strictly a matter of consciousness; awareness."

Space

Although time becomes eternity in the spirit realm, so too is space infinite. In the spirit realm one may view in the distance a city, fields and woods, from a window, and yet "far beyond the range of my vision, and far beyond and beyond that again, there are more realms and still more realms that constitute the designation 'infinity of space'." [20]

Homes

Some people wonder if there are houses to live in on the other side. Springer spends much time describing the elegant homes, built according to the owner's choice. They are constructed of various materials and contain rooms much like the homes here on earth. In one home that she visited she saw a picture of Jesus Christ. She describes it: "Only one picture hung upon the walls, and that was a life-size portrait of the Christ, just opposite the couch. It was not an artist's conception of the human Christ, bowed under the weight of the sins of the world, nor yet the thorn-crowned head of the crucified Savior of mankind; but the likeness of the living Master, of Christ the victorious, of Christ the crowned. The wonderful eyes looked directly and tenderly into your own, and the lips seemed to pronounce the benediction of peace. The ineffable beauty of the divine face seemed to illumine the room with a holy light . . ."[21]

Halls of Learning

For those who believe there is life after death, it is probably the rare individual who accepts the idea that learning takes place there. Some folk think we sit on a cloud for eternity and do nothing when we reach the other side. Nothing could be further from the truth. We learn, study, play, and pray there. There are magnificent halls of learning described by Borgia for us:

Hall of the Art of Painting is described by Borgia: "On the walls . . . were hanging every great masterpiece known to man . . . arranged in such a way that every step of earthly progress could be followed in proper order . . . Every style of painting was represented . . . (our guide) told us that what we had seen in earth's galleries were not the originals at all—but we were now seeing the originals for the first time." [22]

This was such exciting news to hear! We know that everything on earth comes from spirit; therefore the human artist must express himself through the medium of physical paint, with the limited colors and hues available here on earth.

"The things of earth
are patterned in a realm that lies above
And all the things that men have wrought below
Are copied from the Unseen and the Real.
This Real is essence from which all things proceed." [23]

Hall of Literature
This hall contains history of all the nations of the earth—the true history. In addition to the written histories, there are actual histories, written by the people themselves after arriving on the spirit plane. Other rooms contained volumes of writings to be read by anyone interested. There are books on 'psychic science'.
"I was astonished by the wealth of literature under this heading. Upon the shelves were books denying the existence of a spirit world, and denying the reality of spirit return. Many of the authors of them have since had the opportunity of looking again at their own works—but with very different feelings! They had become, in themselves, living witnesses against the contents of their own books." [24]

The Library
It would be impossible to mention literature without indicating the presence of a library, without which any avid reader would be lost. For anyone deprived of learning while living on Earth, it is heartening to know that in that great beyond there is an opportunity available to 'make up for it.'

From *Return from Tomorrow*, by G.G. Ritchie, we read, "Next we walked through a library the size of the whole University of Richmond. I gazed into rooms lined floor to ceiling with documents on parchment, clay, leather, metal, paper." [25]

Springer describes the library in such detail that one could almost replicate it:

> It was a glorious apartment—the walls lined from ceiling to floor with rare and costly books. A large, stained-glass window opened upon the front veranda, and two large bow windows, not far apart, were in the back of the room. A semi-circular row of shelves, supported by very delicate pillars of gray marble, about six feet high, extended some fifteen feet into the spacious main room and cut it into two sections lengthwise, each with one of the bowed windows in the back, leaving still a large space beyond the dividing line, where the two sections united again into one. The concave side of the semicircle of shelves was toward the entrance of the room; and close to it, not far removed from the bowed window, stood a beautiful writing desk, with every thing ready for use.[26]

Hall of Fabrics

In the Hall of Fabrics are found scores of beautiful materials and cloths "woven throughout the centuries, and of which practically nothing remains upon the earth-plane . . . A room of tapestries contained some superb examples of the artists' genius, the earthly counterparts of which have long since gone out of existence. The essential characteristic of human activity on the other side is creativity. In his *The Unobstructed Universe*, White relates: "We do creative things here. There is not much original genius on your side; sometimes there is, but more often what you call genius is a dipping into what individuals here accomplish." [27]

Borgia makes note of another part of this hall: "Annexed to this apartment (Hall of Fabrics) were smaller rooms where many happy, industrious souls were studying and practicing the art of tapestry weaving." [28]

Every discipline conceivable by us is represented in that Summerland. The Hall of Science reminds me of the day Gabriel told us that a new energy would be discovered, eliminating the need of gas, oil, and coal.

Hall of Science

> Here every field of scientific and engineering investigation, study, and discovery was covered . . . the earth world has the spirit world to thank for all the major scientific discoveries that have been made throughout the centuries . . . The laboratories of the world of spirit are many decades in advance of those of the earth plane. And it will be years before many revolutionary discoveries are allowed to be sent through to the earth world, because the earth has not yet sufficiently progressed.[29]

As the authors take us through all the halls of learning we realize the vast store of knowledge and talent that has accumulated through the centuries and is preserved on the other side for our education and edification when we pass over.

Hall of Music

"The library contained books dealing with music as well as the scores of vast quantities of music that had been written on earth by composers who had now passed into spirit . . . We were extremely interested in the many instruments that have no counterpart upon the earth-plane. They are, for the most part, specially adapted to the forms of music that are exclusive to the spirit world, and they are for that reason very much more elaborate." [30]

Hall of Healing

This hall is for people who had long illnesses before transition and those who 'died' a violent death. Attendants are constantly with them until the acceptance of their new surroundings.

Business

The first time I saw the word 'business' in regard to the heavenly realm I was taken aback. What business could there be in a case where there is no commerce as we know it. It was stunning to know 'business' exists on the other side! When we think of business we think of money, and of course, there is no currency on the other side, for there is no need of it. 'Business' there means products and their production.

"There were vast business houses of many kinds . . . many colleges and schools; many book and music-stores and publishing houses, several large manufactories . . . art rooms, picture galleries and libraries; many lecture halls and vast auditoriums." [31]

With all these halls of learning available, we might assume that there were many teachers and guides available for individual assistance and tutoring. Teachers per se were not mentioned. However, Springer mentions the names of two speakers who had appeared in the auditorium. They were Martin Luther and John Wesley.

> Spirit guides constitute one of the grandest orders in the whole organization and administration of the spirit world. They inhabit a realm of their own, and they have all lived for many centuries in the spirit world. They are drawn from every nationality that exists upon the earth-plane, . . . A great many of them are drawn from eastern countries, and from the North American Indians, too, because it has always been the case that dwellers in those regions of the earth world were, and are, already possessed of psychic gifts themselves, and were therefore aware of the inter-relationship of our two worlds.[32]

Daily Life

Clothing
After wearing earthly garb for a time, spirit robes were worn. The substances of which earthly clothes are made are non-existent in the spirit world.
All outward appearances are produced, not by the texture of the material, but by the kind and degree of light that is the essence of a spirit robe. Those that we now saw were in 'flowing' form and of full length, and the colours—blue and pink in varying degrees of intensity—seemed to interweave themselves throughout the whole substance of the robes. They looked very comfortable to wear, and like everything here, they require no attention to keep them in a state of perfect preservation, the spirituality of the wearer alone accounting for that." [33]

Springer offers a more feminine description: "The white robe was soft and light and shone with a faint luster, reminding me more of silk crepe than anything I could recall, only infinitely more beautiful. It fell about me in soft, graceful folds." [34]

Language

When Springer describes her experience in the Temple and the singing of hymns, she noted that although the words were sung in a strange tongue, they were easily understood and no language was spoken there that everyone could not understand.

Occupations

Borgia provides some insight into the occupations on the other side, noting that all tasks were done willingly and there was never an attitude of having to do something; no one was ever compelled to perform an undesirable task. How comforting to know that no one has to 'work' on the other side. Joy prevails everywhere, unlike life on this plane. "LIFE IS BEAUTIFUL [ON EARTH] BUT NOT AS NICE AS THIS—YOUR WORLD IS FILLED WITH SO MUCH HATE." Boss, 91-93.

Recreation

Theater includes comedy, historical pageants, and any activity that is not competitive. Any sport using a ball is not possible, because there is no gravity there. This reminds me of a poster I once saw in a restaurant. It was a photo of a billiard table, with the caption, "If there is no pool in Heaven, I'm not going".

When the sea is described (as above), Springer relates that she sees passengers on board the ships, "clad in the spotless garments of the redeemed. Many among them had golden harps and various instruments of music, and whenever the boat touched the shores and its inmates were welcomed by the glad voices and tender embraces of their beloved ones in the throng, the harps would be held aloft, all of the golden instruments would sound, and the vast multitude would break forth into the triumphant song of victory over death and the grave." [35]

Holidays

The other side is such a peaceful, loving, beautiful place that it does not seem likely they would have any 'holidays' there. But there is one mentioned by Borgia: The only holiday mentioned was Christmas: "Christmas, however, is celebrated simultaneously with the earth because "there rises throughout the earth world a great force of goodwill and kindliness . . . and is always preceded by thoughts of pleasant anticipation . . . it is common enough to hear one person say to another: 'Christmas on the earth plane is drawing near' . . . On this special occasion we are always visited by great souls from the higher realms."[36]

This brings to mind a comment Gabriel made to us at some point in his visitations. He said that the times the heaven world draws close to Earth to celebrate with earthlings are Christmas and Easter. Would anyone question why?

Swimming
Perhaps this is not the proper title, because Springer describes walking into a river with her robe on, sitting on the bottom and gazing at the lovely pebbles. Breathing was not an issue there, of course. She tells us, upon leaving the water that, "My flesh, my hair, and even my beautiful garments, were soft and dry as before the water touched them". [37]

Communication and Travel
"We spoke just as we had always done upon the earth; we simply used our vocal chords and spoke." [38] Travel is done by thought alone. If you desire to be in a particular place, you think about it and—bingo—there you are.

Arrival on the other side
"As soon as a soul arrives, the first thing the angels do is show them the light. Now some souls readily go into the light and others say, 'Oh, I can't.' It depends on their belief system when they were here upon the earth. If they believed in hellfire and damnation a lot of them are so filled with fear of this belief that they create it around them. It is a thought form that follows them about and then the angels have a more difficult time with them." [39]

Explanation of a thought form: When a person believes in a certain image and focuses on it over time, the thought itself becomes an image. Also, when many people feed energy into an imaginary character it becomes a thought form. An example of this is Mickey Mouse. It is an imaginary character, but the thoughts of millions of people have created from it a thought form.

Special arrivals in the spirit world
There is a nursery of Heaven, for the babies who are born 'dead,' or 'die' in infancy. They are tended by loving persons. Children, too, live in small cottages, surrounded by small trees and buildings, and playgrounds. Teachers are there to instruct them. "Children who leave the earth plane in their early years will continue their studies from where they left off, eliminating subjects of no further use, and adding those that are spiritualistically essential." [40]

Other names for the heaven world are 'morning land,' 'house of many mansions,' 'Summerland,' 'the thither shore,' 'the great beyond,' and 'pleasant land.'

It was especially fascinating to me to read about the connection between earthlings and the spirit world. Humans who are prone to prayer and meditation often reach, in their consciousness, to a higher realm, a higher plane for answers and assistance in their lives.

Earth/Heaven Connection
"It seemed to me that at every step we took in the divine life our souls reached up toward something better, and we had no inclination to look behind to that which had passed or to try to solve what in our mortal life had been intricate or perplexing questions or mysteries.'[41]

There are a few places in her book where someone on the other side, upon greeting a newly arrived loved one, would inquire about another person still on earth, saying 'Are they coming soon?', as though they couldn't wait to show them around in Heaven. The author, in a psychic reading in 1979, at the age of 49, was told that her father stood behind her and said, "I'm waiting for you. I want to show you around. The light is different here; the colors are different." This was an incredibly welcome comment, since he had passed into spirit in 1934, when I was only five years old!

Many people think there is no connection between the way we live on Earth and life on the other side. Still others believe they will go to 'hell' if they are not 'good.' Springer mentions this in her book: "If only we could realize while we are yet mortals that day by day we are building for eternity, how different our lives in many ways would be! Every gentle word, every generous thought, every unselfish deed, will become a pillar of eternal beauty in the life to come. We cannot be selfish and unloving in one life, and generous and loving in the next; the two lives are too closely blended—one but a continuation of the other." [42]

Those who wait

Gabriel told us that there are many in the spirit world lying down, awaiting Judgment Day. Angels are sent to tell them that they can rise and carry on with their life; that there is no 'Judgment Day,' but to the angels they inquire, "Is it Judgment Day yet?" And when the angels say, 'no,' they lie down again and wait, wait, wait.

Earthlings Who Believed

Joan of Arc (1412-1431) Maid of Orleans, servant of God.

Emanuel Swedenborg (1688-1772) "Swedenborg came to believe that God had called him to bring a new revelation to the world, and from 1745 until his death twenty-seven years later he spent the bulk of his time adding theological works to his already lengthy scientific and philosophical writings." *A Compendium of Swedenborg's Theological Writings*, Preface, xxiii

---

Many eminent individuals are reported to have had communication with the spirit world. The following persons are mentioned in *Spirits and Spirit Worlds* (Danbury Press, 1975). **All page numbers following refer to that book, unless noted.**

Queen Victoria (1819-1901) 'John Brown, her personal manservant reportedly was also a medium who enabled the widowed Queen to communicate with her beloved Albert (deceased husband) . . . the Queen certainly believed that he had genuine premonitions of the future, and relied on him greatly.' 21

Abraham Lincoln (1809-1865) was given (by a young medium named Nettie Colburn Maynard, while in trance), a lecture about the necessity for emancipation of the slaves. Mary Lincoln, his wife, veiled in mourning for her late husband, sat for a photograph. When the photographer, W. Mumler, produced the print, an image of the president stood behind Mary. She agreed and said, "I am his widow." 22

Sir Oliver Lodge (1857-1940) English physicist, contacted his deceased son, killed in World War I, through Mrs. Gladys Leonard, 141

Johannes Greber, authored *Communication with the Spirit World of God*, 'Personal Experiences of a Catholic Priest', written in German, translated into English and published by Johannes Greber Memorial Foundation, 1974 (fifth edition).

Frederick Myers, later known as F.W.H. Myers, Psychologist and one of the founders of the Society for Psychical Research. Thousands of pages of transcripts were written of messages received from Dr. Myers after his death in 1901, through several individuals using automatic writing. The SPR researched the mass of information which he gave to the mediums, and in *Evidence of Personal Survival from Cross-Correspondences*, H.F. Saltmarsh discusses it. 142

Sir Arthur Conan Doyle, twentieth century writer, creator of Sherlock Holmes. 'Was a convinced Spiritualist for nearly 30 years of his life, and largely gave up his writing to travel and lecture as a kind of spiritualist missionary.' 80

Doyle related his experiences on the other side after his transition. The reader is directed to a book titled *The Return of Arthur Conan Doyle* (White Eagle Publishing Trust, Liss, England. 1963)
Dr. Alfred Russell Wallace, the naturalist who with Darwin enunciated the principles of evolution and one of the early scientists to investigate Spiritualism. After many experiments at séances and in his own home, he

concluded, "Spiritualist phenomena are proved, quite as well as any facts are proved in other sciences." 41

The Fox Sisters. In 1848, in their farmhouse in Hydesville, New York, the Fox family was contacted, through a series of rappings, by the spirit of a man who had been slain and buried in their basement. This precipitated the belief and practice of Spiritualism in the United States. A shrine was begun in 1955 by John Drummond, who placed a stone in Hydesville inscribed:

THE BIRTHPLACE AND SHRINE
OF MODERN SPIRITUALISM

Erected by the most generous contributions of spiritualists and their friends the world over in honor of every gifted spiritual medium from the time of the Fox sisters in 1848 to our spiritual mediums of the present and future. This corner-stone was purchased and laid by the Ministry of Spiritual and Divine Science and friends on July 4, 1955. 6-9

Sir William Barrett, physicist and a founder of the SPR, at first skeptical of the more flamboyant activities of the séance room . . . was finally convinced of the existence of a spiritual world by his experiments. 50

Thomas A. Edison (1847-1931), inventor of light bulb and phonograph. "He shared the enthusiasm of many of his generation for contact with unseen forces, and worked on a device that would locate a frequency between long and short waves to be used as a telepathic channel between the worlds of the living and the dead.", 97

Historical Belief in Life after Death.
The Neanderthal (Stone Age) grave of a mother and her child was found in which pottery and storage jars were beside the bodies, to provide food for their afterlife.
Royal death pits (2500BC) have been unearthed in Ur (now Iraq), where the Queen was buried with 68 others—women of the court and soldiers armed with spears, as though to continue protecting their Queen after death.

An Incan (11th to 16th century) Emperor was buried with wives and servants to serve him in the next world.

A Cayapa Indian from Ecuador was laid to rest in a boat & supplied with food for the long journey . . .

An Egyptian model of a boat carved in about 1400BC was placed in a tomb to provide a safe passage to the next world. 28-29

Scripture

Furthermore we have had fathers of our flesh which corrected us, and we gave them reverence: shall we not much rather be in subjection unto the Father of spirits, and live? Heb. 12:9

While we look not at the things which are seen, but at the things which are not seen; for the things which are seen are temporal; but the things which are not seen are eternal. II Cor. 4:18

There is a stubborn refusal of many people to even consider the existence of a spirit world of God, much less possible communication with it. Yet in I John 4:1-1 we find:

Beloved, believe not every spirit, but try the spirits whether they are of God: because many false prophets are gone out into the world.
Hereby know ye the Spirit of God: Every spirit that confesseth that Jesus Christ is come in flesh is of God . . .

"The doctrine of eternal damnation, so loved by orthodox religion, and of the everlasting fires of so-called hell . . . is one of the most outrageously stupid and ignorant doctrines that has ever been invented by equally stupid and ignorant churchmen." (from a monsignor, son of Archbishop of Canterbury, told to a Roman Catholic priest in 1954 in England.)

Jesus' Message to the World

Jesus himself resurrected and appeared to many on earth to prove the continuity of life. In the apocryphal book 'Infancy', Jesus raised a playmate from the dead. Jesus raised Lazarus from the dead, as revealed in John 11:48.

Why would those in the Spirit World Wish to Contact us earthlings?

1. To inform their grieving survivors that they are all right.
2. To assure us that we will continue living after so-called death.
3. To impart knowledge to us about our future; warn us of pending danger etc.
4. To remove any fears we might have of 'dying'.
5. To open our minds to the possibility of communication between the worlds.
6. To prove such communication.

Some Messages from the spirit world to earthlings

Spirit guidance in wartime.
Archangel Gabriel told us a most wonderful story about a planned invasion from the English Channel by the Germans in World War II. Most of the Englishmen were off to war. Some mediums got wind of the invasion, and gathered all the mediums and old people available. They collected stove pipes and brooms and mops, and proceeded to line the cliffs and the shores with them. As the bright moon struck the items, it appeared to be weaponry—and that is what the submarine's periscopes saw. They called retreat, believing that they were overwhelmingly out-numbered by the armed forces with guns and cannons. Had they attacked by day, the outcome would have been far different.

Accidents explained after the fact:
On October 5, 1930 a "huge British airship, the R101, had crashed in flames on a hillside in Beauvais, France—killing 48 of its 54 passengers—the hesitant, anxious voice of a man claiming to be its captain spoke through the lips of a medium in London. In short disjointed sentences he described the horrifying last moments before his incineration. His account of the crash included a wealth of technical information that was confirmed six months later by an official inquiry." 76

Accidents explained before the fact
'William T. Stead, British editor and convinced Spiritualist . . . The image of a sinking ocean liner occurred frequently in his writings, and in 1893

he wrote a fictional story about the collision of a great liner with an iceberg in the Atlantic. He himself was on the maiden voyage of the ill-starred Titanic, and was one of the many drowned.' 136

Spirit and modern technology
"Friedrich Jurgenson switched on his tape recorder one day in 1959 expecting to hear the recording of bird calls he had made in a Swedish forest. Suddenly the voice of his dead mother addressed him. He heard her saying: 'Friedel, my little Friedel, can you hear me'?" Others have since captured voices from the other side. 92

Fine Arts from spirit.
An accordion played music without human hands, even when it was placed in a cage. 129.

In Lily Dale, a spiritualist-owned village in southwestern New York State, there is, in the hotel, a spirit-painted picture, created without the use of physical paint, according to living witnesses.

The most significant comments from the other side are those made by individuals there who have spoken about God and Jesus the Christ. S. E. White relates a message he received from his son who had committed suicide in his twenties: "*I haven't met him [Jesus]. They talk about him—a mystic, a seer, yes, a seer. Oh, but, Dad, they don't talk about him as a savior. As an example, you see? . . . You see, I want to tell you, I would like to tell you, Jesus is triumphant, you know? But it's not like that . . . not a savior, that's the important thing—an example.*" [43]

J. Boss reports a message she received from the other side:
"GOD WANTS US ALL TO HAVE FAITH. SO BELIEVE, MY CHILD! BELIEVE THAT HE IS WITH YOU AND IN YOU AND IN EVERYONE. HE SURROUNDS YOU WITH THE BEAUTY OF THE UNIVERSE AND THE MAJESTY OF SOULS THAT OCCUPY IT. HE IS AS CLOSE TO YOU AS YOUR HEART AND YOUR NEIGHBOR! HE IS HERE! . . . HE WANTS YOU TO BE HAPPY AND HE WANTS FOR YOU TO MAKE OTHERS HAPPY. THAT IS YOUR MISSION IN LIFE. THAT IS EVERYONE'S MISSION IN LIFE." [44]

For those who doubt the existence of a spirit world of God and communication between it and Earth, no argument will compel them to believe. For those who have experienced any of these phenomena, no argument will dissuade. For those who long to know the truth about the spirit world of God, may this chapter reassure them. Truth needs no defense.

"Come home . . . This world is not where you belong. You are a stranger here." [45]

CHAPTER 2

God's Messengers

Every visible thing in this world is put in the charge of an angel. St. Augustine

Archangel Gabriel's seminar on July 27, 1991, was titled *Angels, Aliens, and Earthlings.* Herein is an abbreviated description of the angels and archangels. Gabriel also provided us with the various groups of angels and their assigned tasks. In the Bible we find the following references to these angel groups: seraphim, cherubim, thrones, dominions, principalities, and powers.

Biblical references to the angel groups

Seraphim are mentioned in Isaiah 6:2: *Above it stood the seraphims: each one had six wings, with twain he covered his face, and with twain he covered his feet, and with twain he did fly.*

Cherubim are mentioned once, in the New Testament, over 60 times in the Old. I chose verse 8, in chapter 5 of Chronicles: *For the cherubims spread forth their wings over the place of the ark, and the cherubims covered the ark and the staves thereof above.*

From the New Testament book of Colossians, 1:16:
For by him were all things created, that are in heaven, and that are in earth, visible and invisible, whether they be thrones, or dominions, or principalities or powers: all things were created by him, and for him: And he is before all things, and by him all things consist.

Thrones. The word 'thrones' appears in the Bible nine times, five times in the Old Testament and four in the New Testament. They all, however, seem to apply to worldly thrones of rulers.

Dominions. The word 'dominion' (supreme authority) appears many times in Scripture. The word 'dominions' is found only once in the Old Testament (Daniel 7:27) but refers to a kingdom of authority, also. Only once does the word appear in the New Testament: See Colossians 1:16, above.

Principalities is found once in the Old Testament: *Say unto the king and to the queen, 'Humble yourselves, sit down: for your principalities shall come down, even the crown of your glory.'* Jer. 13:18
The New Testament contains this word six times. From Ephesians 3:9-10: *And to make all men see what is the fellowship of the mystery, which from the beginning of the world hath been hid in God, who created all things by Jesus Christ: To the intent that now unto the principalities and powers in heavenly places might be known by the church of the manifold wisdom of God.*

Powers. This word does not appear anywhere in the Old Testament. Fourteen times it appears in the New. In Romans 13:1: *Let every soul be subject unto the higher powers. For there is no power but of God: the powers that be are ordained of God.*

Virtues. The word 'virtue' is found in the Bible, referring to a human characteristic, but 'virtues' is not found anywhere in Scripture.

Gabriel's descriptions of the angel groups

Seraphim
Seraphim are the angels of First Cause.
Their essence is light, love, and perfection.
They assist in bringing forth divine essence into spirit form, or life.
They exist for the purpose of praising God, which brings forth more into creation.
They are unaware of earth or humans as such; they see humans as holy, a unique part of spirit life.
They are above gravitation of earth and any other planet.

Cherubim
The purpose of the Cherubim is to record everything perfectly.

They are aware of everything, everywhere, all at once.
Their essence is eternalness, divinity of life.
They are aware of earth only as an energy of divine form.
They are aware of humans only as divine expression.
They never come to earth.

Thrones
(This does not refer to throne of God)
Their purpose: keepers of the flame of life.
They represent steadfastness, holding steady in the Light, perpetuation of the is-ness of divine essence.
They do not come to earth.
Four of the archangels go to the Thrones for steadiness and sustenance: Michael, Gabriel, Raphael, and Metatron.
The Thrones also give the archangels authority to come to earth.

Dominions
Dominions give all other angels (not archangels) their duties.
There are layers and layers of Dominions, like the levels of workers in a large corporation.
There are dominions within dominions. They are more in number than humans could comprehend.
They form groups to work with various types of things.
Their essence is to help humans, earth, and other planets.
Dominions have a vibrational rate that is similar to form.
Dominions come to earth.

Principalities
They provide spiritual pathways of all life—human, animal, plant.
They send forth inspiration, for humans to pick up on.
They work with world leaders; government, religious, legal.
When world leaders gather anywhere, the ethers around them are filled with angels, to influence, guide, inspire, direct—by pushing, flapping their wings all about.
When any soul steps onto the spiritual path, they get help from principalities, which are waiting in huge numbers to come to assist and guide you—to direct you and give you all you need.

Powers

The first level of angels to take form, and that depends on what they are asked to do.

They are aware of earth and all its life forms.

Purpose: Evolutionary progress of earth plane (except humans).

They come to earth—earth devas, fairies and gnomes are all forms of the Powers.

Their primary interest: changes of the earth: flowers, trees, sky, planets.

They communicate with humans only as a 'fringe benefit'.

They are concerned with earth evolution, things outside the human influence.

They send forth thunderstorms, snow, flowers, trees etc.

Virtues

Virtues come to earth, and to other planets.

They bestow their purity upon humans; their purity filters down to earth and is seen as a miracle.

They bring about the totality of life on lesser planes, throughout the universe.

They work in groups, as the Dominions.

Humankind enters into their plane. Above the virtues, humans do not enter.

Virtues work with patterns on earth (such as weather patterns), with vibrations within patterns; with people, animals, vegetation, star influences.

Angels of Destruction

Purpose

There are NO angels who engage in negative behavior.

They are called angels of destruction because their function is to wipe out everything you ask of them (*not humans*): negative thoughts, habits, behaviors, attitudes.

They are powerful, obedient and have no desire to harm.

They do not reason 'why' or consider consequences.

They are only aware of your desire to destroy and the object to be destroyed.

Historically, they have destroyed Lemurea and Atlantis. they destroyed Sodom and Gomorrah. Angels went three times to Sodom and Gomorrah to ask the inhabitants to change their ways; three times they were answered, 'no'.

They create hurricanes, earthquakes, cyclones etc.

Angels of destruction should not be called upon lightly. Serious consideration should be given before calling on them. They can help us grow spiritually if we identify our shortcomings and error perceptions and sincerely, ardently, seek their help. These are the steps Gabriel gave us in order to consciously request their assistance:

1. Identify any blockages that you have which keep you from awareness of your Higher Self, such as fear, anger, communication problems, money problems, relationships, inability to accept love from another.

2. Create a positive to replace the negative which will be destroyed, i.e., replace fear with fearlessness, anger with calmness etc.

3. Be absolutely certain you want the change to take place.

4. Be precise in what you ask.

5. Be totally willing to: let go of the blockages.
    accept the love of God.
    accept total abundance.

Archangels

It was at this seminar that Archangel Gabriel revealed his true identity to the Springwell Metaphysical Studies students. Previously he told us to call him Lucas. After he described the seven archangels, this author approached the microphone and asked Lucas if he was an archangel. He said, "Yes". As I stood there in amazement, he asked me which one I thought he was. I tried to recall all the descriptions, stammered, and he then said, "I am Gabriel, announcer of the ages."

Descriptions of the Archangels

Gabriel said "All the archangels are equal in their power; they are all equal in their abilities. There is no contest between angels. They all love and revere each other."

Michael
(Not to be confused with Mick-ay-el, who is not an archangel). Mick-ay-el gives succor to those who mourn, heals the wounds of the emotional body). Michael has access to the Throne of God, from where he brings his power.

Channeling: Michael does not channel, for his power is so great that it would destroy a human form. However, lesser angels under his dominance do bring forth, by channeling, the message he cares to have spoken.

Protector: When in dire need of assistance quickly, call on Michael.

Warrior: Not with a sword as we think of war, but with the sword of truth, to fight away all of our error perceptions and bring them to the light of God. Through every war Michael and his legion of angels have come to disperse the enemy—not the people we consider the enemy—but our thought forms that have promoted war, destruction, death, pestilence; any form that is not of God.

Gabriel said, "He is terrible to watch in action for he is vaster than your mind can comprehend. You think of him as a singular form with great wings and a sword. Indeed not. Michael is a power, the likes of which your earth could not contain. And he is one of the holiest and one of the mightiest of all angels."

Vision: He sees past your errors and into the truth of your being & is willing to go into the depths of the hells which you have created, to fight the devils you have made; to free your soul of the error thoughts which you have perceived to be truth.

Gabriel

Functions: He is equally powerful as Michael, but Michael is the action and Gabriel is the spirit of truth. He is the birthing angel of the intellect. He is the spiritual urging that you get to pray, to meditate, and to know more.
He is the message bearer, the angel of annunciation. He precedes every age that comes on earth. He is in charge of the mental and spiritual planes of man's evolvement.

Presentation: He comes softly, quietly, with profound love, with 'truth in his wings' to lead us to the path of light.

Messages: It was Gabriel who announced the birth of the Virgin Mary, John the Baptist and Jesus Christ. He comes to those who seek him, even though they may not call him by name, as they desire in their hearts to learn, to grow and to be more. He has legions of angels who help him.

Raphael

Raphael is the healer. All healing vibrations are of Raphael. He and his angels soothe the wounds of mankind, visit hospitals, and create healing places. Whenever you give a healing, you are working with the vibration of Raphael.

Channeling: He does not channel any messages in words. His is a gentle, loving power. He brings healing, not only to the body but all aspects of your being.

Presentation: The power of Raphael goes to sacred centers where people go to be healed.
Raphael brings the infants into the world, those who are troubled of body or in some way in need of help.

Uriel (pron. you-ree-el')

Uriel is the angel of repentance. Whenever a soul becomes aware of its error thoughts and wishes to change them, praying, 'Dear God help me to change my ways', it is Uriel who comes to the rescue.

It was Uriel who went to Noah to warn him to prepare for the impending deluge. Uriel guided John the Baptist in his ministry on earth.

He brings a feeling of regret and desire to be more. Uriel brings the succor that would turn a stony heart into a heart of love.

Zadkiel

Gabriel said, 'He is a very wondrous angel indeed.—he is filled with mercy and benevolence.' It was Zadkiel who stopped Abraham from sacrificing his son, Isaac.

He shows mercy to them who themselves are merciless.

He interferes with those who come to earth to destroy.

Zadkiel worked closely with Michael to preserve the U.S. from destruction in 'this past war.' (Author uncertain which war Gabriel meant)

He is filled with love, compassion, and forgiveness; works ardently with those who work on forgiveness. He also brings laughter, for he knows that true forgiveness is lighthearted and filled with joy. "So when I speak of mercy, I would not have you think of him as tearful or mourning, but rather as light and joy and bringing laughter" . . . Gabriel

Metatron

Metatron has powers similar to Michael's.

It was Metatron who led the Israelites through their years of desolation in the desert. He expressed himself as a pillar of light in the darkness to lead the Israelites to safety.

He assisted Moses in getting the Ten Commandments.

He is extremely steadfast in his devotion to mankind, he cares greatly about it.

"Metatron is perhaps one of the most powerful of all angels and probably one of the least known". Gabriel

Ariel

Ariel is the angel of baptism; he works with water—physical water and the fluid movement of the universe. Ariel often assists Michael; Raphael and Gabriel.

He makes himself available to any other angel requiring his assistance.

When one is baptized, Ariel takes the cleansing waters of the spirit of truth of you and pours them over your error thoughts and washes away your perceived sins.

Ariel brings tidal waves, storms at sea. He loves to play with water and he has a sense of humor. He will splash you as you walk along the ocean shore, or dump you playfully into the water—not to drown, but to play.

"I have watched Ariel, with all the tenderness there is, take a bird into the water and bathe it and cleanse away the parasites, and then lift it up and let it fly free.

"I have watched him swim with whales and sing their song with them, and stroke the dolphins.

"He is the light beneath the surface of the water that the old mariners used to call the mermaid.

"He is the song upon the ocean wind."

Call upon Ariel when there is a drought, and if you are inundated with water, ask him to assist and he will come.

Lucifer

For thousands of years on the earth plane, there has been an error perception of Lucifer. The truth is that he made the greatest of sacrifices for humanity. Mankind descended, in its consciousness, to earth and lost awareness of what it was (part of the Divine Essence which is God).

Mankind came to believe in limitation, illness, death and believed that he was bound to earth and separate from the Father, God. Recall in Genesis

3:21 *And the Lord God caused a great sleep to fall upon Adam.* Now, nowhere in Scripture (stated by Gabriel and also found in *A Course in Miracles*) does it say that Adam woke up! So, here we are, still asleep to the truth of us: that we are divine in essence and eternal in existence.

Angels have come often to get mankind to see the error of its thinking, but mankind would not listen. Then, Divine Essence [God] decided that an archangel would be sent to earth, to help all mankind to see the error thoughts they were living by. One archangel would have to be all the error thoughts of mankind to help it out of its world of illusion.

Five archangels approached the Throne of God: Michael, Gabriel, Raphael, Metatron & Lucifer. Lucifer said that he would be the one to come to Earth to mirror humankind's perceived evil in others and understand; to become willing to change their thinking. Gabriel and Michael asked him if he was sure, since mankind would call him the Devil. But, out of his love for humanity, Lucifer took the task on. He did not FALL. There are no 'fallen angels'—for angels cannot comprehend any realm except the Divine Essence, Love, which is God.

Lucifer came willingly, to help mankind lift itself up in its awareness to recall its source—God. Michael said to Lucifer, "I'll help you."

Lucifer's future: When all mankind is redeemed, he will return to the Light of God. Do not call on Lucifer for help until you are ready to change your ways. The author recommends listening to all the audiocassettes/CDs of this seminar.

For he shall give his angels charge over thee, to keep thee in all thy ways . . . Ps. 91:11

Authors' personal experiences with angels' intervention

1. In the 1980s I was going to meet someone to go bowling. I didn't own a bowling ball, and didn't want to admit that I didn't. So I went to the Salvation Army, picturing in my mind a green ball. Not only was a green bowling ball there, but it fit my hand! Since bowling balls are drilled for personal use, it was to me a miracle.

2. While attending a Springwell Metaphysical Studies weekend in Greenville, NY, I lost my checkbook before I was to pay the balance for the seminar. It rained very hard that night and the next day I figured if I did find it, it would be soaked and illegible. After breakfast, someone gave it to me and said she had found it on the grass. To my utter amazement it hardly had been dampened. An angel must surely have put a little umbrella over it for protection.

3. I wanted to get a dog when I moved from an apartment into a house in Greenwich, NY. One day as I went to work I asked myself what I would like if I could have any dog in the world. I asked for a mature, black female, neutered toy poodle, trained. My daughter had owned one and we loved Melody greatly. Two weeks later a co-worker said she had a dog to give away. It was a 10yr. old black female, neutered toy poodle!

We had six wonderful years together before I had to put her down. (rather I sent her up; for I know that one day I will see her again, on the other side).

4. I greatly desired a new auto, but my credit was poor. Three times I paid a deposit, went home, and thought 'it won't go through'—and it didn't. Then, one day at a Gabriel seminar (though he rarely gave personal advice), he told me to picture a car in my mind and picture myself washing it, putting gas into it, etc. without concern about financing. I pictured the car I wanted, without any thought about debt. In two months I purchased the car I had pictured, and the credit went through without a hitch.

5. I took a broken gemstone necklace to a Psychic Fair in Albany and asked a woman who designed, made, and sold gemstone jewelry to repair it. She opened the envelope in which I had placed all the pieces from the necklace. She pulled out the necklace, which was in one piece, and said, 'What's wrong with it?' I was stunned, and word of the miracle spread quickly throughout the Fair.

Gabriel's Lessons

There is no way that I could present this topic without including some of the phrases of Gabriel explaining his visitations, his role, and the role angels play in our lives. Following are comments made by him regarding these topics.

Gabriel's earthly visits

"I was here 2,000 years ago. I come every two thousand years because it takes you that long to really take in and live the lessons that are brought to the earth not only by myself but by other teachers as well who come and teach truth to you. Then you have to take it in and sow the seeds of truth." [1]

The significance of 'every 2,000 years' is that it represents the turning of the ages, as the universe we know revolves around the Central Sun, which revolution takes approximately 12,000 years and the Zodiac applies to it. Jesus came at the beginning of the Age of Pisces; hence a fish was and remains a symbol of his presence.

There is a divine plan by which angels enjoin us and much preparation is made, as explained by Gabriel:
"I started about 500 years ago to draw near to the earth to get used to the concepts of humankind and to see where my teaching was needed the most. You know, we don't just randomly go anywhere." [2] In another seminar, Gabriel explained that he had been working with Beloved Woman for 500 years to prepare her for her mission of channeling him and Jesus the Christ.

Gabriel on his recent visitation

When Archangel Gabriel began his visitations in 1987 he told us to call him Lucas. In 1991 he revealed himself as Gabriel, Announcer of the Ages. He said the word Gabriel means messenger of light. So does Lucas, he said.[3] He assured us that his teachings are valid and useable at this time: "It would be of little benefit for me to teach you something that you couldn't attain for several lifetimes. I would be wasting my time." [4]

He added, "There was a time when Beloved Woman, if she stood up here and said, 'I am going to channel an Archangel,' she would have been burned at the stake or hung or beheaded, which is why we didn't do that with her before." [5]

Gabriel proceeded to explain why this was the right time for him to come to Earth to teach us. He also noted the prevalence of angels:

"Upon your earth plane at this time, there is a great concentration of angel energy . . . for they are going about making their presence felt, some in little ways, some in larger ways . . . Most of us present wings only to denote that we are angels, for those who may not know it, but we do not have wings. *Real Courage,* 4.

"Now you see angels all over the place. People have them on their modes of transportation, little advertisements across the back that say, 'I believe in angels,' or something of that sort. You see it all over. Now what does that tell you about you in your life? Doesn't that tell you that you are living in a time of spiritual awakening, of spiritual reality, when spirit is no longer something that you can't talk about?" [6]

Archangel Gabriel was the only archangel who came to Earth at that time. (1987-1999). However, he told us that eleven master teachers also came to Earth, in various places. "There is one in France, there is one over in England; there is another down in Australia. They are all over the place." [7]

At another time he mentioned Ramtha (channeled by J.Z. Knight) in California and he said there was one in the southwestern United States. I recall asking him if these centers would someday be in contact with each other and he said yes, they would, but not in this particular incarnation of mine.

Angels and humankind

"When God brought you forth, one of the first things that came into our awareness was that we needed to watch over you . . . We needed to guide you through your error perceptions and to guard you from your own fears. We need to help you see and recognize that everything that has happened to you has ever been of your own choice, your own doing and to help you know that there is no condemnation in God, none, ever." [8]

We often think of angels randomly appearing when we have some kind of emergency or experience some kind of trauma. The activities of the angel world are divinely directed constantly.

Gabriel explained angels' purpose: "When God created angels, He created each of us for a specific purpose and it is only unto that purpose that we can abide. We do not have free choice like you. We are free within the realm of what we were created for, but we are not free as you are free." [9]

Writing this brings to mind the day Gabriel told us that we humans are greater than angels! He explained that we have made vast choices by creating and creating. When we return to God and redeem each of the realms of existence, we will know a joy beyond anything the angels can know. A parallel of earthly experience may be that those who have created for themselves a 'hell on earth' (such as the depths of addiction); there is great joy in finding sobriety and an honest life.

Gabriel said that within the realm of angels there is no fear. "The difference between humans and angels is that we know nothing that is not the Will of God. We know the Will of God completely and that is all we do know. We have to concentrate to become aware of your frailties and to become aware of the things concerning human beings that trouble you so . . . we know nothing of what troubles you at all." [10]

Regarding the duties of angels, Gabriel told us," Angels do a lot of things and one of the things that they do is go about gathering up the unused blessings . . . and hold them until you are ready to open the door and let them come in . . . They do this because sometimes you are not aware of your blessing when it comes . . . you are looking all around elsewhere." [11]

Focusing only on the *now* is essential. So is listening to God, Who speaks to us throughout the day—whispering suggestions to do the 'right thing,' words that come from the mouth of another, words found in books or heard on TV. Busying ourselves with worldly activities prevents our hearing. Meditation opens the door to all wisdom.

In response to a question about the sex of angels, Gabriel replied,

"[Angels] are perceived as male and female by humankind. Actually, we are neither one. We present ourselves according to . . . who we are dealing with. When I dealt with Daniel, I presented myself as feminine because Daniel was male. When I dealt with Mary or with Beloved Woman I presented myself as male because they are female and there has to be a balance [of energy]." [12]

With all the talks and seminars presented by Gabriel in the twelve years he visited us, he made it clear that only one lesson was brought forth: "We [angels] always have taught only one lesson. Love. But because people are so diverse and have different levels of understanding, we present the same lesson in a thousand different ways so that everybody has a chance to learn it." *How Things Come to Be*, 31.

Gabriel and our Guardian Angels

"The Guardian angels who are with you came to me and said, 'We need some help here. They are wonderful people and we love them dearly, but . . . ' Then I listened to a list and it all came down to pretty much the same thing. You don't realize that every thought you think is going to bring results. Every thought. You think: 'But sometimes I just need to swear in my mind.' Well, be my guest, but be prepared to reap the results. The thing is, Beloveds, that you can cancel out a negative thought with the power of a positive one just as surely as you can do it the other way around." [13]

In my memory is a vivid picture of that night in Albany when Archangel Gabriel gave his farewell message. Two hundred people were in attendance in an auditorium. There is an interesting story about that night. In the same building is the New York State Nurses Association office. A nurse entered the building to attend a lecture and made a turn down the wrong hallway. She sat listening to Gabriel before she realized it was not the room she had sought. But she stayed, and she heard Gabriel's last message.

"We strew your path with all manner of things waiting for you to fall on your face and then we say, 'Ah, there it is, right in front of you.' That is how guardian angels work. They take things there for you to discover, as it were, and learn thereby. They guide you that way. We are never, ever allowed to interfere with your free will. Not even the angels can interfere with your free will. If Beloved Woman were to say to me, 'You cannot enter my body this night,' I could not. Even though I be more powerful than she, I still could not. It is her body." *The Power of Thought*, 26-27

This writer recalls a talk that Gabriel gave one evening in Schenectady, NY. A man approached the microphone and asked Gabriel if we had more than one angel to guide us. I don't recall Gabriel laughing out loud as hard as he did that night. He said something like 'you would drive one angel to distraction!'

"Oh, everyone has many, many angels. You never have just one. You have many angels who assist you in your personal life, many angels who assist you in your business life, angels who assist you with your children, and angels who assist you with everything." *Why we are Here Now*, 32.

From *At This time*, page 6, Gabriel explained the power of the mind:
"Everything that happens upon your earth is the result of the power of the mind . . . I urge you to call upon Saint Michael, for he is a warrior. He can dispel with great power the vibration of war. I also urge you to call upon Raphael, for he is the healer . . . I urge you to call upon Uriel because Uriel has the power to bring about great storms. It is pretty hard to hold a celebration of war if there is a thunderstorm, down pouring rain, lightning flashing all about and everybody is getting drenched!"

Gabriel on his departure

"I will be gone in 1999. I am allowed a certain length of your perceived time in which to come and bring unto you these truths . . . So we come, and we saturate the earth with the vibrations of love and learning . . . and then we allow you time to absorb, and then we withdraw . . . There are other angels who come and minister unto you, but they do not teach as we do. So when I leave, it isn't that you are left with nothing. You're simply left without me and the other eleven who came, some of whom already have left." [14]

Some excerpts from his last lesson in truth:

"It is the night that I leave the earth for 2,000 years . . . My influence will remain and angels who work with me will remain . . . I loved teaching. I loved being with you. I loved bringing you truth and watching you grow, seeing your lights get brighter, seeing your fears dispel, watching you come into your own, as it were. It gave me great joy." [15]

The profound effects of his teachings were explained: "These last twelve years are on the ethers. Every word I have spoken to you, every intent of the lesson that I have brought to you is on the ethers and will remain there always. Just as everything that happened 2,000 years ago is still on the ethers and is still used and learned and benefited from this day in your time." [16]

As Jesus and his message of Love has permeated the Earth, so too will Gabriel's teachings continue to inspire and guide generations to come. At one time Gabriel told us that it takes humanity about 2,000 years to accept a new idea.

"Long after I leave this earth, the words that I have given to you . . . will travel throughout the world. In generations to come . . . that which was done through her by me will still be alive and well upon planet earth. Why? Because that is how we bring the consciousness of humankind up. That is the reason we taught you how to read and write." [17]

Gabriel's One Message

I recall a seminar in the year 1997 when Gabriel said that he came to bring one lesson. Then he said that he could see us all thinking that we spent all that time and money for one lesson when we perceived he had brought many. But his farewell message included the following:
"Beloveds, in my twelve years of your time upon the earth, the one true lesson that I desire greatly for you to know is how beautiful you are and how meaningful your life is . . . the greatest heroes of the world are the simple, everyday people who live their lives trusting God and knowing the goodness that is in them." [18]

Angelic help for humankind

Angels have been around ever since humans have. They help us when we ask, but they cannot ever interfere with our free choice. It is essential to acknowledge their presence, albeit we cannot see them. They unerringly respond to our every prayer and desire.

"Back when we started working with you, when we would appear to you, you would immediately fall down to worship us. You would build an altar right there. It wouldn't matter what we were saying to you. It was, 'shut up and let us build an altar!' So the messages were frequently lost in the appearance. That is why this time we chose not to do any phenomena . . . We would lose what we were teaching you because you would become caught up in the phenomena, just as you used to do." [19]

There has never been a time in history when angels were not present. "We have been with you through great and terrible wars. We have been with you through everything that you have created. We walk beside you in every moment of your pain, and we have ever lifted you up. This is why it says in Scripture, *And He gave the angels charge over them lest they dash their foot against a stone*." [20] (Matt 4:6 and Heb 13:2)

At one time a friend said to me, "Pray for me—you are closer to God." I was stunned. No one is 'closer to God' than anyone else. Gabriel emphasized this: "You think angels are the ones who directly hear the voice of God, and indeed we do because it never occurs to us that we can't. And therefore, we do. It is a part of the way we are. But no less so is it a part of the way you are, because that is how you were created." [21]

Angels can and will help us at every turn. Gabriel said when a prayer is heard, angels do not argue about who is going to respond!
"Now if you ask us, we will gladly show you the causes of your problems. We will gladly assist you . . . And we will gladly assist you in not creating any more." [22]

[Angels] are here all around the earth helping us to let go of our fear. "Fear is a great illusion. Nothing can ever happen to you." [23]

From God's love he created all humans to be healthy, joyous and have abundance. God would not give us anything that is not a blessing. But when we plan a lifetime of stress, pain or fear we choose it to learn a specific lesson. WE choose, not God. Angels serve us in this self-created earthly journey.

"You have angels at your command even as he [Jesus] did. You are the Son of God. The angel world is your servant. Remember that." [24]

Communicating with angels
"Just talk to them. They love to be talked to. They do indeed. When you talk to your angels, it brightens them right up . . . they love to be recognized. They love it. That just fills them with joy. All you have to do is just talk to them. Just say, 'Angels, I love you and I would like you to help me with thus and so.' And you will get all the help that you could possibly want." [25]

I can speak from experience about this, because I have called on angels to help me in many ways: to find a parking spot at a busy restaurant on a busy evening, to find a new home when I planned to move, to indicate what aisle to walk to find a desired item in a store, etc.

Everyone has many angels. There was a time when Gabriel told us in one of his seminars that *each* one of us has 144,000 angels. That number staggers the imagination, but he said they are here to help us with all our requests, from choosing clothes and fixing our hair to choosing a career or employment. "We are only the guiding light. We are not *the* light. Ever listen to God's Voice." [26]

Earth changes

Angels are with us always, and will ever be, until we return to our natural habitat, Heaven. This is essential to remember in the days ahead.
Gabriel explained that major earth changes are coming because Mother Earth is very tired of being treated so badly. It is not necessary to explain the ways in which we have abused her waterways with refuse and chemicals, her face with mining and forest cutting, our genetic engineering of the plants and animals of the earth.

Gabriel compared Mother Earth to an old woman who stands and shakes her apron. Mother Earth will shake herself as a means of cleansing herself. The earth changes are coming as a result of our behavior toward this planet and our very thoughts. Our negative thoughts of fear, anger, violence, and war impact negatively on Mother Earth. Gabriel did not come to alarm us, but rather to tell us that there is nothing to fear. We must be calm in the midst of the seeming chaos, for many will act chaotically and those who know the reason must keep a cool head.

"Most of your profound {earth} changes will begin in your perceived year of 1995 . . . Most of the deep or profound changes will have concluded by the year 2011. From that point on it will be a matter of adjusting to what has already taken place. By the year 2020 civilizations will have settled in once more to a saneness, as they always do after a change. This is why we are upon the earth now teaching you so that you will not all panic!" [27]

Who, if I cried out, would hear me among the angels' hierarchies? and even if one of them pressed me suddenly against his heart: I would be consumed in that overwhelming existence . . . Rainer Maria Rilke

CHAPTER 3

Leaving God Behind

Beyond Darwin

Archangel Gabriel explained to us that there are no 'fallen angels,' and humankind did not 'fall away' from God, except in its consciousness. It is impossible to be separate from God for there is no life anywhere, in any universe, without God.

At various times Archangel Gabriel reminded us of our origin as being at one with God—when we knew God loved us, knew that we loved each other, and knew that we were divine portions of God. Our lives didn't begin upon the earth, Gabriel told us. "When God called you forth into beingness from the Divine Flame of Himself/Herself, He called you forth in the eternalness of His own nature." [1]

The *Encyclopedia of Religion* defines evolution from the standpoint of biology, sociology, anthropology, and metaphysics. "In metaphysics the term is applied to the cosmic process in those philosophies which regard the universe itself as exhibiting a pattern of growth."

Many skeptics, deniers, and cynics remain on earth. They continue to believe that 'seeing is believing.' The lesson we are here to learn is that 'believing is seeing.' Then we will come to believe in life as an eternal experience and 'see' the purpose for life on earth as it relates to our spiritual journey back home to God and Heaven, our natural habitat. "If your life on earth is all, why bother with it? Why bring children into the world? Why plan ahead for coming generations? Fundamentally you know that the I AM of man is in evolution, and must go on." [2]

This truth is precluded by humanity's belief in Darwin's theory of evolution. The theory, as described in *Origin of Species and the Descent of Man,* is appealing because there is a unique correspondence between man and other mammals, such as explained by Darwin: that all the bones in his [man's] skeleton can be compared with corresponding bones in the monkey, bat, or seal. So it is with his muscles, nerves, blood-vessels, and internal viscera. The brain, the most important of all the organs, follows the same law. Darwin reminds us this law was shown by Huxley and other anatomists.

At one of his seminars, Gabriel told us the story about the monkey world being upset when they heard about Darwin's Theory. The head monkey asked for an audience at the Throne of God and received it. He went to the Throne of God and complained that humans were thinking that they had evolved from the specie of monkeys, and they were angry!

Another reason Darwin's theory is appealing is because we have accepted the idea that we are 'separate' from God. "Mankind has always had the picture of two entirely different states of being, separated from each other as by a wall—the "on earth" and "in heaven" idea. That division has been expressed, of course, in all sorts of terminology. But the concept is always the same; in every age, by every race, through every creed." [3]

However, there is a problem with Darwin's theory. It is called "the missing link". This means that there is no one specie that represents the transformation from ape to human. It will never be found because *there is no missing link.*

Some who disagree with Darwin believe that God created everything in seven days. "Everybody thinks God created everything in seven days, and that from then on He didn't make anything new. Not true. When life goes forth, it goes out to become, ever to become more, and more, and more, and expand. Your universe is expanding very rapidly." [4]

At the Scopes trial in 1925, William Jennings Bryant said: "There is no more reason to believe that man descended from an inferior animal than there is to believe that a stately mansion has descended from a small cottage." And in 1964 Disraeli told the Oxford Diocese, "The question is this: Is man an ape or an angel? I, my Lord, am on the side of the angels. I repudiate with abhorrence these new-fangled theories."

Most people come to a time in their lives when they begin to ask the age-old questions about why we are here, and is this life all there is. This usually occurs sometime during young adulthood. "I am sure that . . . you have wondered from time to time what you were doing here and what on earth made you choose to come to such a place of difficulties, challenges, adventures, and so forth. The purpose behind anyone coming onto the earth plane is for you to learn how to recognize the divine self of you, even when that divine self is contained within a limiting, physical body." [5]

In addition, Gabriel reminded us of our true Source: "You came forth from Divine Flame, all of you looking pretty much the same . . . beams of light, glimmering, shining . . . You lived within the . . . wisdom, the love, the joy of having come forth from Divine Flame . . . Yet you never lost your centerdness, the light within you, the beginning part of you." [6]

Beginning of our Descent or Devolution

Eons ago (by earth's calculations), we decided to create from this God-Self of us, something 'different' from the perfection we enjoyed. We began our descent downward away from God—in our consciousness. We were totally unaware of the implications of our decision—completely unaware that we were going to a 'far country' (as the Prodigal Son) from which it would take eons to return. Gabriel said watching us go was the hardest thing the angels ever did, because the angels knew that we had no idea of the ramifications of that decision.

Yet God has provided us with the means to return unto Him. "From God you came forth and at the point of your separation, at the point when you became the spin-off of God, at that connection point there came the Holy Spirit. The Holy Spirit is the bridge, the connecting point between you and God. The Holy Spirit knows the full potential of God, the truth of God, the love of God, the perfection of God, the eternalness of God." [7]

The first stage of our descending or involvement away from God was the idea that we could create something other than the perfection we lived in. So we created a mental plane and we created a mental body for ourselves to abide there. Then we lived in the mental plane. It has two parts: Causal and concrete. The causal plane is where we think in terms of generalization: animals, plants, and birds. The concrete plane is where we think in specific terms: a particular animal, a particular plant, a particular bird. At this stage we still did not have a physical body.

The second stage: We began, from our thoughts, to feel separate from each other, and we created an emotional (astral) plane in which to live, and we created an astral body to reside there. We still did not have a physical body. There are two realms in the astral plane: the higher astral and the lower astral. Which one we enter upon 'death' depends wholly on our attitude, how we live our lives, and our expectations of what life will be like upon our transition.

"For God and His beloved Son do not think differently. And it is the agreement of their thought that makes the Son a co-creator with the Mind Whose Thought created him".[8] As co-creators with God and with our God-given free choice and imagination, we descended further down, in our consciousness. We decided to create a physical planet. It was lush and green and beautiful. It was what we know now as Lemuria. Over time humankind destroyed it Gabriel addressed the issue thusly: "You created other planets . . . you created them out of the knowingness that you were a part of God and with your wondrous gift of creative imagination, of which humankind is the only specie thereof who has it. You forgot that was a gift to you from God, and you used it very unwisely." [9]

Then we created Atlantis. It was another beautiful, lush, and green planet. We destroyed it, also. Gabriel told us that its remnants lie off the East coast of the United States. "The Atlanteans were a very cruel lot. They were extremely intelligent but they had no feelings . . . They had not developed their loving nature at all . . . they became very wise as far as how to do things, but they did not become wise in the spirit. Therefore they caused a lot of suffering. They did a lot of terrible things in the name of science that I would not like to see occur again."[10]

Gabriel always took questions about his lessons; sometimes during the session and sometimes just before the breaks. We broke after an hour and a half or a couple hours of channeling by Gabriel. At the seminars there would be a morning break, a lunch break, an afternoon break, and then final questions before closing. Every seminar and every lecture ended with Gabriel offering a prayer.

At one of his seminars, Gabriel was asked if Atlantis would rise. "As to whether Atlantis rises, probably the ruins, pieces of the ruins thereof, will. But Atlantis full blown completely populated, thank God, no." [11]

Our next creation was the planet Earth. It also was lovely and lush and green. All this creating took millions of years. We did all this creating, as co-creators with God. Regarding our planet, Gabriel said, "She IS a sacred planet. Mother Earth was created in holiness. She has never lost her holiness. She has been violated greatly by humankind's misperceptions, but that too is changing. She is casting off the old, rigid, limited ways. That is why you have earthquakes, tidal waves, and all things that you perceive to be negative. They are not negative." [12]

All the stages of our involution downward into physical form—planet earth and mortal bodies—are expressions of the ethers and their vibrations. Everything vibrates. We learn this in grade school.

> Ethers are the extremely fine vibrations from which come physical form . . . there is a vibratory rate that is spiritual, one that is mental, one that is emotional and then you have the ethers which collect all of the above and bring them down into solid form. So the ethers are the unseen, but very real, very powerful vibratory rates that are just above the physical and they are composed of the vibration from all of the above. The spiritual, the mental, the emotional all vibrate upon the ethers. [13]

We admired the planet Earth and decided to create creatures to populate it. We began with birds and fishes. (Gabriel told us that it took three people to make one bird.) What a variety we created—the bird species alone give us an idea of the breadth and scope of our creative ability, as co-creators with God. The diverse varieties of trees, plants, and fish also exemplify the vast panoply of creation.

Then we decided to create animals: dinosaurs and other creatures. We had great fun watching them cavort about. Then we began to wonder what it was like to be a dinosaur. Have you ever watched a pet and wondered what it would be like to be a cat, or a dog, or a horse? So we decided to take our spirit self into a creature, just to have that experience. Then we withdrew our spirit and returned to the astral plane. This seemed like a lot of fun, so we created more and more creatures and continued the game of entering an animal form and retreating back to the astral plane. As we created a great variety of animals we improved on their agility, the brain size etc., until we made the apes, with opposable thumbs so they could pick up things around them and hang on to branches of the trees.

"The divine energy that is within them [creatures] is God, but the forms that they take were brought forth by people. Now, you are still changing the forms of creatures . . . If you do not believe my words, go to any breeding farm." [14]

All this creating was very enjoyable; and inhabiting the bodies temporarily was also great fun. Then we thought how fine it would be if we created a form of our own. Now this posed a problem. If we were to produce as the animals did, we would have to separate our still-androgynous forms into two separate energies. This is where the two energies of creation took on the names of male and female. Gabriel said that in marriage ceremonies where it states, "What God hath joined together let no man put asunder," relates directly to the time when we separated ourselves into male and female. We continued to inhabit and leave these physical forms at will, until one day we forgot our way home. Thus began our belief in earthly life and the concept of a life-ending experience called "death".

We created the human form, as co-creators with God that we occupy on Earth. As a model, we used the last animal form we had created—the ape.

> When you came to earth to take form you were very undeveloped. You had great long arms and short bodies, very short legs. You were not monkeys but you were just one stone's throw away from that. You had a very short life span. If you lived to age 20 or 25 years of age, you were considered very old, and most of you passed on, through whatever, when you were probably about 14, 15 years old. You proceeded

on like that with very little evolution, very little change for perhaps several thousand years. You just sort of stayed there and didn't go forward. There is an intelligent life that came from another planet, observed earth for quite a length of time, and decided that you needed help. And so it taught you how to make fire. It also artificially inseminated some of the females of the species, to bring up and get away from the four legged, crawling type of thing that you did. [15]

Regarding all this creation, Gabriel assured us, "If you were to go back billions and billions and billions of years, you would find a source of humankind upon the earth. Not earth only but other places in the universe as well." [16]

The many gods spoken of in mythology are explained by Gabriel this way: "A lot of what was thought to be gods back then was simply space people traveling. If you are only evolved to the point where you don't know, don't see in color, and you aren't even sure you are separate from the banana that you are eating, something coming out of the sky that is filled with light will of course make you decide it's a god." [17]

As earthlings we had to survive. The first situation that arose for us was that the animals we had created saw us as a good meal and they chased us and ate us. We made new bodies because we still knew how to create from the God Self of us. We fell off cliffs because we didn't know they were there. We made new bodies. "When you chose to take form, you did it carelessly with little thought of the outcome of that form. When those forms began to be destroyed, you accepted that as a natural outcome. You think it is nature's way. If that were a truth, then why think you that the Master Jesus came to teach eternal life and to prove eternal life?" [18]

So we decided we needed to design a way in which we could inhabit a body without losing it and re-making another, which we then considered very wasteful. We needed a warning system to sound the alarm, so to speak, when a cliff was ahead, or a wild animal came after us. So we created the ego as a warning system. The ego is not part of God. We created it to help us, but over eons we have given the ego more and more power until now it holds a great deal of power over us. Refer to Chapter 4.

As newly created beings in human form, we grunted to communicate, because in physical form we lost our ability to create with mere thought, as we had done in the spirit world. Also, as new earthlings, we had no idea that there was a connection between the sex act and a baby being born. "People in general . . . did not understand the concept of conceiving yet. They had no idea how a child was conceived within the woman. For a long time, they believed it was the favor of the Gods . . . It wasn't until probably abut five thousand years ago that the people woke up to the fact that the male had to have contact with the female for there to be a birthing." [19] Eventually we figured out that the sex act was the cause of the tiny new creatures coming forth. Families came into being and tribes formed, then villages etc. The rest of the story of humans joining into groups is history.

"Back about thirty to fifty thousand years ago your society was predominately female and then it was at peace. This is a grand truth. Whenever the Goddess rather than the God is worshipped, there is no war. Why? Because the female energy of the worshipping of the Goddess is supportive, nurturing, loving, birthing. There is no aspect of the female that has to dominate excepting when she is defending her territory, her home, her children, her young, or when she perceives herself to be threatened in some way." [20]

The male dominant society, on the other hand, is explained by Gabriel: "Always man has been interested in conquering: conquering other people, other countries, outer space, and never has he turned inward to learn of himself. In the Tao Te Ching, a sacred book of the Orient, there is a statement, 'To rule the lives of others takes intelligence. To rule the life of oneself takes wisdom. To know how other people think takes concentration. To know how the self thinks takes surrender.' Those words are very wise." [21]

One could almost sense a feeling of frustration when Gabriel told us, "I, and others too, have been with you for more centuries of your perceived time than you can comprehend. We have watched you play this little game over and over. Sometimes masses of you get together and create great holocausts . . . We have watched you go from planet to planet destroying them as you left. Now you have come to Earth." [22]

It is a common belief that when Jesus came to earth people were spiritual because they followed him, listened to him, and saw the miracles he performed. "The consciousness of human kind upon the earth 2,000 years ago was very dull. It was not at all awakened. It was very slow, sluggish, and very much grounded in the earth. The people concerned themselves with camels and sheep, with whose wives were where, and so forth. They gave very little actual thought to spirituality. I know that if you were to read your Scriptures, it would appear that they were very spiritual minded, that they constantly sought to find God. Well, they didn't." [23]

The story of the Garden of Eden is an allegory. It represents the 'sleep' of humanity, for it is asleep to its own divinity. Gabriel and *A Course in Miracles* both draw our attention to the fact that whereas Adam slept in the Garden, nowhere in Scripture does it say he woke up. God awaits our awakening to our God Self, dormant but eternally existent within each of us. "The sleep of Adam in the Garden becomes a symbol of the human condition on earth. The alien man or woman waits for the call, amid the noise of the world, to wake and to return." [24]

Now we are destroying the earth, with the pollution of water and the air, with clear-cutting of the forests, with total disregard for creatures. The Bible speaks of man having 'dominion' over the animals. We have taken this to mean we can manipulate them by producing all kinds of hybrids, like we do with the plants and creatures. Gabriel explained that "dominion" meant we should live in harmony with all life. Indigenous peoples have always respected Mother Earth and all life within it. Mother Earth provides food and healing herbs for all of our needs. We did a good job of creating a nurturing planet that we might survive in physical form, but we have misused our power in genetically engineering plants and creatures at will.

Humankind has engaged in war after war and this is another example of unwise choices we have made as earthlings. "Because war has been upon your earth for such a long time, the vibration of it is a very strong one and very difficult to completely eradicate. Until all hearts turn to love and brotherhood, the vibration of war will be very easy to resurrect and bring back to life. And this cannot happen, beloveds. Trust me; it cannot be again." [25]

Most people profess to desire peace on earth. Most people live honestly, abide by some moral principles, and care for their families. But Gabriel said, "There are many upon your earth who would love to see a war come for lots of reasons. For one, while that war is going on, they can do their dastardly deeds without being noticed. The second thing is that everybody gets rich when there is war . . . look at your world financiers. They are the ones behind a lot of your wars. Whenever their finances begin to get a little questionable, they find a war somewhere." [26]

Overall, Gabriel gave us words of comfort and assurance that no matter how terrible circumstances seem to be, no matter how far down the scale humanity has slid, there is hope for tomorrow and hope for a return to Heaven, our natural habitat. But the journey back is more complex than simply awakening to our true, spirit selves and going back to God. As explained earlier in this chapter we made a decision to 'leave God' by creating other realms. We 'dropped down,' so to speak—or more specifically we slowed the rate of vibration to a mental plane, then an astral plane, then the physical plane of Earth. In our homeward journey back to God each one of these realms must be redeemed. To 'redeem' is to get back, to win back, and to restore, to release from captivity. The first realm to be redeemed is the earthly realm; the realm of physical form. The problem with moving up through the realms in rapid sequence is that we have gotten stuck in the wheel of karma. We believe that we must return again and again to earth to 'make things right.' Each time we 'die' and go to the astral plane we review our earthly existence and determine what lessons we learned and what lessons we desired to learn but did not. Then we plan another visit to earth to try again the unlearned lessons.

This is why the teachings of Archangel Gabriel and others is so appropriate at this time. Forgiveness and love are the lessons we must learn, and we must learn them at this level of vibration, physical form, so that we can then move on up to the next realm, and the next etc.

Reincarnation
Gabriel once said to the audience, "You have only one life." The cringing fear of the group was palpable. Then he said that it is the life of our Spirit, created by God in the beginning and as eternal as God, but that we continue to choose many earthly experiences, or incarnations. Gabriel said that we

have come to earth so many times that we have *met everyone else now living on the planet.* Clearly, this would entail hundreds if not thousands of lifetimes. When queried about reincarnation in the Bible, Gabriel told us that all references to reincarnation in Scripture were purged by the early church fathers. It seems they missed a few, such as:

1. Psalm 90: *Thou turnest Man to destruction, and sayest, 'Return, ye Children of Men.'*

2. Proverbs 8:22-31: *The Lord possessed me in the beginning of His way, before His works of old. I was set up from everlasting, from the beginning, or ever the earth was. When there were no depths, I was brought forth . . . when He prepared the Heavens, I was there . . . When he appointed the foundations of the earth, then was I by Him, as one brought up with Him. And I was daily His delight, rejoicing always before him, rejoicing in the habitable part of His earth. And my delights were with the Sons of Men.*

3. Matthew 16:13: *When Jesus came into the coasts of Caesarea Phillipi, he asked His disciples, saying, 'Whom do men say that I, the Son of Man, am?' And they said, 'Some say that Thou art John the Baptist, some Elias; and others, Jeremias, or one of the Prophets'*

4. Luke 9:7-8: *Herod the tetrarch heard of all that was done by (Jesus); and he was perplexed, because it was said of some that John was risen from the dead; and of some that Elias had appeared; and of others that one of the old prophets was risen again. And Herod said, 'John have I beheaded, but who is this of whom I hear such things?'*

In *The Way of the Essenes*, p. 39, a disciple of Christ describes the Way of the Cross, and adds: "For two thousand years now, my soul has been keeping the secret of these images, for two thousand years these sentences have been waiting, longing for expression at the tip of a pen, little chains of pointless words that could never really tell . . ."

It is possible for individuals to become so entranced with the idea of reincarnation that they begin a life journey seeking to know what their past lives were. Gabriel made it clear that it really doesn't matter what our previous lives consisted of, because today we are the accumulation of all past experiences. He told us that we all were murderers, we all were saints, and we all were homosexuals.

This current life is the one to focus on, and learn its lessons. The adage 'you reap what you sow' is a truism and it is important to realize that concept, not only in relation to this lifetime, but as an application to all of one's lifetimes. We wonder how bad things can happen to good people. First, there are no 'good' and 'bad' people. Secondly, we cannot know what their previous lifetimes consisted of, what lessons they chose this time around, or why they chose them.

A Course in Miracles states: "In everything be led by Him, and do not reconsider. Trust Him to answer quickly, surely, and with Love for everyone who will be touched in any way by the decision. And everyone will be. Would you take unto yourself the sole responsibility for deciding what can bring only good to everyone? Would you know this? "[27]

Sometimes groups of people will participate in group karma, returning as a group for chosen reasons. *Many Mansions* by Cerminara mentions this.

"Many people were given a similar historical background; in fact, the outline of people's past lives seemed almost to fall into a pattern. One common sequence was: Atlantis, Egypt, Rome, France in the time of Louis XIV, XV or XVI, and the American Civil War. There were variations, of course—including China, India, Cambodia, Peru, Norseland, Africa, Central America, Sicily, Spain, Japan and other places; but the majority of readings followed the same historic lines." [28]

Gabriel mentioned that many people gather to bring about a 'holocaust' and the same individuals who are the victims in one become the perpetrators in the next. *Edgar Cayce on Reincarnation* includes a chapter on group karma in which groups of people who have interacted in a past era or several eras return again and again to interact with each other until they learn to forgive and love one another. In *Past Lives, Future Loves*, Dick Sutphen states: "Reincarnation is the cycle of rebirth on the earth plane, and we will continue to be born over and over again until we evolve beyond the need of earthly experiences. Karma . . . is a belief system . . . It states that we and we alone are responsible for everything that happens to us. We created our circumstances by what we did in the past and how we live our present life will dictate our future." [29]

Evolution is the process of returning to our Source. The journey takes eons of time, in human terms. The soul holds the memory of our beginning, when we all were at one with God. When our journey is on the outward swing we find a religion. But the religion tells us that God is out there and we are down here, and never the twain shall meet. We are not, nor ever have been, separate from God. When we begin a conscious homeward journey we turn within. We seek within and we find within. We find that divine spark that first propelled us outward and is now calling us homeward.

There is a tendency in the East to believe in reincarnation which is not shared in the West. "If the reader should question why reincarnation seems to thrive more in the Oriental and primitive societies, let him compare the permissive and tolerant upbringing of, say, a Tlingit Indian child with a child born in U.S Colonial Salem, possessing an equal aptitude for recalling its previous life. This would (for the latter) be instantly labeled as the work of the devil and zealously exorcized. Some of the women who were hanged were hardly more than children." [30]

A major problem with acceptance of reincarnation is the many misconceptions that surround it. One misconception is that there can be a change in species. This is not so. Gabriel told us that reincarnation is *always* specie specific. Dogs are always dogs, snakes are always snakes, and humans are always humans. Likewise, angels are always angels. Reincarnation is an exercise we have developed to learn various lessons. Karma is a distortion of the basic law of cause and effect. The immutable law of cause and effect is that there must be a balance. Karma is belief that we have been guilty of something and must suffer for it; that others are guilty of harming us and they must 'pay for it.' Karma is man-made. Gabriel explained that all guilt we perceive—all guilt—is sourced in our belief that we 'left God,' and He will never take us back. We are guilty of nothing; we have merely forgotten our origin and our soul longs to return to it. No one ever harms us without our permission and we never harm anyone without theirs. See chapter 6.

On January 2, 1994, Gabriel gave an overview of the cyclic journey of humanity over eons:

> Man evolves upward. He learns to walk upright . . . to form words . . . to capture these words upon your scrolls, upon your papers . . . to send these sounds and these words through the air where they might be heard and seen by others miles away. And then he learns to send his messages out into the universe. And at that point, man becomes arrogant, wasteful, and feels he does not need a Divine Source. At that point man begins again. He begins to swing through the trees . . . eating fruits . . . making fire. He begins learning that he is a separate entity from the saber toothed tiger. And he begins again to learn a language, to create. He works his way up into the universe, and he thinks again he does not need another source. And man begins again!
>
> Now, beloveds, you are on the brink. [31]

Gabriel often referred to Scripture, and regarding reincarnation he said this: "It tells you in Scripture, if you were to paraphrase it, through Adam the wheel of karma was begun and through Jesus Christ the wheel of karma was obliterated." [32]

We do not recall past lifetimes and that is likely a blessing. What we are now is the important time on earth. Seeking experiences of my past incarnations came in the form of mere curiosity, but several have been told to me, without me being hypnotized. It seems appropriate to share the past lifetimes that I incarnated upon the earth, as described by psychics and mediums through my adult years. In none of these cases did I personally, consciously 'relive' the time described. Some of those described below are on cassette tape, but some brief portions are given here:

In ancient Greece or Rome I was the wife of a man who 'made the laws,' and died of grief when he was slain by an opponent. Details of the murder were described by the medium.

In Ireland, prior to the invention of spittoons, I was the wife of a tavern owner and cussed as I scrubbed the floors of the tavern. I had two young children and I died of a burst appendix as a young mother.

In France, near Paris, I lived with an aunt and grandmother until my father came to take me to Paris to live with my 'other grandmother' to be brought up in wealth. My husband was killed by a horse and I returned to find that my grandmother had passed and I took my aunt back to Paris to live.

As a two-year old I accompanied my parents to America so that my father could be a missionary in this new land. As a teenager I would write down my father's sermons as he paced, and received them intuitively. I must have had a great admiration for my father in that lifetime to the point that I desired to emulate him. As it turned out, I became an ordained minister in this lifetime, and soon became an inspired speaker.

I was a schoolteacher in Missouri, and later went down the Mississippi River to live with a sister there, and married there.

Another medium told me there was a lifetime which ended when a snake wrapped itself around me and suffocated me.

At one time I was a Native American chief [male], and one of my current daughters was my daughter then. She was greatly loved and admired by the tribe.

The lifetime described to me by Archangel Gabriel is the one I am most certain of. And it was the one most difficult to hear. Gabriel did not give personal 'readings' because he reminded us that we have psychics and mediums for that purpose. And prior to all seminars we were advised not to ask personal questions. But one night when Gabriel presented a question and answer session (occasionally he would come to answer any questions we might have about his teachings, but he did not give a talk on those evenings), Gabriel told us that the life we are living now is based on an issue from a past life. One of the women in the audience approached the microphone and said, "Will you tell me what issue I am working on and from what past life?" Gabriel responded with, "Beloved woman, if I were to tell you, I will have to tell everyone else in the room." To a person we all (15 or 20 present) called out, "Yes, tell us".

So Gabriel told Joe to turn off the mike, knowing that what he was about to relate was personal and private and should not be included in future recordings or writings of his lessons.

When he came to me he said that I was Queen Mary, the one known as Bloody Mary. I cringed. As an active alcoholic a bloody Mary was one of my favorite drinks. He said I was also known as the Queen of the Guillotine. It was a terrible thing to hear, and substantiated the idea 'be careful what you ask for.' Days later I sought information about Bloody Mary, and learned that she was the Queen of England from 1553-1558. I also queried my son who is interested in history and asked him what he knew about the queen known as Bloody Mary. He said, "She sent 167 people to the guillotine, including women and children. Why?" Unwilling to tell him what Gabriel said I merely responded, "I just wondered."

I don't know if Robert Frost believed in reincarnation, but in his poem *Birches,* he writes:

"I'd like to get away from earth awhile
And then come back to it and begin over."

What we are today is what is important, not our past lives, although some people hotly pursue knowledge about their past experiences on earth. Today each of us is the culmination of all that we have ever been. We have all learned many lessons and we all need to learn more lessons. But there is only one lesson, Gabriel told us, that he came to give us: that we are all children of God and made in His Image. We must wake up to that fact and live life from the Lord God of our Being, expressing as God's children all his attributes of love, harmony, peace, and joy. That is when we will ascend—take our physical bodies with us to return to Heaven and stay there; not return again on the karmic wheel. In 1994, at Easter time, the Master Jesus addressed those of us in his audience, who had come to hear him speak:

> . . . I would address the issue of the resurrection. Not from the
> stand point of what took place on your planet two thousand

years ago, because I did that last time. This time I would address the issue of the resurrection concerning you. For it is that which you are journeying toward and that which moment by moment of your lives is unfolding for you.

Resurrection is something that has always been greatly misunderstood. It is something that is thought of as happening to a great savior, a great teacher and not to ordinary people. It is also thought to happen of a suddenness, and it does not happen of a suddenness. It happens over lifetime after lifetime, as you perceive them to be. From the time that you first turned yourselves around in your downward journey away from the consciousness of God and began your upward journey into the knowingness that you are; from the time that you decided that you had gone far enough away from your awareness of your own divine flame and decided that you would return home to that state of consciousness which you were created in; from that moment your resurrection began.[33]

Emmanuel's Book provides us with an overview of our journey away from and back to God, in poetry form:

Who would leave the Oneness
If not to serve that Oneness through the leaving?
As you have roamed through centuries of unknowns,
always moving into the next moment of nothingness
to create light,
you have fragmented from this journey
and have forgotten who you are
and why you have come.
And in the forgetting
you have taken on human personality
and gone to the particular
and in that particular
you find yourself now seemingly disconnected
from the Source,
reaching to return
through agonizing slowness,
back to the Oneness again.[34]

CHAPTER 4

So Much More

Beyond the Physical Body

This Age of Spirituality upon us is the time when we are ready to hear the wisdom of the ages, or Archangel Gabriel would not have come to educate us. We are reminded of the phrase in Scripture: . . . *for there is nothing covered, that shall not be revealed and hid, and that shall not be made known.*[1]

Also, in Paul's first letter to the Corinthians he tells them: *Therefore judge nothing before the time, until the Lord come, who both will bring to light the hidden things of darkness, and will make manifest the counsels of the hearts, and then shall every man have praise of God.*[2]

We have become accustomed to believing that our physical body is all there is, except for those of us who also believe we have another, finer self that is called spirit, or conscience or something else. Archangel Gabriel included in his teachings all the unseen aspects of humankind. One of these aspects is the energy centers, called chakras. Also we have subtle bodies such as the etheric, the astral, and the mental bodies. These aspects are true but largely unknown or named but not fully understood. We also have the following aspects: the mind, the ego, the soul, the spirit and the personality. An abbreviated explanation of all these attributes is presented to show the complexity and magnificence of ourselves as children of God. The aura is also described.

Gabriel told us: " . . . As a human being you contain millions of units of energy . . . units of energy that produce the growth of your hair, units of energy that produce the circulatory system, units of energy that produce your breathing, the growth of your bones, the condition of your innards, and so on. And within those units of vibrations are even more vibrations. Combined with and interwoven into all of that would be the vibratory rate of how you think . . . how you feel, what your emotions are." [3]

Prana

The word 'prana' means to breathe forth. "'Prana' is a Sanskrit word, derived from pra (forth), and an (to breathe, move, live) . . . the word 'prana' has been used for the Supreme Self, the energy of the One, the Life of the Logos. Hence, Life on each plane may be spoken of as the Prana of the plane, Prana becoming the life-breath in every creature . . ."[4]

In the readings of Edgar Cayce one can find the chakras mentioned, as well as prana energy. "The primary premise of the Edgar Cayce readings is the oneness of all force. The One Force is the Spirit of God and all that we know or experience is a manifestation of that force." [5]

The interconnectedness of the physical, mental, and emotional bodies is explained by Edgar Cayce:

"The principal of oneness requires that the activities of the spiritual body and the mental body be reflected in the physical body. Thus, at the level of the physical body, conscious processes are experienced through the cerebrospinal (sensory) system; at the level of the mental body through the autonomic nervous system; and at the level of the spiritual body through the endocrine system." [6]

Endocrine Glands and the Chakras

There are seven endocrine glands in the human body. Each has a related chakra (energy center). Endocrine (ductless) glands excrete hormones directly into the blood stream. Each hormone has its distinct function. The word hormone means 'to arouse activity.' The reader is directed to a biology text for more information about these glands. The chakras are not visible to the human eye, but have been identified for centuries as the body's energy centers. They play a very important part in our spiritual development

> The system most capable of bringing about the proper balance of all the atoms in the body is the endocrine system.

When quickened, attuned, and aligned, and working in accord with one another under the direction of the higher centers, especially the pituitary, these glands may send out hormonal messages to all the cells of the body, awakening and instructing them in their proper functioning. In turn, the cells may be responsive to these instructions for healing in such a way as to affect all the molecules and atoms within each cell.[7]

The System of Chakras
The word 'chakra' means wheel. Each chakra has spokes like a wheel and many colors weave in and out of the spokes as they whirl around, but each chakra has a predominant color. The chakras are funnel-shaped discs located in the spine of the etheric body and are points of contact at which the prana vitality force flows. The large end of the funnel receives the energy flow, where it whirls around and enters the spine from the small end of the funnel.

The chakras are about a quarter of an inch outside the skin of the body. In a new-born baby they are tiny, hard little circles, barely moving & faintly glowing. When they remain undeveloped they move sluggishly and glow dully. In developed people . . . The chakras glow & pulsate, blazing with blinding brilliance like miniature suns. They vary in size from about two inches in diameter to about six inches. Each chakra has a certain number of spokes. The root chakra has four spokes and the seventh chakra, at the top of the head, consists of 960 spokes. The chakras have two functions:

1. Absorb and distribute prana (vital life energy) from the astral to the physical body.
2. Bring from the astral to the physical a conscious memory of astral experiences. (i.e., we dream on the astral level; when we awaken we recall the dream).

The seven chakras
The name and location of the seven chakras:

1. Root (base of spine)
2. Navel

3. Spleen
4. Heart
5. Throat
6. Third eye (between the eyebrows)
7. Crown (top of the head)

The First Chakra: The Root Chakra

This 'base' chakra is located at the base of the spine and is defined as the chakra which governs understanding of the physical dimension. It is the energy center through which one experiences 'fight or flight.' It contains four spokes and its primary color is red. Physically, it is out-pictured as the adrenal gland, which governs the kidneys and the spinal column. The adrenaline it produces gives the physical body extra strength in emergencies. There is the story of a woman who lifted an automobile which had fallen on her child. A lot of adrenaline was obviously required to accomplish this.

The Second Chakra: The Spleen Chakra

This chakra is located in the sexual organs (ovaries in women, testes in men) and is the chakra of creativity. It governs attitudes in relationships, sex, and reproduction. It dispenses the vitality which comes from the sun. This vitality is poured out from six spokes. The colors which are radiant and sun like are: red, orange, yellow, green, blue, and violet. Each one represents a different quality from the sun which is used in various ways throughout the body. The hub is pink, which is an elevated red representing the physical vitality touched with a spiritual awareness. This is true only of those people who have become awakened to their spiritual selves. For those who have little or no idea of the spiritual aspects of themselves, this color is very dull, being almost gray, tinged with pink here and there. The primary color of this chakra is orange.

The Third Chakra: The Navel Chakra

This chakra is located behind the solar plexus (sun network) and has ten spokes, each with a different radiation governing feelings and emotions. The solar plexus is the receiving station of all psychic influences and the emitting station of all physical phenomena (sight, hearing etc.). The colors are of several shades of red (emotions) with large amounts of green (healing, love of nature) throughout. Physically it externalizes as the pancreas, which governs the action of the liver, spleen, stomach, gall bladder, and aspects of the nervous system. It is the clearinghouse for emotional sensitivities and issues of personal power. Yellow is its primary color.

The Fourth Chakra: The Heart Chakra

This chakra contains twelve spokes. It is the center (I'm sure it comes as no surprise) through which we feel love. The related endocrine gland is the thymus gland, which governs the heart, blood, and circulatory system, and influences the immune system and the endocrine system. Its color is green. One might wonder why the heart chakra is green. At one time Gabriel told us that "healing and love are the same." Green is the healing color.

The Fifth Chakra: The Throat Chakra

This chakra contains 16 spokes. It is the center of expression, communication, and judgment. It is the power chakra and the power of the spoken word is very potent. Anyone who has ever met up with a salesperson (and who hasn't) knows how the spoken word can be made to influence another, sometimes even against all logic to the contrary. An extreme negative example of a charismatic person is Hitler. He used—rather misused—the power of the spoken word by influencing others to perform in a negative way. At the other end of the spectrum, an example would be the U.S. President Franklin D. Roosevelt. He had a very charismatic personality, but he influenced positively millions of Americans, by encouraging them and giving them hope when they were suffering through the Great Depression. This chakra balances spiritual growth. The related endocrine glands are the thyroid and parathyroid, which govern the lungs, vocal cords, bronchial apparatus, and metabolism. Its color is blue.

Interestingly enough, Gabriel commented at one time on the relationship of this chakra to the ego:

"It is at this chakra that the ego . . . does its greatest damage. It is there that it closes off your power center. It is there that the ego gets a stranglehold on your creative ability and instead of allowing the full flowing of it, allows little droplets to come through from time to time. Have you ever noticed that when you are in your greatest fear, your throat gets very tight? That it is almost impossible to swallow?" [8]

The Sixth Chakra: The Brow Chakra
This chakra is located in the center of the forehead. It contains 96 spokes and is known by many as the 'third eye.' In the booklet *Star of Bethlehem* (12/5/93) we find Archangel Gabriel saying, "The phenomenon that is known as the Star of Bethlehem also is symbolic of that star which is within you . . . The star in the sky was a star, yes. But that which is within you is not a star. It is a state of consciousness. It is a point of awareness. Its location is between your eyebrows. You call that your 'third eye,' but it resonates to the same vibratory rate as what the Star of Bethlehem did." [9] Through this center we consider our spiritual nature. Spiritually it represents a combining of all forces for the fulfillment of spiritual man. It is the harmonizer of the spiritual body, bringing into focus man's true potential and giving meaning to his life. The related endocrine gland is the pituitary gland, which governs the lower brain and nervous system, ears, nose, and the left eye, the eye of personality. It is located in the brain. It is the master gland of internal secretion. It is the pituitary that causes the other glands to respond to a given need. 'Pituitary' comes from the fact that it secretes pituita or phlegm (mucous). Its color is violet.

"Becoming aware and consciously using this center within you is very important in the days to come and this day in your age right now. The breaking of so many things upon your earth is taking place now . . . Look at your own continent . . . The old systems are breaking. New ones are coming in. As these change, you can either be a part of them and go with them, or you can perceive that there is a lot of turmoil, a lot of unhappiness." [10]

The Seventh Chakra: The Crown Chakra
This chakra is located at the top of the head and contains 960 spokes. Books in India refer to it as 'the thousand-petalled lotus' and it could in fact contain 1,000 spokes, since it vibrates so fast that only the most discriminating psychic could begin to count. It differs from the other chakras in that its center is a whirlpool of purest white with a gleaming golden center. This center itself has 12 spokes. Through this chakra one may ultimately reach the feeling of integration with God: the At-one-ment. Needless to say, it is the last chakra to be developed. The Bible refers to it as the golden crown. [11]

Pictures of Jesus often show a brilliant light above his head; a halo.

The related gland is the pineal gland, which governs the upper brain and right eye. Its color is white. No wonder it baffles the scientific community. From a book published in 1982, The Brain, I quote: "Projecting down above the back of the brainstem, the pinecone-shaped pineal gland poses an enigma. People once considered it a vestigial third eye. Now, research suggests rather a light-sensitive clock affecting sleep and sex glands." [12]

Keep in mind that focusing on energizing one chakra in particular is not advised. Archangel Gabriel reminded us that this is not beneficial and said, " . . . to concentrate on one [chakra] without the full knowledge of it can be a little unsettling because you can throw yourself out of balance . . ." As we develop spiritually, through our thinking & behavior, our prayers & meditation, our attitudes and understanding, our chakras become more activated automatically." [13]

The chakras in meditation

> The physiology of meditation involves all of these systems—physical, mental, and spiritual—and is related to a hierarchical direction of the flow of energy from God into the earth through us. The reason we must be still and quiet is so that the sensory motor system related to our muscles and senses will not rule the flow of the process. If our body is the primary focal point of consciousness, then that will work against any directing force which may come from within. If we can get the senses and muscles to be quiet, then we can go deeper to the autonomic or mental level. There we still the thoughts, the heart beat, the respiratory rate. Then our purposes and ideals awaken the spiritual center in the endocrine system . . . [14]

The subtle bodies

Each of our subtle bodies became the form we used to exist on each level, or realm, in which we resided. When we 'left' God we developed a lower and lower rate of vibration. From spirit to mental, from mental to emotional (astral), and from emotional to physical form—the earth. The earth has the lowest of vibrational rates in the all of creation. In that sense, we have nowhere to go but up! Each realm requires redemption. These forms will continue to exist until we no longer have need of them. That time will come when we are fully, consciously aware of our oneness with God. The flow of energy from God through us, as His beloved children, as well as the origin of our fears, is explained by Gabriel:

"Now that energy [from that divine center of you] then goes into the mental body, and it becomes a thought, a state of awareness, a consciousness. It becomes your reality. In that mental body, it is quite safe. Nothing attacks it there. It isn't until it comes down . . . into your feeling nature, into your emotional body that you run into trouble. Because at that point is where fear comes in . . . your ego dwells . . . in your emotional body . . . it is alive and well and dwelling in the emotional body." [15]

Our subtle bodies do not suddenly exist because we have become aware of them. The subtle bodies have been recognized for centuries:

"We look at it and we do not see it;
Its name is The Invisible.
We listen to it and we do not hear it;
Its name is The Inaudible.
We touch it and do not find it;
Its name is The Subtle . . ." [16]

In addition to our physical form, we consist of four subtle bodies—bodies which our moral eyes cannot discern. They are the etheric, the astral (emotional), the mental and the spiritual bodies. These bodies were confirmed by Archangel Gabriel and have been noted in various publications in recent years.

The etheric body
The etheric body is an unseen band around the entire physical form. It is sometimes called 'the etheric double,' since it duplicates the body in all aspects. The sensations of touch, pain, pleasure etc the etheric body transmits this information to the astral body and on up to the mental body. In the same way when we have an idea or an inspiration, it is the

etheric which transmits this information to the physical brain. Thus, the etheric body acts as a two-way street. If an organ or limb is removed from the physical, its etheric counterpart remains intact. It is for this reason that amputees often complain of pain in a limb which has been removed, or an extracted tooth still hurts.

If the etheric body is forced away from the physical body by unnatural unconsciousness, such as a blow to the head or being anesthetized, it will wrap itself about the astral body and cling there until it is drawn back to the physical. As it is clinging to the astral, it dulls the consciousness of the astral body and so the person, when awakened, will not remember anything that happened. Also, it is the etheric body on which an operation is performed in psychic surgery. This explains the absence or paucity of blood in the procedure.

"In recent years there have been increasing reports of 'healers,' many of them in the Philippine Islands, who claim the phenomenal ability to perform psychic surgery. These practitioners claim that the human body is opened for surgery without the use of instruments; only bare hands of the healer touch the patient. The psychic surgeon uses no anesthetic. The patient remains fully conscious but feels no pain." *Psychic Surgery*, the book's jacket.

The astral body

This subtle body lies outside the etheric body and does not duplicate the physical form. It is the body of emotions. There is a difference between emotions and feelings. Spirituality is a feeling; love is a feeling. If they could be diagrammed, feelings would appear like a wavy pattern of up and down, like a gently rolling ocean. Emotions are the extremes of feelings. If they could be diagrammed, they would be seen as sharp variations, peaking and dropping severely to a nadir point. Humans are feeling creatures but we have a choice whether to acknowledge our feelings and express them, or let our emotions run rampant without control.

The astral body is part of our makeup while we are on the earth. When we transition to the astral plane, after 'death,' we leave the physical form behind and continue on with our spirit now expressed in the astral body. The astral plane is the plane of emotions and instant gratification. Upon thinking of something it suddenly appears. The astral plane holds some mesmerized and they stay there for a long time, before returning to earth to learn more lessons. The astral plane is not Heaven but from earth it is the only heaven we can know. There are other realms to attain before we find ourselves once more at one with God. All realms must be redeemed. Eventually we will attain to the "seventh Heaven".

The mental body
The mental body is oval in shape but not evenly distributed throughout the oval. The greater part of it is within the physical and especially in and around the head. The mental body consists of two distinct parts: the high mental body which is pure intellect. It deals with particulars, such as a particular car, house, book, or chair etc. and the causal body, which deals with abstract thoughts, such as houses in general, cars in general.

The particles of the mental body are in ceaseless motion, yet these particles form a kind of loose organization. There are in it certain striations which divide it more or less irregularly into segments; each of these corresponds to a certain department of the physical brain, so that every type of thought should function through its duly assigned portion. The mental body is as yet so imperfectly developed in the ordinary person that there are many in who a great number of special departments are not yet in activity. That is why some people have a head for mathematics and others are unable to perform a simple mathematical equation. It is why some people can understand and enjoy music while others do not know one tune from another. Present day psychologists have some insight into this when they say that we use only about ten percent of our brain.

Good thoughts tend to produce a finer vibration and these will float to the upper portion of the mental body, while negative thoughts will be drawn downward toward the lower part of the oval. The mental body is very powerful. Placebo medications work because our mental attitude is that we have taken medicine and we will feel better. Placebo surgery has been performed—by nicking the skin—and fifty percent of those so treated wanted more surgery! Biofeedback is another example of the power of the mental body.

The spiritual body

This body has been referred to as the Higher Self, the Divine Self, or the Spirit Self. The spirit of us is the eternal Self which is an individualized portion of God, with no beginning or end. The spiritual body wears the bodies of the mental, astral, etheric, and physical as we wear our clothing. The spirit is perfect in every way; divine and in tune with God at all times. Our other bodies allow us to experience life and sensations of different kinds on the lower plane. However, we can turn anytime to the spiritual body and ask it to manifest itself in our thinking and feeling aspects. The spiritual body will respond to the extent that we are willing to quiet the other bodies and allow it to 'shine through.' This takes some effort on our part, since we are more used to using the other bodies. Each time we 'will to do the will of God,' we are calling on our spiritual selves to manifest in any given situation. It will never lead us into any action which is not wholesome or holy. It can be trusted without exception. The key is to practice the stilling of the other bodies and allowing the spiritual free rein. This takes some practice and the best practice is meditation. When the spiritual body has free rein in our consciousness, it guides us by intuition. Intuition is the Voice of God speaking to us. One may call it a 'gut hunch,' sudden idea, a revelatory thought. It seems to come from nowhere and yet we know it is truth coming to us.

Although the spiritual body is beyond our physical eyesight, it has been described as a beam of pulsating energy whose brilliance is so great that it would blind the physical senses. There were times when Archangel Gabriel, as a person approached the microphone to ask him a question, would address the person as 'beloved light.' The outer bodies dilute and dull the glory of the spiritual body until the time when the upper planes come into our awareness.

Our willingness or unwillingness to seek guidance from the spiritual body is described in *A Course in Miracles:*

"Who hangs an empty frame upon a wall and stands before it, deep in reverence, as if a masterpiece were there to see?. The masterpiece that God has set within this frame is all there is to see. The body holds it for a while, without obscuring it in any way. Yet what God has created needs no frame, for what He has created He supports and frames within Himself.

His masterpiece He offers you to see. And would you rather see the frame instead of this? And see the picture not at all? [17]

The aura
There is an energy that surrounds every living thing. It is called the aura. The term has become so well accepted that it is found in many crossword puzzles. Trained eyes can see the aura. Flowers, creatures, humans all have an aura. In humans it is egg-shaped and completely surrounds the individual for a distance of two or three feet. It is said that Jesus' aura extended hundreds of feet.

The aura is thickest near the body and so is most visible there. It is the aura's energy that we can feel when we are near others, and this explains why, without reason; that we like or dislike a person upon meeting them for the first time.

Although the aura is colorless, it is flooded with every color of the spectrum as it reflects our mental attitude and emotional state. The aura changes shape as well as color. A calm, peaceful feeling of well being and love will leave the aura in its egg shape with lovely hues of blue, green, pink and various shades of pastel beauty. However, thoughts of anger, hatred, envy, or any unkindness will change the aura in a fraction of a second to a raging, fiery inferno of leaping flames shooting out in all directions and sending startling vibrations out into the ethers. Gabriel once told us that if we could see our aura as it appears when we are angry we would never want to be angry again.

Our aura can be affected by others if we are not careful. When we are around people who are ill or depressed they 'draw on us.' This means that without their conscious awareness—or ours—they pull our energy to them for healing. This explains why we feel depleted after visiting someone who is ill. We can avoid this by consciously pulling our aura in closer to the body to conserve energy. Simply say, "I surround myself with the pure white light of protection. Keep from my aura any negative vibrations I come in contact with, and bless the other person."

The thoughts we have affect our aura, our attitude, and our experiences. There was an interesting scene in a television show on November 21,

2000, called "St. Elsewhere". One character said to another, referring to the dangers of rape, "I have a calm aura, and I don't invite being a victim".

Care of the aura is important, as well as awareness of it. We can cleanse the aura as we take a shower, just by desiring it in our thinking.

"The moment that you recognize that you are in [a negative] frame of mind, that is the moment for you to . . . take a moment and you cleanse your aura. You picture your aura flooded with white light. You invite your guardian angel to come and assist you and you affirm:

'I shall dwell in the light this day. My mind shall bring in truth thoughts. My emotions shall feel love and I shall take action that is of the spirit,' or words to that effect." [18]

To view your own aura, sit comfortably with your hands on your lap on a dark cloth, palms up. Look at your hands through squinted eyes. You will see a small, bluish line around your hands. You can also see another's aura by using a squinting view of them. The colors of the aura are manifest on the astral plane, thus they are sometimes called astral colors. As in the physical, the colors are formed from the three primary colors.

Understanding colors
Use the colors to flood your aura with the energy you desire.
The wearing of any color represents the energy you wish to draw to you. The color you are wearing does not emphasize the characteristic, but rather the characteristic creates your desire to wear the color.

Red represents that which has to do with physical life. Crimson denotes love and is usually seen on Valentine's Day cards. A dull red denotes anger. Pure, unconditional love is a rose tint.

Yellow represents the intellect; reasoning; logic. Use yellow when you are approaching any kind of learning experience, such as taking an exam, or reading something to memorize.

Pale blue represents spiritual peace, reverence, and faith. Flood your aura with this calming color before and after meditation to bring into your awareness a peacefulness, or at any time when you find yourself in a situation which you expect to upset you in any way.

Green is the color of nature; hence the earth is covered with vegetation. It is also the color of balance, healing, and abundance. Use this color for healing or to bring abundance to yourself. I do not mean money and material things. For Scripture reminds us*, But rather seek ye the kingdom of God; and all these things shall be added unto you.*[19] When we habitually go within, in meditation, and acknowledge the Kingdom of God there, all abundance flows to us.

White contains all colors, as can be easily demonstrated using a prism in the sunlight. It represents spirit. Flood your aura with brilliant light prior to meditation, and when you feel in any danger. Picture others surrounded with pure white light for protection and enlightenment.

Various shades of colors represent the spectrum of emotions. For example a murky red represents jealousy, a murky green is greed. The darker colors, such as brown, gray, and black represent negative thoughts and emotions, such as revenge, violence, hatred, and depression. Always remember that your aura is part of you. Your moods, feelings, and emotions color it, and as it is colored it sends out that vibration from you. That is why your words are heard as meaningless if your feelings are not reflected in them.

The Soul, ego, mind, spirit, and personality

These aspects of us have been named and described in human terms. Gabriel offers a definition from his holy perspective that enables us to appreciate the wholeness of our being and better understand the role each plays in our daily lives.

Soul
And God said, Let us make man in our image, after our likeness (Gen 1:26). Think on those words, beloveds. You are the image and likeness of God. You are not the physical vehicles that you wear. Those are only the garments of your soul.[20]

Ellen Wallace Douglas

Gabriel reminded us of what we believed in the past and the truth of the soul:

"It used to be believed that you could lose your soul to the Devil. Well, we already know he doesn't exist. But what the older people were reckoning with was this tumultuous feeling within themselves; that they were out of control, that something was terribly wrong. So they perceived that Satan was afoot and was after their soul. Actually, the only thing after their soul was themselves, just as with you.[21]

The reader is directed to *Getting to Know Your Soul*, which is a compendium of selections from Archangel Gabriel's teachings. Briefly the functions of the soul are:

1. Your soul is the perfect memory of everything you have ever done; all of the personalities that you have created, and all of the actions and reactions of those personalities. Your soul records truth & error without discrimination. Whatever you believe to be, that is what your soul records. If those experiences are recorded in truth, by you, then they are remaining in your memory as a truth. If they are recorded in error, then they remain in error in your memory. That is why you have memories that cause you to be fearful in circumstances that make no sense to you.[22]

The author has a fear of snakes. The fear may be in my soul because in a past incarnation (as told to me by a medium) I was suffocated by a snake that wrapped itself around my body. I understand that anacondas do this. Also, shortly after I was ordained as a Christian Metaphysical minister I began having pain in my left leg. Over time the pain led to a continuous limp and then total hip surgery. Based on Gabriel's teachings I came to realize that my soul still had the memory of an incarnation in about 500 A.D. when I was killed for heresy as I preached Jesus' teachings. The ego, using the soul's memory, reminded me this could happen again. On the other hand, when I began my writing career at the age of 69 I had no doubts or fears about my ability. This is probably due to the fact that I had never been a writer in the past and therefore had no doubts or fears about succeeding at it. The reason for that is explained *in Getting to Know Your Soul:*

2. "Because the soul of you knows that nothing can happen to you, it does not take an attitude of right or wrong, good or bad, dangerous or

safe, holy or unholy, sinful or innocent, or whatever. It does not take that attitude about you at all. The Soul's attitude about you is that you are a living, experiencing, sentient being who can go forth into life and experience anything and everything that it chooses."[23]

3. "So the soul of you is what calls you to be a spiritually aware individual. It is the soul of you that urges you to attend church or temple . . . believes in life after death . . . teaches you how to reach out in love, for that comes down from the spirit of you and is processed in the soul of you."[24]

In order to calm the soul we need only to start back into the flow of the Godness within, and the soul immediately calms down and becomes obedient to our will. "The soul is a very real aspect of you. It is very precious, very sacred, and holy. It is a gift from God so that nothing that ever happens in your lives, whether it be the present one or future ones . . . nothing is ever lost to you. It is held in holiness in the soul of you." That is why Gabriel admonished us for our negative thoughts: "Think before you speak a word of anger, 'What will this do to my soul?' Before you say an unkind word or think terrible thoughts about someone, think of what it is going to be doing to the soul of you. And you will have to deal with that. Indeed you will." [25]

Gabriel explained that the subconscious is the voice of the soul from the perspective that the soul has every memory within it that we ever had. "Subconsciously you conjure up all kinds of doubts and fears. What do you think is going to radiate from your mind? Chaos, depression, anger, self-hatred, fears, all of the armies of 'what ifs,' and all of the negativity. Then you are going to be sending out vibrations that are going to collect from the ethers like vibrations and you are going to attract to you negative influences from all over the place." *Vibrations,* 11.

Ego
Gabriel explained that when we were created in the spirit world, we knew that we were one with God and with each other. There was no status, no differences between us. We loved each other equally, as loving siblings, with full knowledge that we were all one in God and all offspring of our Creator, God. As we descended to the earth plane and took physical form, the creatures we created chased and devoured us. And we fell off cliffs,

unaware of them. So humankind created the ego in order to protect us, which it did do for centuries. That was its function. Unfortunately, over time, we have given it more and more power over us.

The voice of the ego will always fill us with dread of some kind; it always has grief of some kind in it. We must learn how to tell the difference between the voice of the ego which fills us with fear, and the Voice of the Higher Self which always guides us lovingly. It's not difficult to know the difference. "All you have to do is recognize its (ego's) voice and keep it in its proper perspective. You don't have to do anything with the little bugger! Leave him be. Just know for yourself that you are in very good hands." *How Things Come to Be,* 17.

The ego tells us that we are separate from each other and therefore we are less than some, better than others. The ego tells us that our differences are more important than our similarities. It tells us to fear each other, and by fear it controls us. Gabriel reminded us that all fear is of the past.

The ego works very subtly. It brings into our awareness such ideas as:

— "You can do anything, but nobody else can".
— "Listen to what they are saying about you; you better change".
— "You should be afraid of anything you don't understand".
— "Life is always risky and dangerous."
— "Don't trust anyone until they prove they deserve it".
— "You are better than they are because you have more money, a better education, a larger home, a higher salary, more material things."
— "If you put yourself in God's hands, you don't know what He will ask of you."
— "You are just one person; what difference can you make?"
— "What makes you think you deserve that job/person/home?"

And on and on the ego goes, putting fear in our every thought and idea. Rather, it is essential for us to believe—to know—that we are God's children and therefore entitled to every good thing. "The ego dwells in your emotional body." [26]

It is common when one begins upon a conscious spiritual path to have problems suddenly arise that seem to hinder our progress. "When you begin . . . on the spiritual path, the ego gets very nervous, very worried. What if you get smart and don't need it anymore? What is gong to happen to it?" [27]

Our response must be governed by vigilance. "The moment that you surrender to God, your ego is going to start fighting for its life. It is going to present to you in every manner that it can think of why you should not follow your spiritual path. It will use smoking (cigarettes) or whatever weakness it perceives you have and it will beleaguer you with it. [28]

The ego will lead us into endless circles that take us nowhere.
"You must learn how to tell the difference between the voice of the ego which will fill you with fear and the voice of the higher Self which always guides you lovingly, with no fear, into a betterment. It is not hard to tell the difference." [29]

Because we created the ego we can uncreate it. "The hunger in you for God has to become greater than the satisfaction that the ego self will give you. When that happens, you then will change in a twinkling." *Temptations of Jesus,* 14

To deal with the ego as we set upon a conscious spiritual path, "You say to the ego, 'I bless you to your proper place.' Then you take yourself up and you say, 'Thank you, Holy Spirit, I know your work is complete,' and you stay in that state of accepting that the Holy Spirit has indeed done its work." [30]

Gabriel assures us that speaking thusly to the ego works. "The ego must respect your command. It might argue a tad with you, but it must respect your command. What you do is say to it, 'Beloved ego, I love, and I appreciate all you do, but I need you to step aside for I must work from the Spirit Self of me now. I will call upon you later'." [31]

Mind
Thoughts are things and if we do not experience love, peace, and joy, it is because our thoughts are getting in the way. We often say 'what goes around comes around,' and it is a grand truth. Ella Wheeler Wilcox wrote a poem about this circular action of thought in *The Heart of New Thought:*

"You never can tell what your thoughts will do
      In bringing you hate and love,
For thoughts are things, and their airy wings
Are swift as a carrier dove.
They follow the law of the universe—
      Each thing must create its kind,
And they speed o'er the track to bring you back
      Whatever went forth from your mind." [32]

Also, regarding the power of thought, Wilcox wrote:

"Our thoughts are shaping unmade spheres,
      And, like a blessing or a curse,
They thunder down the formless years
      And ring throughout the universe." [33]

Our minds are individualized portions of the Divine Mind of God. We have constant access to it because it is part of us. It is our choice whether we listen to it or not. As we turn our conscious attention to God's Will for us, we can and do receive the guidance we need for our highest good. The intuitive thought that guides us, the words from others' mouths that inspire and direct us, words we read and hear at the perfect time; these are the ways that God guides us. God also puts words in our mouths that we need to listen to. Life is not as complicated as we would like to think. There are only two voices to hear; only two ways to live. We can choose to do the right thing at all times and ask God's guidance—through prayer and meditation—or we can allow our ego's ideas to rule us. When we listen to the ego's fearful warnings we allow our self-will to run riot in our lives. We always pay the consequences.

Divine Mind is the unmanifest from which all ideas source. All discoveries, all inventions, and all creations come from Divine Mind. It is accessible to all at all times. When humans discovered atomic energy, God did not say, "Wow. Look how powerful man is now!" For God knew and always knows that we have the power of Divine Mind at our disposal. And He knows that we have often abused the power. Each of us has the choice to use the power of Divine Mind. History shows the many negative choices humankind has made, choices that altered history, enslaved peoples, destroyed nations, crippled societies.

Divine Mind is accessible to everyone. One must be motivated, have an intention to succeed; and be willing to focus completely on an idea. Such a desire (de-sire means from the Father), success is inevitable. Successful individuals are those who move ahead with their idea, certain of success. Whatever seems to deter them is put aside in favor of the desired goal. They are not easily discouraged. Gabriel told us of a man who once concentrated on a peanut, desiring to learn everything about the peanut that he could. By virtue of his intent, his desire, and his concentration, he discovered peanut butter! Electricity has always existed, but man 'discovered' it by tapping into Divine Mind as he desired to know, was motivated to learn, and concentrated on what he already knew. Then, from Divine Mind, the idea sprang forth. Edison tried dozens of materials to find the appropriate material for a filament in an electric bulb. Had he meditated on an answer, he would not have had to use the 'trial and error' method, which science so insistently demands.

Emmanuel Swedenborg, in the 17th century, envisioned a submarine and an airplane, but they remained unmanifested for 200 years. Someone had to come along with the necessary knowledge and willingness to access Divine Mind, to bring them into existence.

All knowledge is gained from previous knowledge. A third grader does not understand calculus. Arithmetic, geometry, and algebra are forerunners for the understanding of calculus. Divine Mind is not equal to analytical thinking. Analytical thinking is based on experiential learning and text book knowledge. Divine Mind is ageless wisdom.

> Because the mind of you uses its discernment in a negative way and causes there to be judgments placed upon form, the form follows the dictates of the judgment that you give it. The judgment that you give it is that there is such a thing as limitation, illness, poverty, and ultimately death. Because you embrace these ideas to be truth, although they are not, you have fed into the cell forms of your bodies the dictates

of these things. Your bodies, following that which is desired of them, become ill, limited and ultimately die.[34]

Gabriel provided us with an overview of the awakening of our consciousness:

"The consciousness that is God in you knows that everything is already yours. God gave you a mind to use to come to recognize that . . . Remember, God dwells in the mineral world. God awakens in the plant world. God walks about in the animal world. But God thinks in the human world." [35]

Spirit

Our spirit is the true essence of our being. It is the original form, the first form we took from God. It is unmarred by any thought or action of any past lifetimes. It is perfect and eternally so. It is as immortal as God. "Because of the way in which you came forth into beingness, breathed forth in joy and love from Divine Flame and made a conscious knowing, feeling expression of that divinity, you have all of the glory and all of the joy and all of the love within you with which you were first created. However, you have taught yourselves that the presence of God is far removed from you." [36]

Archangel Gabriel made it abundantly clear that the Presence of God never leaves us, but for eons we have felt separate from Him: "It has become unthinkable to humanity that God can care about you enough, love you enough, and forgive you enough, and be with you constantly. It is not an acceptable thing to humankind because after all, humans are down here and God is up there and there is a big space in-between. That is the way people feel about God, but that is not the way it is at all, not at all. The Presence of God is with you as profoundly this moment as I am with you and even more so than this. The Presence of God never leaves you." [37]

In reviewing the many lectures that Gabriel gave, it is amazing to me that he said so many times, in so many ways that we are divine in essence and perfect and eternal as God Himself. He said, "Spirit by its very nature is limitless and changeless . . . At no point does spirit ever need to become more for it is ever all that it is ever designed to be; perfection, completeness, limitless, boundless and eternal." [38]

Gabriel also said, "You have within you that God Presence and in that is all wisdom, all beauty, all truth and you have access to that within yourself". [39]

Turning within we can not only know but feel the truth of Gabriel's words: "From that center of stillness within you, that God within you, there comes forth power, there comes forth vibrations, and there comes forth an energy that is a living energy. That energy comes into the very spirit of you and causes you to be an individual . . . the spiritual aspect is your own individual divinity. Now in that divinity, you know anything and everything you need to know on all levels . . . you realize that there are choices to be made, and that you have the right to choose." [40]

In his infinite wisdom and his vision beyond form, Gabriel knew what we were thinking at all times and even answered a question one time before a woman at the microphone had even asked it! He also used our vernacular at times, knowing we would identify better with those words. "You think circumstances overpower you . . . But I tell you a truth. You have more power in you than any circumstance or thousands of circumstances could ever wage against you. You are the child of God, made in the image and likeness of God. It doesn't get any better than that!" [41]

All the great spiritual teachers who have come to Earth followed a spiritual path, and Gabriel acknowledged that: "That is why your great teachers—Buddha, Jesus, Moses, and all of those who brought a difference to your earth plane never got locked into wealth, possessions, owning." *Desires of Personality,* 13.

Spiritual path
"When you become aware of that spiritualization within you, then you come into unity or into harmony with all living things and especially with one another." *Giving and Receiving,* 17.

It was always exciting for me to hear Gabriel quote Scripture, and sometimes provide us with detailed explanations, such as Moses and the burning bush:

> When Moses approached the burning bush, he said to himself,
> 'This is a great phenomenon . . . ' so he approached it farther,

and he realized that what he was looking at was the symbol of Divine Flame in form known as spirit. It was showing him that the consuming fire of the spirit dos not destroy life but rather destroys illusion . . . It was here that Moses first became aware that he was indeed on sacred ground, for he had taken a step up in his consciousness and could know that God was beyond form, that God was not a man sitting in judgment upon the throne, that God was, is ever, life. The flame that burned around the bush and did not destroy it is likened unto the flame that is your awareness, your life, your energy, that which is you . . . As Moses stepped away from the bush, he had been transformed . . . He had stepped into the realm of awareness in which he became consciously aware that he could know of the presence of God.[42]

Gabriel told us that he brought nothing new to the earth. He said we already knew everything he taught, and he came only to help us remember it. I recall a time when I took a list of questions to a lecture and when I approached the microphone I told Gabriel that I had written a list of questions but had lost it. Then he said to me, "You lost it because you already know the answers." I suddenly desired to see the list so I could know what I knew! But another time he made this situation clear to me: "Now the outside world; teachers, myself, books you read, things you hear, awaken truth in you. Everything you learn from the outside is something you already know and it is simply being brought to your remembrance. That is what learning is. It is remembering. It is remembering . . . from your own God self. That is when it becomes your truth." [43]

When Gabriel equated thoughts of lack and limitation with cursing God, it was a profound lesson to hear. "When you see yourselves as limited and lacking and ill and out of tune with your own divine center, that is a form of cursing God . . . But to see yourselves as God created you, in the joy and the unspeakable beauty that you are is a form of worship . . ."[44]

The spirit Self of us, Gabriel explained, never touches the earth. He said, "Remember, you are on the earth; you are not *of* the earth, and whatever is going on in your physical world is bound to get better". [45]

There was another time when Gabriel referred to the ubiquitous phrase in Scripture, 'It came to pass,' telling us that it does not say that 'it came to stay.' He was explaining that God is ever becoming more, ever changing in expression even though God is immutable and the same forever. It is the energy that God is that is changeless, but manifestations of the energy are constantly changing.

Meditation makes us aware of our true value. "When you are aware of the true value of your existence, there comes into your awareness a sense of well-being, a sense of wealth, a sense of nurturing, a sense that you are love. You are loving and you are loved." [46]

In this context 'wealth' does not mean material possessions or money, but rather an abundance of love and wisdom as they flow from the Father to us. "The attunement in the divine self of you opens the doors that you have closed and have blocked to the flow of life. Now the flow of life is never poor. The flow of life is never ill. The flow of life is never dead. That vibrational rate will bring into your experience anything that you are able to accept. Once you have opened the doors to acceptance, you will find that anything you perceive you desire is there." [47]

All problems disappear when we focus on the Spirit Self of us: "Keep your thoughts centered in the spiritual reality of you, and you will find that all of the little things that seem to beleaguer you will drift away".[48]

Later the same year, Gabriel told us of the harmony of all life that naturally follows when we center in our spiritual reality: "When you become aware of that spiritualization within you, then you come into unity or into harmony with all living things and especially with one another." [49]

There have been writers who recognized the Will of God for us:
Emanuel Swedenborg, mystic writer of the eighteenth century, wrote in his Divine Providence: "In everything it does, divine providence focuses on what is infinite and eternal from itself, especially in the intent to save the human race." [50]

In the same book Swedenborg speaks of the change in our lives which must occur on our spiritual path: "When we are regenerated, the whole pattern of our life is inverted. We become spiritual instead of earthly, since what is earthly is contrary to the divine design when it is separated from what is spiritual, and what is spiritual is in keeping with the divine design." [51]

This is expressed also in *A Course in Miracles*:
"To have, give all to all.
This is a very preliminary step, and the only one you must take for yourself . . . but it is necessary that you turn in that direction. Having chosen to go that way, you place yourself in charge of the journey, where you and only you must remain. This step . . . is the beginning step in reversing your perception and turning it right-side up." [52]

Various current religious teachers have accepted and acknowledged the divinity that is inherent in humankind. "Sri Satya Sai Baba has an ashram near Bangalore . . . [his] message is that everyone must realize his or her divinity. [he said] 'You are all God only you do not know it'." [53]

We have a tendency to think that a spiritual path is very dreary, very limiting and outside the activities of everyday life. But Archangel Gabriel addressed these thoughts of ours: "Beloveds, everyone thinks a spiritual journey is some solemn, narrow path that you walk where you don't lift your eyes up. No. A spiritual journey is recognition of the holiness within you, the holiness within your neighbor, the blessings of each day, your freedom to be who you want to be. A spiritual journey is thanking God, even if it is quietly within your heart for just being, for the opportunities that are placed before you." [54]

Religion and truth
Lest the reader think that Gabriel came to discount the sacred writings of the various religions, please note his comment regarding this topic:

"You have had upon your earth all these generations the secrets, the answers, the keys . . . of the innate within you. All of your profound religions have contained this truth. And if you will go past the adulterations that man has put upon the truth and seek to find that central core, you will find that every religion brings you a truth." [55]

Personality

"The personality doesn't want to be bothered with God. You would be surprised at the number of people who are walking about the earth who don't want to hear about God. They associate that with religion and they associate that with 'Thou shalt not'. So the personality has a bit of a problem. It doesn't want to know they [urge, need, desire] belong to God. So the urge, the need, the desire manifest as a driving need to have bigger and better and more of whatever." [56]

In order to grow and mature into a responsible person one must undergo a complete personality change. Gabriel made it clear that our personality is not of God but of our own doing. "Because the personality is something that evolves and changes and becomes, any idea that you have set for yourself is also changeable. So you are not trapped. You are not. None of you are; ever; for any reason, by anyone, by anything, at any point in all eternity." *Desires of Personality,* 5.

Gabriel said that anything the personality desires is temporary because we are evolving, ever becoming more. Buddha came from a wealthy family. When he came to recognize the difference between the illusion of the personality ego self and the reality of the spirit Self, he released and let go of his perceived needs, wants and desires.

"Now there is a peculiar thing about the personality. When it creates a desire, the desire is two-sided. The desire brings a craving. The craving is painful until it is satisfied. Then it becomes a pleasure momentarily. But when the pleasure aspect of the craving has faded, then the desire becomes a memory. Once it becomes a memory, it is the seed for future desires which bring pain, then pleasure, then memory, then pain, then pleasure then memory and you are locked into a cycle that goes and goes and goes." [57]

Our personalities began eons of time ago and it is a coming together of the perceptions, the truths, and the errors, of all the things that we have brought together and stored in our soul memory. "All of you created your personalities that you use. Each incarnation that you have upon the earth, you build that personality, and that personality comes forth . . . [it] has already begun before you enter the physical body that you intend to occupy." [58]

Gabriel addressed the wall that the personality represents: "Your creation, your personality, the limited self that you have made and come to believe is real, is the only thing that stands between you and your holiness" [59]

CHAPTER 5

Lies of the Ego

Source of error perceptions

Error perceptions are perceptions which we gain from our five senses. They are accepted as real because we have accepted our physical bodies not only as real, but as our only reality. Our bodies are temporal as is everything else on the planet. The truth of us is our spirit Self, created by God and therefore eternally perfect and whole.

In Scripture (John 8:58) Jesus says, *Before Abraham was, I am.* He was not referring to Jesus the man, but the Christ Love that he demonstrated in his life. Christ Love is timeless. As our elder brother, Jesus came as an example (John 13:15), to show us how to awaken to our own Christ Self.

It is a conscious awareness of that spirit Self of us which is the goal of learning on the earth plane. Teachers and prophets and writers are now explaining how to awaken. *A Course in Miracles* is a spiritual guidebook. Archangel Gabriel and Jesus the Christ came to teach us, from 1987 to 1999. The people who attended the seminars and lectures planned to do so, before our birth. We were not a 'chosen few,' but rather we chose to be there for our own reasons and as a result of our experiences through time, through all of our incarnations on earth.

Error perceptions can be—must be—replaced by true perception. True perception is ours when we see with eyes that reveal only truth. " . . . see through the eyes of Christ [love], and then you will behold a world in perfect forgiveness and perfect love". [1]

We think people are complex; that a life is complex. It only appears that way because we choose to see it that way. There are only two ways to see life and its experiences. There are only two ways to see ourselves and others. One is with love and the other is with judgment. "Every time you looked past someone's error, someone's mistake and you loved them anyway, every time you didn't judge someone by what they have said or done but rather recognized inside there is a good, wholesome, loving soul. Every time you look with the eyes of love, you are living from the God Self of you. You are expressing in you and through you the love that God has for others." [2]

Emanuel Swedenborg puts it another way, "*The good that love does is actually good only to the extent that it is united to the truth that wisdom perceives, and the truth that wisdom perceives is actually true only to the extent that it is united to the good that love does.*[3]

Some error perceptions:
Time and space
Communication as limited to humans
Judgment vs. discernment.
Illness
Grief

Time and Space
Time as defined in *Encyclopedia of Religion:* "Anglo Saxon *tid*—origin of tide. As quantity, the 'measure of change.' (Aristotle) . . . Augustine attempted to define time . . . As essentially psychological . . . [and] inferred from this theory that time does not apply to God . . .", 787.

More recently we find Eckhart Tolle writing, in *The Power of Now* "Time isn't precious at all, because it is an illusion . . .", 40. And in *A Course in Miracles,* "Time does not really exist." [4]

Archangel Gabriel explained that time and space are illusions. We do need them in order to keep track of our activities, but in the spirit world they do not exist for there is no need of them. "Time and space are both illusions. They are the manifested thoughts of humankind brought into being in order that you might regulate your lives, so to speak." [5]

Gabriel referred to the illusion of time thusly: "The past, the present, and the future are all states of consciousness that you have created, for God only created the present moment. When you learn to live in that present moment, from the God of you, you will find all of the nightmares and illusions that have haunted you in the past are nothing, and you will know it." [6]

Regarding angelic perspective of our time frames, Gabriel spoke of the view from the spirit realm: "For we in spirit realms realize that every moment is a new expression of divinity that is all life. But because you have decided to mark off your years, and your centuries, and your orders of time, we honor that." [7]

From the other side, we have this statement: "TIME IS A CONCEPT THAT IS DIFFICULT TO DEFINE IN OUR WORLD. IT DOES NOT EXIST. OUR WORLD IS OPEN TO EVERYTHING. YOURS IS SO VERY LIMITED." [8]

Jesus the Christ explained the effect of the illusion of time: "Time is the illusion that binds you to your past and causes you to doubt the surety of the present and the future." [9]

Gabriel gave an example to help us understand the illusion of time. If one stands on a train that is traveling 60 miles per hour, and bounces a ball on the floor of the train, how far does the ball travel? He added that in addition to the speed of the ball hitting the floor and returning to the thrower's hand, the speed of the train must be considered. Also, the speed with which the planet earth revolves on its axis, plus the rate of earth's revolution around the sun are to be taken into consideration. It was a fascinating concept to me and having a natural love of numbers and calculations, I decided to work it out. Referring to an almanac and using one second of time as a base, the calculations arrived at the distance the ball traveled—18.8 miles! This calculation is not exact. Surely it is not designed to launch a space vehicle, but the message is clear.

Relating human consciousness to time, Gabriel said, "The past, the present, and the future are all states of consciousness that you have created; for God only created the present moment. When you learn to live in that present moment, from the God of you, you will find all of the nightmares and illusions that have haunted you in the past are nothing, and you will know it." [10]

The following words of Gabriel astonished us: "These words I speak to you I spoke long ago, but you are just now hearing them because you are now just understanding them . . . The greatest illusion is limitations—especially of time . . . You speak of 'telling time,' but you never tell time anything.

It runs your life . . . The past, present and future are simultaneous. Everything that will ever be has already happened . . . Your finite mind could not comprehend the limitlessness of space . . . Space is a state of consciousness." [11]

Einstein said that time is not at all what it seems. It does not flow in only one direction, and the future exists simultaneously with the past. He said, "The distinction between past, present, and future is only an illusion, however persistent."

Gabriel told us that timelessness will come to earth with the New Age. Without providing any details about location or motivation, He told us this story:

"Some years back three men decided they would each go to a single room, with food and comforts and books if desired, but no method of communication with the outside world. No clocks were allowed; no way of knowing day or night. They could do anything or nothing, but had to keep a log of thoughts and activities. At the end of six weeks one man became mad, saying monsters had come into his room, he was in a storm at sea; needed treatment. [All of negative past came back to him, Gabriel explained]. The second man busied himself with a project he had brought. He slept when he wanted, ate when he wanted. He worked 48 hours without rest, slept for twelve. He ate less and thought he was there only ten days. The third man read books—all he had ever wanted to read. He read for fifty hours and slept for 20 hours. He ate less food. He thought he was there only three days." *Illusion of time* [12]

Regarding space, Gabriel explained that our galaxy is one of millions of galaxies. Our galaxy and all others are ever moving outward, expanding—that is creation.

Interspecies Communication
Gabriel once told us, " . . . All life is in the process of recognizing itself as divine." [13] The key word here is 'recognizing,' which says clearly that all life is divine but does not recognize its own divinity. So it is not only humans who are becoming aware of an innate divinity, but all life forms. As interspecies communication is developed all life will come to recognize its true essence

of spirit, which is divine. In scripture we find a suggestion to communicate with the animal kingdom and the earth itself: *But ask the beasts, and they shall teach thee; and the fowls of the air, and they shall tell thee:*

Or speak to the earth, and it shall teach thee: and the fishes of the sea shall declare unto thee. Job 12:7-8

Birds

Longfellow referred to communication with birds in *The Song of Hiawatha:*

Then the little Hiawatha
Learned of every bird its language,
Learned their names and all their secrets,
How they built their nests in summer,
Where they hid themselves in winter,
Talked with them whene'er he met them,
Called them "Hiawatha's Chickens".

Plants

The method whereby one may communicate with animal or plant life is to become very still in their presence and calling it by name. Send a mental picture of self and say, "I'd like to talk with you today. I have some things I'd like to ask you." Ask the question one by one and await an answer. The answer will be received mentally, not with mortal ears. When communication is over, it is important to say, "You were very helpful, you're beautiful, I admire you". This communication with plants was clearly experienced and written about by members of the Findhorn Community in Scotland. Plant devas instructed the residents about what seeds and fertilizer to use, and when and how to plant. The garden thrived in sand where no one expected it possible. Another example of deva communication is Perelandra, in Virginia, where Ms. Wright desired greatly to emulate Findhorn in the U. S.

Not only can plants communicate but they display an understanding of life in all its forms and their existence as stemming from One Source. Ms. Wright gives us the words she received from the Lilium Auratum Deva.

Although the conversation was extensive I present only a portion of the words expressed by the deva:

We feel it is high time for man to branch out and include in his horizon the different forms of life which are part of his world. He has been forcing his own creations and vibration on the world without taking into consideration that all living things are part of the whole, just as he is, placed there by divine plan and purpose . . . The theory of evolution that puts man at the apex of life on Earth . . . leaves out the fact that God, universal consciousness, is working out the forms of life. For example, according to generally accepted regulations, I am a lowly lily unable to be aware of most things and certainly not able to talk with you . . . There are vast ranges of consciousness all stemming from the One, the One who is this consciousness in all of us and whose plan it is that all parts of life become more aware of each other and more united in the great forward movement which is life, all life, becoming greater consciousness. Consider the lily, consider all that it involves, and let us grow in consciousness, unity and love under the One.[14]

In recent years we have read about hugging trees as a way to thank nature for its loveliness. Gabriel explained that when one desires to communicate with a tree, it is important to keep in mind its stationery nature, unlike our mobile form.

The Psychic World of Plants provides us with many examples of people talking to their household plants, such as the clergyman in London who noted, "I speak to them as if they were pets. They grow well on it. This is the secret of green fingers." [15]

A New Yorker said that she couldn't have a fight with her husband because it upset their plant so much. "I can't say bad words—the plant doesn't like it . . . the leaves sort of shut up, curl up, and if I get very mad, the plant vibrates, or reacts, to my feelings, my thoughts." [16]

An artist remarked, "When I paint a plant I turn the picture around in different lights so the plant can see what I'm doing. The plant likes the pleasure you get in painting it; it likes the attention and the fact that you think it's beautiful." [17]

Animals

In *Communicating with Animals,* we find four ways in which we may receive communication from animals:

1. Getting words or a sentence.

2. Getting a mental picture. i.e.: a lost animal will have in its mind a picture of the surrounding scene, the communicator picks it up psychically.

3. A kinesthetic sense—drawing your attention to one area of your own body, and feeling the animal's sensations, which can be physical or emotional.

4. A knowingness; an intuitive impression.
   From *The Psychic Power* of *Animals,* p. 30 " . . . animals are endowed with a sensitive psychological awareness comparable to our own; and . . . behind their alert bright eyes lies an acute faculty for judgment and appraisal that we ordinarily do not think about because it does not manifest itself in human speech."

And in Wright's book she says, "The animal kingdom functions as a full partner within nature by serving both the planet and mankind as one of the buffers . . . Dogs and cats, for example, will absorb the raw emotional energy that is released during an argument and then act on it by coming to the people involved and insisting on attention—kind, caring attention—something the people arguing needed to do for themselves." [18]

Cats are psychic and have a tendency to assist in healing. The author once received a gemstone healing and the healer's cat jumped up and lay on the bed beside me. She remained there throughout the healing episode. The healer explained that that particular cat (she owned three) frequently did so with her patients.

Small dogs feel insecure when they are outside, according to an animal communicator, "Little dogs are the insecure ones and they often tell me, 'I risk my life every time I go outside'." [19]

Kimball, the animal communicator, once was asked to find out what was wrong with a horse that excellent veterinarians could not find the cause of an ailment. The horse said, "I backed into a rough board in my stable and drove a splinter into my spinal column" The information was given to the vet and examining the horse, found it to be true. The splinter was removed and the horse got well." [20]

Rocks

In *Behaving as if the God in all Life Mattered,* there is a story about a woman in Washington, DC and found, in a park there, a large rock that she loved to sit upon. One day as she sat on it she heard laughter, but no one was near her. She realized it was the rock laughing and she asked it what was so funny. The rock replied, "Human beings are so funny. They race around like crazy, and they miss almost everything." [21]

A woman in a workshop given by Mrs. Wright decided to touch into the consciousness of a stone she had picked up on a beach in Ireland. The stone flashed to the woman an idyllic beach scene where many children were at play. But the impression came to her that the scene was not a contemporary one; it had occurred in Holland, in the late 1800s, where the stone was sitting, until it washed up on the shores of Ireland.

Gemstones

. . ."Rocks and animals 'bridge time' and can tell us of their origin and their last location before we find them. Ms Wright gives the emerald as an example, stating that it originated on Venus and 'has as part of its energy pattern an expanded, dynamic energy of love, which is part of the dynamic of Venus. So by touching in with the emeralds' consciousness, it is possible for us to gain insight into the dynamic of love as well as to experience the planet Venus." [22]

Water

A creative and visionary Japanese researcher, Masaru Emoto, wrote *The Messages from Water,* which describes his worldwide research. "Masaru Emoto's extraordinary work is an awesome display, and powerful tool, that can change our perceptions of ourselves and the world we live in, forever. We now have profound evidence that we can positively heal and transform ourselves and our planet by the thoughts we choose to think and the ways in which we put those thoughts into [action]". www. wellness goods.com

Life in all creation consists of vibratory rates. "The vibration that would produce a tree is very different from the vibration that would produce a flower." [23]

When one tunes into the vibration of plant or an animal, a communication can take place. The story Gabriel told about the origin of peanut butter was a fascinating one. He said the person tuned into the vibration of a peanut, seeking to know all its secrets and from the information he received he created peanut butter. And needless to say, peanut butter has become a staple in most U.S. households.

Judgment vs. Discernment
Judgment is an error perception in that it prevents us from seeing others as our spiritual siblings, as fellow children of God. Discernment is an awareness of the differences in two different things or people. Judgment is a value call that assigns one person/thing a higher value than another. All of God's children are loved equally by God. Only humans assign different values to certain groups, from prejudice to caste systems.

A serious mistranslation in Scripture, as told by Gabriel, was the phrase that describes Jesus the Christ as the only son of God:
John 1:18 *No man hath seen the God at any time; the only begotten Son, which is in the bosom of the Father, he hath declared him.*

John 3:16 For *God so loved the world, that he gave his only begotten Son.* Gabriel told us the only word missing in the translation is " . . . he gave it **to** his only begotten Son.

I John 4:9 In *this was manifested the love of God toward us, because that God sent his only begotten Son into the world, that we might live through him.*

Correctly translated, the phrase would be: [Jesus was] the begotten Son of the only God. As so clearly explained by Archangel Gabriel, the entire race of humankind is the only begotten Son of God.

The difference between judgment and discernment was explained fully by Archangel Gabriel. Judgment infers a value system, placing one person or thing above another. It results in some or many being 'less than,' such as the historic error of humankind believing that the black race of men was inferior to the white. As a matter of fact there are white people who believe all other races to be inferior. In that regard, Gabriel told us at one time that if we were to honestly look at history the only races that ever started wars against another race were the white and yellow races. The black and red races never began a war against another race, albeit they fought amongst themselves.

Discernment, as defined in the dictionary, "to recognize or identify as separate and distinct". This does not impose a value system. For example, we can discern that one person is wearing red and another is wearing green, but place no value judgment on the color, the clothing, or the person. We merely recognize and identify the distinct observable differences.

Illness
"The acceptance of peace is the denial of illusion, and sickness *is* an illusion." [24]

Hearing or reading this for the first time gives one pause. Pain feels real, and pain is real to our senses. Sickness is an illusion in that we create it by our belief in it. We create it for a reason. We plan with intent. It is our belief, our reason and our intent that are not in our consciousness. No one ever consciously chooses illness, and everyone desires to be 'well again.' But unconsciously we desire illness for specific reasons.

"Some of your illnesses are temporary, passing things, results of negative thoughts, results from 'I'm not worth it,' results of 'I guess I better be punished, and this is a good way to do it' . . . others have decided that you would leave the earth . . . [with] an illness that your current medical associations cannot reverse. However, you can reverse it. That decision is yours." [25]

Anger will bring illness because our innate nature is love, peace, joy, and harmony. In truth anger is not a natural feeling. Anger is the antithesis of love, peace, joy, and harmony. Therefore it disrupts our body's mechanisms and can cause high blood pressure, ulcers, and various other maladies.

Guilt and fear will bring on illness because we think the guilt demands payment of some kind necessary. In truth, we are guilty of nothing. God breathed us forth and willed for us love, peace, harmony, and joy. If these attributes do not exist in our lives, it is our own thinking, attitudes and decisions that deny them to us.

Fear will bring on illness if we dread a coming event. Children become suddenly sick when a difficult final exam is on the schedule at school. Adults suddenly feel poorly when facing an interview for a prospective job. "All ailments come from a fear, and that fear is that you will never find your way back to God. That is not a conscious fear. Most people don't even give it a second thought about their way back to God. But it always comes in on the idea that you are guilty of something. Therefore, you must be punished and what is more punishing than pain?" [26]

Irresponsibility will lead to illness. If we can't do what we are able to do when healthy, then others have to take up the task and do it in our place. "A lot of people choose illness in order to not be responsible for something else that they don't care to deal with and if they are ill, they can't be held responsible. Some people are ill because they know it is the best and most wondrous way to get waited on and taken care of. There are many reasons, but everyone brings their own ailment with them." [27] This reminds me of another time when Gabriel said that those who live alone are not sick as often as others, because they know there is no one to make them chicken soup.

Healing
The Bible tells of the healing given by Jesus to a woman who had an issue of blood twelve years (Luke 8:43).

> "What happened when the Master [Jesus] healed? . . . You are perfect already and the Master knew this. He knew his own perfection . . . you do not receive from out there like you think . . . So all he did was to make a spiritual contact with that person and remind her that she was already whole. She was already perfect. As that spiritual connection was made and the person remembered, it was like, 'Oh, that is right. I am perfect'.
> While it was not a conscious thought, it was within the memory of the soul of that perfection. So he called forth her

memory and she awakened to it, her own spiritual divinity healed her. It poured down through her physical form and removed all of the error perceptions . . . of the illness . . . and set her free." [28]

Gabriel recommended that first it is a good idea to address the soul of the person and ask permission to send the healing. This is done mentally. If one feels a warm acceptance they do want a healing. But if it seems there is a wall between, they do not want to be healed. They have their reasons. Gabriel said that at times angels go to hospitals and ask mentally if the patients want to be healed and they often get a 'no.'

It was wonderful indeed to hear Gabriel say that there is no such thing as a failed healing. The motive of love when one sends a healing is sustained until such time as the patient chooses to use it.

For those who accept the healing: "Now that healing goes to them and they are free to use it however they choose. Some people use it to pass into spirit. Some people carry their healing with them into another lifetime and use it then. But it is never wasted, nor does it ever interfere." [29]

Archangel Gabriel told us that healing and love are the same thing. After pondering this statement I realized that one does not wish to heal unless one cares about the wounded person. And when we love a person we pray for the total health and well-being of that person.

"All healing is divine . . . Divine healing is something that you can do from the within of you. That Divine Force is channeled through the individual, connected into that individual, and goes out into the person requiring the healing." [30]

We refer to the medical community as a group of healers, and there are healers who practice alternative methods of healing. But everyone can be a healer if s/he chooses.

Anyone can send a healing. The only qualification is a sincere desire to heal. Love and healing are the same, Gabriel said. "Trust the Father implicitly. You have to recognize that what you are asking will be granted." [31]

Gabriel explained how cats heal: "Cats are extremely psychic. Even though they have physical bodies, they operate strictly from the psychic realm . . . So therefore, when a person is doing a healing, his or her cat is aware of it. Sometimes a cat will come and absorb some of the energies to work with themselves. Sometimes they are also conductors, and they will absorb the energy, and then they will go into the presence of someone who needs that energy. They will just lie down there and allow that energy to go from them into the other person." [32]

The spirit of us is perfect eternally and never needs healing. But the body, the emotions, and sometimes the mind need healing.

In *A Course in Miracles:* "The body is healed because you came without it, and joined the Mind in which all healing rests." [33]

A healer must not focus on the problem the person is having, regardless of where in the body it is located or the extent of the pain. It is essential to focus on the person as whole and healthy, not focus on the ailment. A person who is terminally ill can be sent a healing. "You can offer her love and healing and she has the right to use it or to refuse it. You cannot alter that. For everyone's death, as you call it, is their own choice of where and when and how and all of that. And only the person can change it." [34]

Grief

There was a time when Gabriel explained to us that all grieving is selfish, for we know in our spirit Self that the person has merely transitioned to another plane. We grieve because we do not have the pleasure of their company or the support of their presence. "You mourn those who leave your physical world . . . This mourning for the empty shell is but part of the sickness of your minds that embraces the ideas of illness and death." [35]

There are many people who believe they will see their loved ones again on the other side, when they themselves pass over. Many individuals receive messages from their lost loves or they 'feel their presence' after the transition. Gabriel rarely gave personal messages to his audience, but one day at a lecture, a person in the audience had recently lost a loved one due to a terminal illness. He said to her, "You never once lost the knowing that the loved one chose to leave when and how they did and it is ok. This doesn't mean that you didn't feel bad or you didn't sorrow, but you kept your spiritual balance and you dealt with it most admirably." [36]

Our error perceptions include the habit we have of missing the spiritual gifts that come to us.

Distortion of spiritual gifts

> You have taken gifts of the spirit and you have seen the negative side of them or you have created negative versions of them and you perceive them to be the essence of your lives . . . You have perceived your life to be difficult or a struggle or somehow not good. In thinking and perceiving that your life is not good, you have denied yourself the blessings of the goodness of your life . . . . There is an innocence that you have that you don't use. You don't see it in yourselves or in one another and that innocence is the enjoyment of life, enjoying the very beingness of yourselves. That is so important because without that sense of yourselves, you are denying God. [37]

CHAPTER 6

Personal Choreography

Planning Our Lives

In the vastness of the cosmos, there is a synchronicity, a rhythm, a predictable schedule that can be foretold centuries in advance. We can look at a prepared chart and determine at what time the sun will rise on March 12, 2115. God's world is a marvel of beauty and cooperation. We enjoy the seasons, the stars, and the migrating birds. All is in tune with nature. People see life on earth quite differently. We do not live in such harmony but rather find fault with one another, separate into select groups, choose special relationships and all of this fortifies our belief that we are all different from each other, and have nothing in common.

Belief in Chaos

There is a commonly accepted and persistent idea that we are some kind of pawns in life, subject to the whims of fate and in danger at all times. It is so generally accepted that we have no problem insisting loudly that it is the truth about our lives. I recall reading, a few years ago, a comment by a sports writer in Albany: "And please remember: nobody—and I mean nobody—controls his own destiny." It is that kind of arrogance on the part of humans that prevents us from 'seeing' and accepting the truth of our being.

Why is this arrogant notion such a comfortable and accepted idea? Perhaps because we have become accustomed to the 'victim' role in our lives. Perhaps it stems from an unwillingness to take responsibility for our circumstances. Perhaps we feel free to dissociate ourselves from life's experiences and choose rather to place blame on someone else, a group, or God. This belief keeps us in a constant state of fear, doubt, and misgivings. Combined, these beliefs have become so accepted that we live out our lives as potential victims of other individuals, other countries, nature's behavior, and our own self-condemnation.

Free Choice

Where, in all of this, does our free choice fit in? Of all known species, only humans have imagination and free choice. If we live our lives out at the mercy of some unknown, unseen 'fate,' how can we explain free choice? Is our free choice limited to rebel against what 'fate' delivers or yield to it? Some would say 'yes'.

God created our spirit selves in the Beginning. We are His beloved children. As His beloved children we know everything, have access to the power of God, and many angels assist us on our journey through life. But through the process of devolution—believing that we left God—we have completely forgotten we have the ability to access all knowledge, to choose whatever we desire, to control our circumstances, and most significantly, we have forgotten that we are part of God, and therefore eternal.

Adults—parents or guardians—take care of us when we are children. They are not responsible for us, because we already planned our lives, including our choice of parents, [with their permission]. However, adults are responsible to their children, and later, as there is role reversal, adult children care for their parents. We each are responsible only for ourselves. Young people have to be taught responsibility because it does not come naturally. The most difficult lesson Gabriel taught, I believe, is the fact that we plan our lives. Like many others, I did not have a great childhood. Born into a middle class family it fell apart shortly after my father's death and became extremely dysfunctional. Yet, after learning that we plan our lives I realized that I had learned much from that early experience. And I planned it in order to learn the lessons.

"Before you came to Earth you decided what experiences you wanted to walk through and what it was exactly that you intended to glean from these experiences. Some of them will be painful. Some of them will be joyous. Some of them will be a boost upward in your evolution. Some of them will be a stumbling block. You create ahead of time the road map of your earthly journey." [1]

Gabriel said it is interesting to watch us gather on the astral plane and decide who is going to be the father, the mother, and the children. And if a woman says she wants to raise a child but not go through labor to birth one, another woman will say, 'I'll have a child and put it up for adoption.' This lesson from Gabriel denies the common belief that we choose our friends but our relatives are thrust upon us.

"Everything that you do, you have planned before you came here, and you will not vary from that. The average person doesn't know enough to change their mind. And so they follow unerringly the path that they chose before they entered the earth plane." [2]

All of this planning does not indicate predestination. This is so because after we come to earth we can change our plan at any moment in time. When Gabriel was asked what happens then to the others who planned to participate in our lives. He answered that we simply, while asleep, tell them we have changed our mind and they have to do with that whatever they desire. "You can change [your plan] at any point. All you have to do is go up to the higher self of you, contact those who are interacting with you and say, 'I have changed my mind. I have decided that I shall do this instead.' Then that causes them to shift their plan and their interaction with you and so forth, and the change is complete." [3]

When Archangel Gabriel came to teach in 1987 we had no idea that Jesus the Christ would also come to teach. Gabriel did say, however, that there would be another one to follow him. On November 20th 1995 the Master did come, and he spoke of our planned life on earth:

> The journey you have selected is an ancient journey of mankind brought to bear upon the individual by the very spirit of their own God self. Each of you selected, always each of you selected, that which you do, the experiences that you would create and experience and then cast off. You each have chosen to be exactly where you are. You each have chosen the woes that beset your path just as you have each chosen the joys that you experience. I challenge you to leave behind your woe . . . For only as you partake of that which is sacred can you aptly recognize that which is not sacred." [4]

Once we accept the idea that we plan our lives, we can review the lessons we have learned and allow the old angers; the old resentments fade away by forgiving anyone we thought had harmed us. "Some of you chose a totally unreasonable spouse . . . parents that abused you . . . work places that are very debilitating to your energy and to your interests . . . physical bodies that will give you . . . every kind of pain or ailment that you can think of . . . And some of you have taken all of the blessings that God pours out upon you, turned them upside down and sent them scurrying on their way so you can sit there and say, 'Poor me, I have nothing'!" [5]

There are many things that our body does automatically without our participation. Our heartbeat, our breathing, the flow of blood, the digestive system, and the elimination system all manage themselves very nicely when we love our body and treat it well. That is a blessing, as noted by Emanuel Swedenborg in *Divine Providence*:

"We know that we do outward things consciously—we see with our eyes, hear with our ears, taste with our tongues, feel with our skin . . . It is enough that we are conscious of these external processes, and manage them for the health of body and mind. If we cannot do this, what would happen if we had control of the inner processes as well?" [6]

The spirit and soul of us knows that we are all on our return journey to God, our Source. Our perceptions tell us it is a rough road. "You perceived in your thought that it [returning to God] was a hard and arduous journey, and so you created a hard and arduous journey. When in truth, all it is, is forgiving, releasing, and knowing where you are . . . The only one you need to forgive is you. As you do, you rise to an awareness where you recognize there is no need to forgive anyone because no one has done anything, not even you." [7]

We find it so easy to blame others, to project our woes on others that it becomes second nature to us. Others agree because they share the same resentments and the same angers. We tell ourselves it is 'justified anger' and seek out others to commiserate with. But Gabriel's teachings turn that idea upside down. "You call into your life those who will interact with you in a way that will allow you to act out that which you have chosen, be they friend or foe, be they comforter or antagonist. You have invited them there or they wouldn't be there." [8]

In typing this I am reminded of one of the phrases Gabriel used that stunned me. There were many. "Nothing will happen to you that you did not plan—for God wouldn't allow it!" I don't recall when or where this was said, but it validates God's love for us and His Will for us to have joy, peace, and abundance in our lives. And when we do not, we have brought about something else. "When one is so poverty aware that one chooses to live out of garbage cans, that is up to the individual to change their thinking and change the value they place upon their own life. When they value the life that is in them, their consciousness changes and as their consciousness changes, they will stop living in a poverty consciousness." [9]

This reminds one of the prodigal son who, when eating the slop he was feeding the pigs he reflected on his father's abundance and knew his family was eating well. That was the point in which his consciousness changed and he realized that he had the choice of giving up his situation and seeking another way. The fundamental plan of our chosen lives is to awaken to the divinity within.

" . . . when you come into the earth's vibration you find it very difficult to retain that connectedness to the God self of you. It is at that point that you begin to see or believe that you are separate from God; that God is someplace far off high above you and you can't reach Him. However, the lives that you have were carefully planned and orchestrated by yourselves in order to present to you certain opportunities to use your realization of how you are indeed the child of God." [10]

Information about the other side has been received by those able and willing to listen. In Boss' book *In Silence They Return*, she quotes an entity in the spirit world. The words coincide with Gabriel's teachings:

EVERYTHING THAT HAPPENS TO YOU ON THIS EARTH IS THE RESULT OF YOUR FREE WILL NOW. WHEN YOU USE GOD YOU WILL BE GUIDED BY HIM—YOU ARE THE ONE WHO MAKES YOUR EARTH LEVEL, WITH OR WITHOUT GOD, DEPENDING ON YOUR CHOICE. TO CHOOSE OR NOT TO CHOOSE GOD

MAKES THE DIFFERENCE. THIS IS WHERE PRAYER COMES IN—IT IS DIRECT COMMUNICATION WITH GOD.[11]

Seeking direction from God is the key. God is ever with us—closer than hands and feet. But we must make a conscious choice to allow Him to guide us and when we do, life becomes much easier. We learn to love and forgive and be aware of the love in others. "You are led moment by moment. Every moment of your lives you are divinely led and guided. Whatever transpires in your life, you chose to walk through for what lesson it has to bring you. Anything that happens to you is momentary." [12]

Because we plan our lives there are no 'accidents.' Gabriel made this very clear. Accidents happen suddenly and so we do not expect them. We have not consciously planned them, but subconsciously we planned them.

"The thing is, Beloveds, you are responsible for you. The Holy Spirit is responsible for keeping you and God connected because it is through the Holy Spirit that you make your way back in your consciousness." [13]

Our plans are only in our subconscious, however.
"The part of you that has the most control over your lives is the part of you that you don't give a whole lot of thought to and that is the subconscious part of you . . . None of you . . . would deliberately choose to become ill or to have a problem or to enter into a situation that would cause despair . . . However, you do rise in the morning quite prepared for battle for the day." [14]

Emanuel Swedenborg wrote about our erroneous belief in coincidence. "Many people in this world attribute everything to themselves and to their own prudence, and anything they cannot claim in this way they attribute to chance or coincidence. They do not realize that human prudence is nothing and that 'chance' and 'coincidence' are empty words." [15]

The Master Jesus said this: "There is no supernatural power sent by God to erase your error perceptions . . . I tell you a grand truth. You are the power that will release forever that which binds you." [16] He also told us, "Beloved lights, your journey is sacred. Your fears are unfounded, and your trust is never betrayed. Believe and as you believe, so it is done unto you . . . It is the Father's good pleasure to lead you into the Kingdom." [17]

Reading this last phrase, one is reminded of Luke 12:32 and one can't help but wonder that Jesus the Christ must have infinite patience to continue telling us the same thing through the centuries. When, I wonder, will we understand, accept, and live his teachings?

Some of the things Gabriel told us about our lives and our journey home as being our responsibility:

— "You are here to learn how to love even when love seems to be absent. You are here to learn that every one of you is a treasure, that nobody is the bad guy." [18]

— "Coming to recognize the divine self within you is not as difficult as it first appears . . . . You are consciousness, and that life and that consciousness had its beginning somewhere far beyond this little limiting body that you occupy . . . Your consciousness goes far beyond what your physical brain allows. Recognizing that is as simple as changing the way you think". [19]

— "Your thinking process pulls in the energy that you require. What things you draw to you, what things you do not draw to you, what thing you repel from you . . . all of these come from the same source. The way you believe begets more of what you believe. Do you see a pattern here? . . . We have told you this ten million times, I guess!" [20]

— "You die, as you call it, when you choose to. No one can vary that, excepting you. Only you have the power to change your mind to live longer or live lesser, as you call it . . . You choose when you will leave, and only you." [21]

— "God allows you complete free will, and you choose when you will go, and that is acceptable to Him . . . Whether you are in a physical body or whether you are free of a body is of no difference to Him. He sees you as that loved expression of joy. Where you have taken yourself doesn't matter to Him. His love and His joy in you never diminishes . . . It is only you who perceive yourself to be at the point of death or at the point of some great adversity." [22]

— "You are never more in charge of your life than you are when you completely surrender to God. At that point your own God self takes over and does everything wonderful for you." [23]

— "Now remember, to exercise your spirituality requires that you must meet certain challenges in order for you to realize that you are able to overcome them." [24]

Whenever we find ourselves in a painful situation—whether it be physical or emotional—we sometimes realize that the day will come when the pain will end. And that day is seen as the day we 'die.' Jesus the Christ demonstrated 2,000 years ago that there is no death. He not only resurrected but appeared to many after his resurrection. Gabriel assures us that there is no death, but rather a freeing of our spirit: "Actually, death is the freeing of the spirit from a particular adventure upon the earth. Life is eternal and death is an illusion. It is the grandest of illusions because everybody believes in it. But death is really a change of form. It is the laying aside of something you are no longer using and going onward. It is not the end of the individual by any means." [25]

The Use of Dreams

"Since ancient times, people have been tantalized and tormented by their dreams . . . Though they differ in their perspectives and goals; this common thread runs through them all: dream work is an unfailing catalyst for self-discovery. It's virtually impossible to work with a dream, your own or someone else's, and not obtain some kind of revelation or insight." [26]

Gabriel explained that " . . . all dreams have a purpose . . . There are dreams that are very prophetic. Then there are dreams that are trying to show you how to look at a situation in a different way. Dreams symbolize a truth that you need to deal with. Some dreams . . . are very literal." [27]

Many dreams are reported in Scripture by many persons. The most famous dream is described in Daniel, Chapter 2. Nebuchadnezzar, king of Babylon, had a dream which troubled him greatly. He sought an interpretation of it from his magicians, astrologers, sorcerers, and wise men. None could interpret it. But David, whom the king held in prison, interpreted the dream for the king.

Perhaps it is this story which convinces people they need a professional to interpret their dreams. "One of the great stumbling blocks to a more intensive and widespread use of dreams is the notion that dreams have a single right interpretation, which the dreamer has little chance of deciphering without highly skilled psychological or psychic help. The attitude that all of us can and must work with our dreams needs to replace the notion that only highly skilled people can properly interpret dreams." [28]

A Course in Miracles addresses the importance of dreams in our lives: "Dreams are illusions of joining, because they reflect the ego's distorted notions about what joining is. Yet the Holy Spirit, too, has use for sleep, and can use dreams on behalf of waking if you let Him." [29]

Working with our dreams helps us to make a connection between the higher self of us and our waking consciousness. "One of the main problems of working with dreams is dealing with unconscious processes, which stand between our waking consciousness and our immediate access to the Divine. Yet when depicted in our dreams, even these barriers become instructive." [30]

When we sleep we vacate the body. "Not as in death. In death, the silver cord is severed and you can't go back. But when you are sleeping, you and your consciousness slip out of your body, and you go where you will and your body, your physical body, rests in slumber . . . angels always watch over your body." [31]

Because we have incarnated many times on earth, our dreams may include scenes from a past lifetime as well as a previous time in this incarnation. "There is no dimension of human life, whether social, financial, emotional or physical, mental or spiritual with which the dream may not on occasion deal . . . What we actually receive depends upon our attitudes, motivations, the measure of our attunement, and the extent to which we have made applicable what was received in earlier dreams and in waking experiences." [32]

One of the confusing things about dreams is that "the priorities set by our internal processes are not necessarily those we think of as important in our waking lives. As we recall our dreams, we may observe those things with which the inner life is concerned. The dreams may reflect the high priorities of the spiritual life or the detours we take, allowing our motivations to get us off the right track." [33]

Humans have a difficult time in concentrating. "You are easily led thither and yon. So usually in your sleep time we try to get you collected up. Sometimes we meet with you as a group. Sometimes we meet with you individually. But we always seek ever to keep you buoyed up . . . keep you with your goal in mind . . . We give you these intense lessons. Then we give you a time of allowing that to be digested and to be incorporated into your thinking, and so on. Then we give you another intensity." [34]

There has been an increasing amount of research in dreams which indicate that not only is sleep necessary for our general well-being, "but also the need to have a certain amount of dreaming sleep. It has been demonstrated that when deprived of this kind of sleep human beings, and other animals as well, become agitated and anxious." [35]

Gabriel explained that we need our " . . . Repose time because while your body is lying down and sleeping, you are off in the spirit world doing wondrous, enjoyable, loving things. This rests you from the heaviness of the earth because while you are lightly flitting about the spirit world, you are being reinvigorated." [36]

Recording one's dreams is the first step in interpreting them. Some dreams are vague and fleeting. We awaken knowing that we dreamed but cannot recall the dream. Other dreams are lucid and easily recalled. They must be recorded as soon as possible. Keeping a pad and pencil by the bed enables one to immediately write down a clear and memorable dream during the night. The next day the interpretation can be made.

Edgar Cayce offers a series of steps that we can apply when we choose to record and interpret our dreams. Cayce explains each step in detail. Here is an overview of the six steps:

1.   Write down your [spiritual] ideals.
2.   Have a seeking attitude.
3.   Write the dream immediately.
4.   Consider the dream from different levels and approaches.

5. Correlate these truths.
6. Decide upon a course of action.

In addition to dreams and the self-knowledge we can glean from them, the dreamless sleep is also spiritually beneficial to us, as explained by Gabriel:

> Now the dream state is that state in which you enter into the astral plane. There you experience the true and the false of it for the astral plane is a mixture of many things. Now the dreamless state is where you have transcended the astral plane and have gone into the higher realms. There you bring back information that is placed in the subconscious of you . . . you are bringing back with you the direction of your path, the outcome of certain things, the fulfillment of your goal . . . Your soul will then direct and guide you into the experiences that you require to fulfill your goal.[37]

In Morris' *The Dream Workbook,* she ends her book with this promise: "There are innumerable possible applications of dreamwork exercises in both our waking life and dream life; the more you explore them, the more you'll discover ways to use them. One thing is certain: stimulating your right brain and gaining access to the avenue between your unconscious and your conscious through dreamwork will enhance your potential for experiencing a full, rewarding life." [38]

Gabriel suggested that before we drop off to sleep we ask our angels to take us to the halls of learning. "We call it the halls of learning in order that your earthly minds might comprehend its purpose. But it is actually you going up [in sleep] to a state of consciousness in which you are able to embrace and understand the higher truths. These become permeated within your mind. When you return, although there is not a conscious memory, there is within the subconscious and super conscious mind of you what you have learned, and what you have remembered." [39]

History of Divination

There are several reasons for this topic within this chapter about our responsibilities. One of them is that Archangel Gabriel came to teach us through a dedicated, spiritually evolved woman with whom he had worked for 500 years to prepare her for the task of channeling him and channeling Jesus the Christ. Disbelieving in spirit communication would preclude us from hearing this wisdom of the ages. At the same time Gabriel was channeling in New York State, he told us there were eleven master teachers coming to centers of light all around the planet earth, all to teach the same lesson: "Wake up to your divinity and live from the Lord God of Your Being. You are all children of God. Walk you in the light; you are the light."

Ever since time began, humans have wondered what the future holds and have sought to know from others who were talented with psychic gifts. Scripture is replete with examples of psychic phenomena, including healing, spirit voices, visions, and many other methods. Some people believe that God only gifted the ancients with these talents. Why would that be so? Jesus said he would not leave us comfortless, and many have found great comfort in hearing from their loved ones on the other side. Knowing there is life after 'death' enables us to look forward to reuniting with loved ones again. Sometimes a loved one on the other side warns us of pending problems. Because forgiveness comes easily after one transitions, earthlings have heard from seeming enemies that everything is fine between them now.

Another reason for this topic is that when the history of a talent is explained, there is a willingness to accept one's current experience with it. Divination has had a bad name in the past only because it was not understood. And no one sought to understand it, so there was no acceptance of it outside the field of believers who accepted it as a gift of the spirit.

> *Now there are diversities of gifts, but the same Spirit . . .*
> *For to one is given by the Spirit the word of wisdom; to another*
> *the word of knowledge by the same Spirit;*
> *To another faith by the same Spirit; to another the gifts of*
> *healing by the same Spirit.;*
> *To another the working of miracles; to another prophecy; to*
> *another discerning of spirits; to another divers kinds of tongues:*
> *to another the interpretation of tongues:*
> *But all these worketh that one and the selfsame Spirit, dividing*
> *to every man severally as he will.* I Cor. 12:4-11

Prophecy and *discerning of spirits* are some of the spiritual gifts that Paul mentions.

There are a few psychics who are charlatans and deceive others about their psychic abilities. When a psychic asks for a large sum of money to provide a message, that is deception, for which the psychic will pay a price. For the most part psychics and mediums are sincere and helpful.

The ancients had their sybils and oracles. The Delphic Oracle was the best known. Kings sought messages and traveled far to learn about the destiny of their realms. Gold and other gifts were stored in many places atop Mount Parnassus, where the oracle resided.

The Puritans, upon establishing themselves in the New World of America, hated and feared the women who could prophesy. And so they tried them and burned them at the stake in Salem, Massachusetts, until cooler heads prevailed and stopped the killings.

In recent history many people—from all strata of society, including government officials—seek and receive psychic readings, "I have sat for many persons in government circles—congressmen, senators, members of the State Department and special agencies; for generals and admirals, ambassadors, special envoys and others in extremely high places." [40]

"Everyone who lives in the great white house, as you call it, has contact in some manner with spirituality through mediums, psychics, astrologers, different things." [41]

Law enforcement agencies have been known to call on the expertise of mediums and psychics to locate a missing body when a murder is known to have been committed.

Gabriel referred to his channeling: "Certainly I am not the only one channeling. I know you all have heard other channelers, most of you anyway." [42]

In *Nothing So Strange* we find a message brought from a former editor of the Bombay Times: "God is the goal, Jesus Christ is the Way. Buddha, Gandhi, everyone can be a Way, or a Way-shower to the degree of their being. You see, God still speaks through people. In this new age the veil is becoming very thin between the seen and the unseen aspects of the universe." [43]

There is great promise for this increasing use of telepathy, as noted by Gabriel: "There is a time coming soon upon your earth when groups of people will meet to develop telepathy. They are already doing it secretly, but soon they will be doing it openly and thoughts traveling through the ethers will be a common way of communication." [44]

In *A Course in Miracles* the Master addresses the issue of psychic phenomena:

"Certainly there are many 'psychic' powers that are clearly in line with this course. Communication is not limited to the small range of channels the world recognizes. If it were, there would be little point in trying to teach salvation. It would be impossible to do so. The limits the world places on communication are the chief barriers to direct experience of the Holy Spirit, Whose Presence is always there and Whose Voice is always available but for the hearing." [45]

CHAPTER 7

Trailblazers

"The decision to consciously step upon a spiritual path is simply a matter of changing our thinking. We will not, we can not, walk it alone. "We do not go alone. And we give thanks that in our solitude a Friend has come to speak the saving Word of God to us . . . An unheard message will not save the world, however mighty be the Voice that speaks, however loving may the message be".[1]

Throughout the centuries, many have come to earth to show us the way. Sacred writings of all religions show us the way.

"Individual religions, like different nations and cultures, have unique characteristics. But these characteristics are only the surface aspects; the fundamental principles at the heart of all religions (like those at the core of all cultures and nations) are universal.
"For this reason, the letters of the law, or the surface meanings found in the words of the teachings, are not as integral as the spirit of the law, which is universal and shared by all religions and cultures." [2]
The Old Testament provides the names and activities of many prophets. Their fellow humans managed to kill them all. Jesus the Christ came to show us a more upbeat way than the 'shalt not's of the Mosaic Law, and couched his teachings in a more positive vein, as shown in the beatitudes of Matthew, [3]

How important to know and understand what Gabriel said about the Master Jesus' life—Jesus was a good Jew, born of faith-filled Jewish parents. He did not come to start a new religion but rather to wake up all humanity to its own divinity. He came to show us the way and in Scripture many references are found describing Jesus as an example to follow, and he often said, Follow me.

Since Jesus is our example, our pattern to follow, it is necessary that we study the way he lived and the things he taught. Gabriel explained that Jesus the Christ came to earth many times before he manifested the Christ

Love in the man Jesus of 2,000 years ago. We also have come to earth many times. Gabriel told us that we have all been saints, we have all been murderers, and we have all been homosexuals. He stated that we have journeyed to earth so many times in history that we have met every other person now living on planet Earth!

Jesus also said, *He that believeth on me, the works that I do shall he do also; and greater works than these shall he do; because I go unto my Father.*[4]
Taking him at his word, we cannot help but wonder what *'greater works'* there could be than those he performed. What could be greater than walking on water, raising the dead, changing water to wine and healing instantly? One day we will know what he meant. *'because I go unto my Father'* may mean that because he ascended after the crucifixion, or it may mean that he frequently went within to the Father in meditation, as he withdrew from the disciples to meditate. As we assume the habit of frequently going within to meditate and ask that our will be aligned with the Will of God, we also can accomplish what he accomplished in his lifetime.

Jesus' Earlier Incarnations

Jesus lived many previous lifetimes on earth, but Gabriel told us only of the ones in which there was a significant shift in consciousness. Gabriel described some of the past incarnations of Jesus in his seminar titled *Master Jesus,* on January 18, 1997. At this seminar Gabriel was asked if Jesus had been Adam, but he said no, there never was a man named Adam; the Garden of Eden story is an allegory. The essential lesson of the allegory is the statement that Adam fell asleep, and nowhere in Scripture does it say that Adam woke up! Adam (symbol of humanity) fell asleep to his own divinity—his connection to God—and as yet humanity has not awakened to its own divinity.

Enoch
The first incarnation of Jesus that Gabriel described was that of Enoch. As noted in the Old Testament: *And Enoch walked with God after he begat Methuselah . . .* Gen. 5:22. Enoch is also referred to in the New Testament: *By faith Enoch was translated that he should not see death; and was not*

found, because God had translated him: for before his translation he had this testimony, that he pleased God. Heb. 11:5

This is a clear statement that Enoch ascended as did Jesus centuries later. Levi, author of *The Aquarian Gospel of Jesus the Christ*, received instructions from the Spirit of Supreme Intelligence: "Write full the story of the Christ who built upon the Solid Rock of yonder circle of the sun—the Christ who men have known as Enoch the Initiate".[5]

Enoch means "Entrance into and instruction in a new state of thought, of understanding. In the case of the Enoch who walked with God the new state of thought would be spiritual consciousness, the new life in Christ." [6]

Edgar Cayce provides us with information about Enoch: "Again it [the soul who became Jesus] was manifested in Enoch, who oft sought to walk and talk with that divine influence; with the abilities latent and manifested in self to find self in the varied realms of awareness, yet using the office of relationships as a channel through which blessings might come, as well as recommendations and warnings might be indicated to others." [7]

Hermes
After Enoch, the Master incarnated as Hermes, who lived at the time of Ra, the Egyptian Sun God, or Amenhotep IV. Gabriel speaks about the problems that Hermes had with his ego, and thus lost his 'magic touch' because of his own self-conceit: "Hermes was famous for his talent of turning anything into gold and was sought by kings to do so, but eventually he got lost in his own creative ability and was so impressed with his own popularity that he never [as Hermes] reclaimed the Christ Love." [8]

Melchizedeck
The next incarnation of our beloved Master Jesus which was described by Gabriel, was Melchizedeck. In the Old Testament we find, *And Melchizedeck king of Salem brought forth bread and wine: and he was the priest of the most high God.* Gen 14:18 Ritual was extremely important during this period. The ritual used basic substances for the people of the time. Bread is the staff of life, could be made anywhere, and would not spoil easily on nomadic journeys. Bread was the symbol of the substance of life force from which everything comes forth. Wine represented blood, or the

continuing flow of life. Gabriel explained that Melchizedeck introduced the idea of Holy Communion to Abraham and Abraham introduced the idea to the people. The idea was thus presented of taking into the body the Essence of God, symbolized by everyday substances.[9]

Joseph

Joseph was the son of Jacob and Rachel. (Gen35:22-24), and was the next earthly life of Jesus which was described by Gabriel. The story of Joseph being sold into slavery by his brothers is found in Gen 37:28. And Joseph's willingness to forgive his brothers their betrayal is found in Gen 4:1-5. Gabriel told us that this forgiving act was the very first expression on earth of the forgiveness consciousness that used love rather than vengeance.[10]

Joshua

Joshua was the next incarnation of Jesus that Gabriel described. Joshua, son of Nun, was Moses' minister and the leader of Moses' army. In his reading 362-1[11] Edgar Cayce referred to Joshua: " . . . Joshua the prophet, the mystic, the leader, the incarnation of the Prince of Peace".

Cayce mentioned Joshua more than once. "Thus . . . may ye use the Son of man, Jesus, the Master, as the ideal in the present, and find a new meaning—if there is the studying and paralleling of the life of Jesus and of Joshua." [12]

"In the Hebrew the name [Joshua] is identical with the name Jesus." [13] This is a very interesting piece of information. Archangel Gabriel told us (1/18/97)[14] that Moses knew what he wanted to do but not how to put it in action. He ardently desired to please God, but feared his actions would offend God. He asked Joshua for help and said to him, "Get these people to the Promised Land". Joshua had a warrior mentality and he had vast power including the ability to read the signs of the earth . . . and so he tuned into the earth's vibration and discerned that an earthquake was coming. When he arrived at the river he heard an angel suggest he had carriers take the Ark of the Covenant out into the water. Ten miles upriver the earthquake stopped the flow of water so that Moses and his people could cross.

After crossing the river, Joshua was faced with Jerusalem's warriors equipped with chariots and their menacing spoked wheels. Joshua knew the chariots could not mount the hills, and so he took the battle to the towns up in the hills. With his huge manpower he ordered the men to 'take no prisoners,' and all the people of all the towns were murdered—men, women, and children. Joseph was the forgiver, Joshua the slaughterer.

This information startled the author—that the man who spiritually grew into the Christ consciousness was capable of engaging in mass slaughter. What is so significant about this story of Joshua is that it represent a time when the Master, in a previous life, killed many people for Moses. In this regard he misused the power of God that was in him. How often do we, Jesus' spiritual siblings, misuse our God-given power? Metaphysically interpreted, the total slaughter represents the elimination of all thoughts of limitation. We must abandon all our thoughts of limitation as we go within and know there are no limitations in spirit. In quoting Scripture, Gabriel said that *Every knee shall bow* (Rom 14:11) . . . means every illusion will bow to the Almighty God.

Buddha

The penultimate incarnation of Jesus was Buddha. Gabriel explained that Buddha was born in wealth and lived a protected life. After marrying and having a child he ventured outside the temple walls for the first time. For the first time he saw death, disease, poverty and hunger. He could not understand how these things could be, and so he left his wife and child to embark on a quest to learn. He rejected all comforts, wore ragged clothes and stopped eating until he nearly destroyed his intestines. Seeing his reflection in a pool he thought, 'I am thin and wretched and I still do not understand.' So he dressed, ate, and concluded that the outside world did not give him an answer. So he decided to 'go within' and meditate. When others saw him sitting in silence they perceived him to be a guru and brought him food and water. He learned one great truth: compassion, respect, love for all life was the only way to leave behind one's karma and not build any karma by negative thinking.

Buddha did not always sit under a tree, as depicted. He walked and helped others. Buddha's teachings are almost identical with Jesus' teachings. When Jesus traveled (from age 12 to 30) he visited Kapivastu, India. One of the priests there said, "Is this not Buddha come again in flesh? No other one could speak with such simplicity and power." [15]

Gabriel further explained that Buddha had a total understanding of human needs—compassion and forgiveness. On the astral plane after the Buddha incarnation, he contemplated how he had brought these aspects of himself into understanding and how he could bring them to fullness . . . . Then, Gabriel said, the Master Jesus spent five hundred years of earth time, surrendering absolutely to the Will of God. Then he incarnated as Jesus. On January 18, 1997, after describing the previous incarnations of Jesus Gabriel gave a summary. Then he said that Buddha considered wisdom the paramount goal in life, but from his perspective on the other side after his transition, he realized that the paramount goal in life is love, and so he came as Jesus to teach it and to demonstrate it.

The Christian Bible's Influence

Christian Scripture has been the source of inspiration to millions, including the great artists throughout history.
"In all ages great men have gone to the Bible as to the very springs of thought and inspiration. This Book lent Milton his Paradise Lost; lent Handel his Messiah; lent Titian his Transfiguration; lent Christopher Wren the plan of his cathedral; lent liberty to Cromwell; lent Lincoln a rule, 'golden' for white and black alike." [16]

The Metaphysical bible

There are many Bible students who insist that its every word is the infallible word of God. Others have concluded that there are hidden meanings in all the stories of the Bible. For them, the metaphysical interpretations offer a richer and deeper comprehension of the Bible stories.

Archangel Gabriel frequently referred to Scripture during his lectures and seminars. He addressed the metaphysical aspects of the Bible and said, "Remember always that everything in the Scripture was written in allegory. Within all things in your Scripture there is a seed of truth . . . So everything is written in allegorical ways in order that those who truly seek to know will find within the Scripture a guidance and a truth." [17]

The significance of metaphysical interpretation of the Bible was emphasized by Gabriel, on April 8, 1996(p.14), when he said, "{symbolism]—it is the only way it [the Bible] could carry any truth. It is through its symbolism . . . Unfortunately, there is very little in it that is worthy of being taken literally. But it is a very valuable book when the symbolism is deciphered and understood

. . . the best way to read the bible is from your heart and do your own deciphering, because all people are right no matter how they decipher. There again . . . the truth will be revealed to he who seeks."

Some current authors have addressed the symbolic meaning of the Bible. Others have indicated that clearly there are supernatural events described in it. Psychic phenomena permeate its pages, for those who are familiar with such phenomena. Two examples are burning bush (Ex. 3:2-4) and the pillar of cloud (Ex. 13:21)

"If ever there was a manifestation of the supernatural, it was in the condition of things out of which arose the New Testament. We have only to take up the Epistles of St. Paul and we find him surrounded, penetrated, permeated with the supernatural. It is, as it were, the very atmosphere which he breathes. He does not assert it. He does not need to assert it . . . St. Paul assumes it as a fact everywhere present to the consciousness of his readers as much as to his own." [18]

A comprehensive view of the Bible was published by Unity School of Christianity in 1931. It provides the metaphysical meaning of all the proper names in the Bible. In the Preface we find, "Apart from its being a book of great historical and biographical interest, the Bible is, from Genesis to Revelation, in its inner or spiritual meaning, a record of the experiences and the development of the human soul and of the whole being of man; also it is a treatise on man's relation to God, the Creator and Father."

For the reader to understand the metaphysical explanations of the Judeo-Christian Bible, some examples of the symbolism are given here:

Adam
"The first movement of mind in its contact with life and substance . . . This Adam is all of what we term soul, intellect, and body. We are continually at work with this Adam; we can breathe into his nostrils the breath of life, inspiring him with the idea of life in all its unlimited fullness. We can lift

up this Adam by infusing into him those sublime ideas, and in no other way." [19]

Eve
"Love, or feeling, in individual consciousness . . . Woman symbolized the soul region of man and is the mother principle of God in expression." [20]

Eden
"A pleasant, harmonious, productive state of consciousness in which are all possibilities of growth. When man is expressing in harmony with Divine Mind, bringing forth the qualities of Being in divine order, he dwells in Eden, or in a state of bliss in a harmonious body." [21]

Egypt
"The realm of substance and life in the depths of the body consciousness. To the unregenerate soul it is the land of darkness and mystery, yet it is essential to the perpetuation of the body . . . We also refer to Egypt as the flesh consciousness, sense consciousness, or material consciousness." [22]

Bethlehem
"Bethlehem means 'house of bread,' symbolizing the abiding place of substance . . . At Bethlehem, the substance center in man, a union of love and wisdom takes place, and the Christ is brought forth in substance." [23]

Nazareth
"Nazareth was despised place [. . . can there any good thing come out of Nazareth? John 1:46] . . . yet in this commonplace village Jesus was reared; and in the seemingly mediocre mind the Christ Truth is received and expressed. Nazareth typifies the commonplace mind of man, but it is a place of development, through which the Christ comes into expression."[24]

Gethsemane
"The struggle that takes place within the consciousness when Truth is realized as the one reality." [25]

Metaphysical Parables
When one considers the metaphysical interpretations of Scripture, it naturally follows that one consider the metaphysical interpretations of the

many parables Jesus presented to the people. We first may ask why Jesus taught in parables in the first place.

Matthew refers to the psalmist's words: *All these things spake Jesus unto the multitude in parables; and without a parable spake he not unto them: That it might be fulfilled which was spoken by the prophet, saying, I will open my mouth in parable; I will utter things which have been kept secret from the foundation of the world.* Matt 13:35

Jesus himself addresses the topic: *Because it is given unto you to know the mysteries of the kingdom of heaven, but to them it is not given.* Matt 13:11-17. This could be interpreted to mean that the multitude was not entitled to know the mysteries of the kingdom. Yet Jesus never devalued anyone, never discriminated against anyone. His teachings were all-inclusive. It is likely that what he meant was that his close followers, by their faith and by their devotion to the Word, would understand the meaning whereas the multitude required parables in order that they might derive his wisdom from experiences of their daily lives.

Jesus' parables, and all his teachings, mostly went over the head of the farmers, shepherds, and peasants to whom he spoke. *Therefore speak I to them in parables; because they seeing see not; and hearing they hear not, neither do they understand.* Matt 13:13 In the 13th chapter of the Gospel according to Matthew, Jesus gives several parables to the disciples, that they might fully understand the Kingdom of God.

Even the learned rabbi, Nicodemus, had difficulty comprehending the hidden meaning in Jesus' teachings. Nicodemus was a wise and educated man of his day. When Jesus said one must be born again, Nicodemus said, *How can a man be born when he is old? can he enter the second time into his mother's womb, and be born?* John 3:4

The esoteric meaning of Jesus' words eluded him. They were beyond the limited understanding of that time on Earth. Only in its advanced stage of comprehension can humanity understand the hidden meaning of the Bible stories. Gabriel explained that it takes humanity 2,000 years to get a new idea in its head.

Other Trailblazers

More current trailblazers for us on our spiritual path are some modern day mystics and sages who have provided us with inspiring words of guidance. "There are lots of them [prophets and seers] on earth at this time . . . Listen with your heart. Do their words encourage you to be all you can be? Do their words encourage you to be free in the love of God and not be bound by rules and regulations?" [26]

Anne Bancroft wrote about some of them in her book, *Twentieth Century Mystics and Sages*. The following page numbers refer to her book, unless noted. Biographies of these men can be read elsewhere. It is their beliefs that are placed here:

Alan Watts

"[*Alan Watts*] became an Episcopalian priest and served as chaplain to Northwestern University. His theory of life and his place in it: "I feel this whole world to be moved from the inside, and from an inside so deep that it is my inside as well, more truly I than my surface consciousness." [27]

Thomas Merton

Merton was a Trappist monk. Upon seeing the many carved figures of the Buddha when visiting the caves of polonnaruwa of Ceylon, he said, "The rock, all matter, all life, is charged with dharmakaya (law and truth) . . . everything is emptiness and everything is compassion. I don't know when in my life I have ever had such a sense of beauty and spiritual validity running together in one aesthetic illumination."[28]

Pierre Teilhard de Chardin

The Jesuit priest, *Pierre Teilhard de Chardin*, in Writing in *Time of War*: "There can be no doubt that we are conscious of carrying within us something greater and more indispensable than ourselves. Something that existed before we did and could have continued to exist without us: something in which we live, and that we cannot exhaust: something that serves us but of which we are not masters: something that will gather us up when, through death, we slip away from ourselves and our whole being seems to evaporate."[29]

What a lucid description of God in us that this priest provides!

Krishnamurti
" . . . A mind which seeks sensation through experience becomes insensitive, incapable of swift movement and therefore it is never free. But in understanding its own self-centered activities, the mind comes upon this state of awareness which is choiceless, and such a mind is then capable of complete silence, stillness . . . It is only the still mind that can know eternity."[30]

Gurdjieff
Gurdjieff taught that the personality should be abandoned to reveal our essence: "When we speak of inner development and inner change, we speak of the growth of essence. The question now is not to acquire anything new but to recover and reconstruct what has been lost."[31]

This quotation of Gurdjieff reminds the author of a statement made by Archangel Gabriel. "I come to teach you nothing new; only to remind you of what you already know but have forgotten. "

Martin Buber
This Jewish prophet states:
"The It-world hangs together in space and time.
"The You-world does not hang together in space and time.
"What is essential is lived in the present, objects in the past."[32]

Aldous Huxley
Author *Aldous Huxley* wrote these profound words regarding the world as illusion. "The world is an illusion, but it is an illusion which we must take seriously, because it is real as far as it goes, and in those aspects of the reality which we are capable of apprehending. Our business is to wake up." [33]

Mother Teresa
Mother Teresa was the beloved practical mystic who saw in everyone a spark of divinity which responded to her own. When asked how she could help so many people as she did, her response: "I can give my whole heart to that person for that moment in an exchange of love. It is not

social work. We must love each other. It involves emotional involvement, making people feel they are wanted." [34]

In *Belief and Immortality* (4/13/96) Gabriel explained that Mother Teresa did not see a wretched, sick human being before her, but rather she had a conscious awareness of her own eternal spirit and saw that same eternalness in those she helped.

Recent Trailblazers

More recently we have read books by *Marianne Williamson, Eckhardt Tolle, Wayne Dyer, Deepak Chopra,* and others that inspire and uplift our thinking as we all travel on our spiritual upward path back to God. The *Dali Lama* offers us the kind of instructions and advice that we can use daily on this grand adventure of awakening:

"According to Buddhist philosophy, happiness is the result of an enlightened mind whereas suffering is caused by a distorted mind. This is very important. A distorted mind, in contrast to an enlightened mind, is one that is not in tune with reality." Dalai Lama (Dalai Lama website) from His Holiness the Dalai Lama's address to the inter-faith seminar organised by the International Association for Religious Freedom, Ladakh Group, in Leh on 25 August.

Many are the trailblazers who have come and continue to come, to show us the way back home to God. Not all trailblazers become famous. We each can recall a person or many persons who have inspired us to do more, to be more, in our daily lives.

CHAPTER 8

Ascension

In the process of going home to God, it is important to remember that there are two aspects of this journey. At any moment in time on Earth we can meditate—go within and touch into that Kingdom within us. In a larger sense we will physically ascend one day and be at one with the Father once more, as we were in the beginning. All humans are God's beloved children, created from Love as God breathed us forth eons ago. Over time—longer than our minds can comprehend—we have lost awareness of God' Light inside of us. When the Master Jesus came 2,000 years ago and told us that the Kingdom of God is within, it mostly went over our heads. It sounded wonderful, but we continued in the darkness of our thinking and responded with 'wouldn't it be nice if it were so.'

Lest one think that ascension is something that will occur centuries from now, please know that at one of Gabriel's seminars he spoke directly to a pregnant woman in the audience and told her, "The child you are carrying will ascend." I know the woman's name but will not divulge it here out of respect for her privacy.

Archangel Gabriel came at this time on Earth to awaken us, aware of the fact that Jesus' words were not fully understood. Gabriel did not perform any visible miracles, such as instant healing or raising the dead. He did not because he said that when Jesus performed miracles, everyone got caught up in the miracles and placed Jesus on a pedestal to be worshipped. In its obsession with his miracles, humanity missed the whole point of Jesus' teachings. He came to awaken all humanity to its God-Self. He came to teach and demonstrate the Love of God. He did not come to start a new religion or to be worshipped. Nowhere in Scripture is it reported that Jesus the Christ asked to be worshipped. Jesus did not call himself a king. In Matthew 27:11 Pilate asks Jesus *Art thou the King of the Jews?* Jesus replied, *Thou sayest.* In Mark 15:2 and Luke 23:3 Jesus responded *Thou sayest it.* But in John 18:37 Jesus answers more fully to Pilate's question. *Thou sayest I am a king. To this was I born, and for this cause came I into the world, that I should be witness unto the truth.* Cleary he denounces the title of king and clarifies for us that his only reason for coming into the world was to witness unto the truth.

To understand our journey back home to God, there are truths we must be aware of, such as the Ages of time. In learning truth we can, as God's children, come to understand our lives, why we are here, and how we are going to return home to God and Heaven, our natural habitat. We must also be aware of the kind of lives we need to live, from a standpoint of love and forgiveness.

The Cycle of Ages

As so well explained in the Introduction of *The Aquarian Gospel of Jesus the Christ,* there is a cycle of ages that exceeds the shorter monthly cycles we know as the astrological signs of the zodiac. In this cycle of the ages the universe we know revolves around a Central Sun and the revolution takes approximately 26,000 years. "It is conceded by all critical students that the sun entered the zodiacal sign Taurus in the days of our historic Adam when the Taurian Age began; that Abraham lived not far from the beginning of the Arian Age, when the sun entered the sign Aries."[1]

Archangel Gabriel said that he comes at the beginning of every age. The only previous age he mentioned was the one when he came 2,000 years ago. At that time he announced to Mary, mother of the Master, that she would bear a male child and call his name Jesus. Gabriel also came to Elizabeth, Mary's cousin, to announce that in her old age she would bear a son. He became John the Baptist. Gabriel came to Joseph, telling him to not abandon Mary because she was pregnant, for she was with a holy child of God.

Then Gabriel came at this turning of the ages. One might readily ask why Gabriel spoke only to a very few individuals 2,000 years ago and to a group this time. Simply put, humanity has evolved to the point where channeling information from the spirit world to earth is more accepted. Not by a majority but by a small, certain minority. We are embarking upon the Age of Aquarius. But more importantly, Gabriel said, it is the Age of Spirituality. Gabriel came to a few dedicated students in Albany, New

York. But Gabriel said that eleven Master Teachers also came to Earth at the same time. Those eleven came to channel through fine channelers—to bring seekers the wisdom they sought and would pass it on to others. Three came to the United States, others to Europe and elsewhere. There was only one lesson taught by them all, which applies to all humanity: Wake up and know that you are children of God. Live from the Lord God of Your Being. Live the light that you are.

Every sign in the Zodiac is ruled by two—a cherubim and a seraphim. The guardian spirits of the Piscean Age are Ramasa, the cherubim and Vacabiel is seraphim. The guardian spirits of the Aquarian Age are Archer, the cherubim and Sakmaquil the seraphim. In the Introduction to The Aquarian Gospel we find an exquisite description of the transfer of dominion from one Age to another. Then the author, Levi, as he was about to write what he heard, was told by Ramasa, "Not now, my son, not now; but you may write it down for men when men have learned the sacred laws of Brotherhood, of Peace on earth, good will to every living thing." And when the transfer ceremony ended, "the goddess Wisdom spoke, and with her hands outstretched she poured the benediction of the Holy Breath upon the rulers of Aquarius". [2]

Age of Spirituality

"The concentration of energies as you approach the year 2,000 is one of the breaking of the old mold . . . the old war-like, the old angers, the old pains, and so forth, and the emerging of a new spirit of truth which will ground people in a sense of joy, of love, of peace, of Godness."[3]

Although unseen, there is now on earth a great concentration of divine influence—a great concentration of angels and a great concentration of an upward spiral of human consciousness. "Fifty years ago of your time, there would not be a group like this . . . You come because you know that there is more to life than what appears to be."[4] Gabriel made a connection between the Master's appearance and our present time on earth. "This time there has come a Christ who started 2,000 years ago because he knew it would take you that long to learn. He knew that the energy had to reach a certain peak of power at a certain time in your perceived years for humankind, as a mass, to become aware that his was a choice that had to be made now, for there wasn't any time left."[5]

Adam, who slept in the Garden of Eden, represents humanity which still sleeps to its own divinity. "Everyone does [awaken], you know. That is why I come back every two thousand years, waiting for the next crop to come up to the light."[6]

Gabriel said we are not made in God's Image, but rather we *are* God's Image—made from the same Spirit that God is. God breathed us forth from Himself. We are his spiritual offspring and the only reason we feel separate from God is because we have brought our consciousness down into the lowest vibration possible—physical form—and believe that life on earth is all there is. God waits patiently for us to return to Him, but at every new age he sends Archangel Gabriel to help us rise in our consciousness above the earthly life.

"You went through the ages, and as you are coming into the new age, you went through all of these states of consciousness. There was a time when slavery was thought to be all right because it was mentioned in your Scripture. Now you all know that slavery is not all right."[7]

In this Age of Spirituality just now dawning on Earth, many changes will take place. "You will witness changes in governments and so forth that will be brought about by the influx of spiritual knowledge."[8]

Change, Gabriel explained, does not come gently. "You are just newly into the Age of Aquarius, and you have that smashing force. Are you not aware of your earth changes? They are already upon you. The floods we told you of have already been and so on . . . as that enlightenment comes forth, there has to be a breaking away. And that balancing force is what comes in and breaks it away."[9]

The importance of the New Age can not be over-emphasized. Gabriel said we are at a crossroads now: "The one fork in the road will take man into a spiritual conquest in which he will find that the place to be conquered and ruled is within. The other fork in the road will take him back to begin again, to start over, to begin to learn to speak a word, to write a word and so forth."[10]

The promise of the new age is the awakening of humanity. "This is the age of the spiritual awakening. This is the age when spirituality is going to be out in the open. This is the time, Beloveds, when you are going to be able to fully see the child of God within yourselves expressed and within others expressed."[11]

Earth as a Living Entity

"When there is a living organism such as the earth and other planets in the universes, they are the out picturing of a higher ideal which comes into a solid form to be used, to be dwelt upon, by the organisms who choose to resonate to that particular vibration. That is what makes you earthlings rather than Martians. Because all things are connected, there is nothing that is spinning out in the universe alone and bereft of any kind of care. For all things work together through a singular life fore. The various appearances are only various manifestations of that singular life force."[12]

Reading this phrase from Gabriel reminded me of the Bible quote: *And we know that all things work together for good to them that love God, to them who are the called according to his purpose.* Romans 8:28

Gabriel noted increased spiritual awareness of humanity: "If you will look about your earth at this time, you will see that the changes that are there are based on a better understanding of human nature . . . Look at how your country is being filled with people from other countries coming here to learn, to grow. Look how freedom and democracy are making their way around the world . . . All of these things, Beloveds, are going on around you and you don't see them as part of the miraculous upsurge of spirituality."[13]

It was promising indeed to hear Gabriel mention the reason for the increasing spirituality at this time on the planet Earth. It is because those entities choosing to come now desire greatly to bring peace. "The age that is upon you will bring a higher consciousness. The souls that are entering into earth form are those of a higher nature."[14] How grand it was to hear these words in the midst of all the violence that is so prevalent on earth. Gabriel also commented on the spiritual development at this time of earthlings:

"The consciousness of your earth at this time is the highest spiritual consciousness that has been attained thus far. You have reached a point where most people, regardless of their religious affiliations, believe in something more. You can call it God. You can call it Buddha. You can call it Christ. You can call it anything you want, but the belief system remains pretty much the same throughout your world . . . everyone believes in something."[15]

Gabriel also made note of the fact that Americans have a religious freedom unknown elsewhere. "When it comes to religious worship, you can't go anywhere else in the world and find the freedom that you have here in your country . . . You have the right to believe in any kind of God that you want to or to believe in none and you are not imprisoned for it or put to death for it. Learn to treasure what you have and to use what you have. Use that freedom to explore new horizons."[16]

When President Franklin D. Roosevelt (12/8/41) told the nation, "We have nothing to fear but fear itself", the nation steeled itself to win WWII. In the coming years we must remain calm to offset the fear mentality of the mass consciousness.

In the chaos of earth changes coming we were reminded by Gabriel to keep calm and not be fearful. The earth changes are merely Mother Earth cleansing herself. He said, "The new energy that is . . . in and is still coming in is a transformative energy and when something refuses to be transformed, it is broken. Now the purpose of it is to get it out of the way to let this new energy in. So what appears to be chaos is merely the stirring up of old negative conditions so that they can be dispersed and gotten rid of so that the new can come in and take its form. Always affirm, 'This has come to bless me,' and ever shall it do so."[17]

Gabriel also mentioned the effect on humans: "You are going to see manifested upon your earth psychological changes and emotional changes—a great surge of hatred and attacks upon one another. The reason being that the old ways are leaving and are dying slowly and with a hard fight . . . . You will witness many changes in governments and so forth that will be brought about by the influx of spiritual knowledge."[18]

Regarding the units of energy that comprise the universes, Gabriel at one time noted their effect on humans in their daily lives: "Within those units of energy are all the vibratory rates of domestic violence that beget more domestic violence, of war that begets more war, of diseases that ravage and kill. These are the vibrations that come in units of energy and beleaguer your physical world, and they are all coming from the higher, unseen, unknown realm of vibrational rates."[19] These words do not mean that God is 'after us,' they mean that we take the Divine Energy of the Creator and with our thoughts we misuse that energy and create chaos here on earth—in our homes, in our lives and in the world. The only chaos in the world is man-made. God does not create chaos.

In addition to earth changes, Gabriel noted there will be changes in the entire universe.

> Whenever a planet is awakened in the Christ, all of the other planets around it are affected as well . . . Uranus also quickened its vibration . . . And in the power of the movement of Uranus, it has a smashing effect on anything that does not yield to its movement. You might wonder why that [destructiveness] be so when the love and gentleness of the Christ Spirit is where the enlightenment would come. Why would there have to be . . . destructive power coming at the same time? Because there has to be something to move the old form of thinking, the old way of being, the old attitude, the old ways of looking at things. So whenever there is an awakening or enlightenment, there is also that smashing force that comes with it.[20]

For pragmatists like me, it was good to hear these words of Gabriel regarding the scientific approach of the universe: "If you wanted to approach this (view of the universe) from a scientific point rather than a spiritual point, you would find that the whole universe is mathematical."[21]

Ellen Wallace Douglas

Learning to Live in the New Age

"The days that lie ahead upon your earth are going to require that you have a center in you that you know is immovable, unchanging, forever. Otherwise, you will join the mass consciousness. Do not join the mass consciousness. Be the God of you. If you could not, then I would not come and tell you this . . . there will be changes of form upon your earth that will come and have their day and be gone. That has nothing to do with you as children of God. That is Mother Earth becoming greater."[22]

How our thoughts affect our lives

Some people believe that thoughts are not harmful as long as we do not put the thoughts into action. But Gabriel explains the effects, short term and long term, of our thought process.
"When you are doing something that doesn't require your rapt attention . . . pay close attention to what is drifting through your mind . . . You will go back to scenarios in your childhood . . . you will entertain thoughts of some kind of violence . . . The idea of what goes around comes around is a powerful truth. And the seeds that you sow, be it a million years ago, are going to bear fruit somewhere, sometime if only in the thought process of your mind."[23]

Negative thoughts have an effect on our bodies, our aura, and our world. We have so many negative thoughts. Anger, resentment, fear, doubt, judgment, criticism, condemnation are some. " . . . depending upon your thinking you will manifest discomfort, pain, whether it is a headache or stubbing your toe or spraining your ankle or smashing your finger or getting intestinal troubles. You get whatever is going to inflict physical pain upon your body . . . Another thing that brings you a great deal of distress is jealousy and envy. [these thoughts will] cause havoc in your life because they are so much a part of the pattern of your thinking. How do you stop? . . . It takes diligence, extreme diligence, but it can be done and is done. People do it."[24]

We often see others as our 'enemies' and sometimes wish them ill fate. But Gabriel said, "You are never angry with someone else. Ever. You are always angry with yourself. Even if your negative thoughts are about someone else, they are produced with the intent of self harm."[25] This was a revealing and surprising statement indeed!

All this negative thinking is the creation of humankind, Gabriel explained. "It is that aspect [of you] which denies God because God is love and positiveness and ongoingness and life sustaining."[26]

Evil was addressed by the dear archangel this way: "The only evil there is is what you believe in. When you believe there is evil, then you draw negative vibrations to you and they will present themselves to you as evil. But when you recognize that in truth evil is an illusion and the only thing that is real is God and truth and love, then you are not at all going to attract anything that you would perceive to be evil."[27]

More strongly put on December 3, 1999, in his farewell message, Gabriel said, " . . . every time you think a damning thought, whether it is to yourself or another, you distance yourself in consciousness from that blessing [of God]. You cannot pray for goodness and then look and see evil."[28]

Negative thinking to positive thinking

"For you have all become very addicted to excitement in a negative fashion . . . when you look at your . . . . picture boxes . . . the most popular are the ones that are violent."[29]

All of our problems are dealt with from one of two places; from the fear aspect or from the spiritual aspect. God provides us with the spiritual aspect. We created the fear aspect and it rules many lives. The key is to keep ourselves spiritually aligned. This does not require spending most of our time on our knees in prayer nor long meditations. It is a matter of keeping our thoughts on positive ideas, treating others in positive ways. Most importantly, it is a matter of treating ourselves in a loving, caring, gentle way. Accepting ourselves as children of God this ought not to be difficult.

Truth vs. Error Perceptions

Gabriel provided explanations for many of our error perceptions and gave us the truth. He brought only truth.

Truth and reality

"Don't' confuse truth with reality. Truth is that which is pure, unadulterated, has no agenda. Reality can have all kinds of other consequences. The thing is that from your soul you get information from your past experiences which are always based on a combination of your experiences, some of which are quite holy and others which are filled with error. So your soul is bringing into your response mechanism a mixed message. You are not getting the clarity that you should have."[30]

Empathy vs. sympathy

Empathy is compassion. "Learning to allow others to be whom and what they are is the first step toward compassion."[31] Another time Gabriel gave a specific instance of the difference between empathy and sympathy: "If you know a dear friend is going through a terrible time and you get down and you sorrow with them, are you of a benefit? But if you can see that it is just a part of a situation they have chosen and that they soon will go beyond it, then you can be of help, can you not? . . . That is what changes the world . . . not getting down and wallowing in sorrow. That accomplishes nothing."[32]

Religion and spirituality

Addressing the topic of religion at one time, Gabriel stated that all religions have some truth but no religion has *all* truth. "There are thousands of expressions of spirituality and all of them are real, all of them are true; all of them are the spirit of the human coming forth to express God according to their understanding at the time. That is why you have so many different religions. There are many different religions right in this room this night . . ."[33]

Fear and trust

Fear, Gabriel told us, is something we have created. "It chases you about, and you flee from it. If ever you were to turn and face your fears, you would find they would dissolve into nothingness. Fear is the biggest illusion. Believe in who you are. God believes in you!"[34]

Trusting in God and ourselves as His beloved children, Jesus the Christ said, on January 9, 1996 (*Trust Yourself*) said, "You must trust if you are to do what you have come to do. That trust must be all encompassing, never doubting, never wavering. You must be willing to take each step as it presents itself to you with perfect trust. There can be no deviation from that."[35]

Fear and trust are diametrically opposed. "When you are in perfect trust, you do not fear. For fear and trust cannot dwell in the same abode. You are either trusting or you are fearful . . . fear takes many forms. Trust also takes many forms. For every avenue of fear that you explore, walking beside you is an avenue of trust begging you to look at it, to see its smiling face, and to take its hand and know that it walks with you. Trust is an absence of fear."[36]

Also, on August 1, 1993 Gabriel said, "The only thing that knocks you down is your fear . . . There is nothing greater than you. Nothing! You were created without limitation. You were given free will. Free will, beloveds, to live however, however you choose." [37]

One of our greatest fears is the fear of change, and yet, "Change brings new growth. Change brings a time when you are allowed to spread your wings and see how high you can fly. There is no sadness in goodbyes. There is always the sense of joy and adventure for that which is coming."[38]

The Course notes that 'change is learning.' Fear of an unknown future intimidates many. When we become aware that we do not desire our current circumstances, and muster up the spiritual courage to change, we can accomplish anything with the knowledge that God is ever with us.

We ourselves have created all the fears we have. They are *all* based on the past. Mostly, our past lives, for how could we fear something we have never seen or known in this lifetime?

"The Holy Spirit deals with fear in this wise: Because fear is a manufactured product of humankind's thinking and emotion, the combination thereof has brought forth the child called fear. What the Holy Spirit does is to go in there and erase the illusion."[39]

Abundance and wealth
"Now there is a difference in desiring abundance and desiring wealth. A lot of people mix the two up . . . to desire abundance means abundance of health, abundance of energy, abundance of understanding, abundance of

love, and of course abundance of funds. So there is a difference. To desire wealth for wealth sake alone, that is of the ego. But to desire abundance, that is of God."[40]

Right and wrong

"There is no right and wrong. There simply is life and energy and adventure. There are no enemies, for all are one in the love of God."[41]

Prayer and Meditation

Prayer

Prayer is talking to God; meditation is listening to God.

"True prayer is not praying out loud, but just being . . . If you will listen to the prayers that I say, I go into that place of mine that is my own divinity. I proclaim that which I know the Father Mother God desires to be so for humankind."[42] Readers please note that every time—every time—that Gabriel spoke to us, in a short lecture or a day-long seminar, he always closed with a prayer.

Some of us say our prayers in the morning and at night before sleeping. And during the day, if something confronts us that we didn't expect, we pray for protection or guidance. Yet God knows at all times exactly what we are thinking and feeling. "It is interesting to us that you feel you must set aside certain times to speak with God. It doesn't seem to occur to you that every thought you think, every feeling you have is known to God."[43]

The way we pray also needs correction. As Gabriel puts it, "From the way you pray, it would appear that you think God is standing up there with all manner of obstacles . . . That is not how it works. This is how it works . . . you bring your idea and you ask God's blessing upon it. 'I will to do the will of God.' Go with the ideas that are coming forth. Follow your internal guidance."[44]

When Gabriel mentioned 'scientific prayer' it sounded very curious to me. He explained it this way: "Whether or not you believe in scientific prayer has nothing to do with the fact that you all are using scientific prayer. What is scientific prayer? Scientific prayer is the recognition and the realization that everything you think has the power to reproduce and give you back exactly what you are thinking. Exactly."[45]

When Gabriel spoke of 'talking to God,' he noted the sincerity which must prevail. "Talking to God is something that you ever do, all of you, only you don't call it that . . . But when you approach with a great deal of respect the thoughts that come into your mind and realize that this is a communion with the divine, then you will know that what you are thinking and asking is a reality."[46]

Regarding our thinking and its consequence, Gabriel said, "Think abundance. In that way, you bring abundance to you. Actually abundance is all around . . . Your consciousness is so tuned to what you don't have that you do not always know what you do have. But when you proclaim, 'I am rich in the ways of the spirit. I am rich in the ways of love. I am rich in the ways of the world,' and rich in whatever ways you desire to be, and you bring in that spiritual energy, it will indeed manifest for you . . . Thoughts of fear keep abundance away."[47]

Meditation
For those who do not meditate, nothing will occur in their lives that would not have occurred otherwise. For those who do take up the daily practice, there are subtle and overt positive results.

When some people hear that meditation is listening to God, they immediately assume that they hear a voice with their mortal ears. Not so. "God's voice to you is like a subtle awareness in your mind. It is a feeling within you that has no external foundation In other words, you can't reason it away. Well you can, but it is unlikely that you would because suddenly you know. It is a rock sure knowing, and that is the Voice of God."[48]

We seldom realize that God's Voice is ever available. "God speaks to you constantly, constantly, but you don't hear Him. You don't listen. You think it can't be because you are not a Moses or a Jesus or a Jacob or a Mohammed . . . But I tell you a grand truth. God speaks directly to every living thing that came forth into creation."[49]

Gabriel once reminded us that in prayer we always look up. Whether we think God is up high above us, or we know that we are focusing on the third eye—the sixth chakra—is immaterial. Gabriel explained how profound our concentration is in meditation, and the wisdom that comes to us: " . . . if you are in your meditation or prayer, and your centeredness is here between your eyebrows, and someone touches you . . . it startles you, does it not? It is because all of your vibratory rate has been gathered here, and is coming forth from this point outward . . . you are then in alignment with your at-one-ment with God. Any action or thought or word you speak from that is pure, very pure; very much in align with wisdom. "[50]

The purpose of meditation was clearly explained by Gabriel: "Meditation is your time to receive from God. It is that time when you are open to receive divine ideas and inspiration, divine words, divine feelings, divine thoughts. That is the purpose of meditation. It is to listen while God speaks to you. I am talking about meditation because I want you to understand how you control your vibrations."[51]

Focusing of the mind is essential. "So the purpose in meditation is to bring your mind into focus so that it is not taking you away from where you want to be in meditation . . . as you bring your mind into focus, you are gathering up the vibrations of the emotional body and of the mental body and you are bringing them into alignment to this single pointedness, to this focus so that the vibrations of your meditation are very even, smooth, unruffled."[52]

The Importance of Meditation was the topic of one of Gabriel's Lectures (6/6/93). Also, he noted the importance later, on January 2, 1994: "Just as all of your colors are contained in one white, so all things are contained in what would appear to be a 'nothingness.' But it is that profound sanctuary that is God. Because you are made in the image and likeness of that, there is within you that center of absolute silence and stillness. It is that center that you must ardently seek, and find, and know, and be at one with. For as long as your ear is tuned to the turmoil, and as long as your eyes behold the chaos, and as long as your mind is filled with fear, you will not know that central stillness. From that center of stillness there proceeds outward absolute peace. It is that absolute peace that you must call forth upon your earth."[53]

We seem to live in a world of chaos. It is a chaos that humanity has created, not God. Humanity has created the chaos from its negative thinking process. The doubts, fears, angers, judgments which lead to dissension and war are those feelings and attitudes of humankind. More seeming chaos is coming, Mother Earth, tired of the pollution and abuse we have perpetrated on her, will shake herself in order to cleanse herself. For the mass consciousness this will seem like Armageddon. For those who understand the reason, peace of mind can be maintained.

"Because of the changes you will be witnessing, it is important for you to know the source of your Beingness which is the God within you, which is the God of all things."[54]

As we regularly meditate on a daily basis, or more often, we raise our consciousness. "As you raise your consciousness, as you return your thoughts to your own source, as you recognize your own divinity, as you see the beauty that you are, as you see these things within yourself, that is coming home to God."[55]

Reminding us of Moses' experience in the desert, Gabriel said, "You are on sacred ground. Remove the shoes of old ways of thinking and allow yourself to approach the Divine Flame within you. Listen and accept the Voice of God that speaks to you daily. Flow with the thoughts that come to you. Go with your successes."[56]

Meditation provides a journey to an awakening of the light within.

Illusion of Illness

Some of things Gabriel taught ring clearly in my ears such as:

Healing and love are the same.

There is no illness that cannot be healed.

We believe that a transplanted organ is rejected by the body. But actually it is the organ that rejects a body which is not aligned spiritually to it. In essence, the organ rejects the body because it [the organ] is out of spiritual alignment with the new body. It is not a matter of 'good or bad' spirituality; it merely means the body and organ are not on the same spiritual level at the time.

Causes of illness:

Our thinking and our own planning bring about any illness or disease that we choose to suffer. Our choosing began before birth. Our thinking is our daily responsibility. We have a tendency to blame others for our illnesses and diseases. We attribute a cold to being in contact with another who suffers and we 'pick up' the germs. If this were a truism, how do we explain the medical helpers who attend to patients who are highly contagious and never 'catch' the disease?

We blame our family tree for genetic diseases. The truth of the matter, as Gabriel explained, is that we choose parents who have the genes to provide us with a disease we think we need to suffer in a particular incarnation.

"Some of your illnesses are temporary, passing things, results of negative thoughts, results of 'I'm not worth it,' results of 'I guess I had better be punished, and this is a good way to do it.' . . . others have decided that you would leave the earth . . . [with] an illness that your current medical associations cannot reverse. However, you can reverse it. That decision is yours." [57]

Teach Only Love, by Jampolsky, succinctly tells a story of a young man injured in an accident so badly that all doctors gave up hope and sent him home. With the constant tender, loving care of his family he not only recovered but the story ends with the patient going skiing!

God created His children, all humanity, to be whole, healthy, joyous, and have abundance. The absence of any of these attributes is the result of error perceptions, negative thinking, or a desire to self-punish. "Never were you created to die; you are eternal. When God called you forth into Beingness from the Divine Flame of Himself/Herself, He called you forth in the eternalness of His own nature. When you chose to take form, you did it carelessly with little thought of the outcome of that form. When those forms began to be destroyed, you accepted that as a natural outcome. You think it is nature's way. If that were a truth, then why think you that the Master Jesus came to teach eternal life and to prove eternal life?"[58]

Grief

Everyone grieves when loved ones 'die.' We sorely miss them because they were so much a part of our own lives and daily activities and thoughts. We usually say, "I lost my mother," instead of "my mother died." The loss is ours. Gabriel said all grief is selfish. The Higher Self of us knows full well that the person who has transitioned has gone back home to the Father in Heaven. For those who still believe in hell, Gabriel made it clear there is no such place. He has been around since the beginning and he has never seen a geographic place called hell, nor an entity that is called the devil. "You mourn those who leave your physical world . . . This mourning for an empty shell is but part of the sickness of your minds that embrace the ideas of illness and death."[59]

True Innocence

In the Bible the disciples ask Jesus who is the greatest in the Kingdom of Heaven. And setting a child in the midst of the, Jesus responded,
Verily I say unto you, Except ye be converted, and become as little children, ye shall not enter into the kingdom of heaven.
Whosoever therefore shall humble himself as this little child, the same is greatest in the kingdom of heaven.[60]

We have a tendency to think of little children as naïve, ignorant, vulnerable, and gullible. It is more likely that Jesus meant they are accepting, nonjudgmental, curious and open to learning.

Gabriel explained the true quality of children: "Know you how it says in your Scripture that you must become as a little child before you can enter into the Kingdom of Heaven? . . . I shall tell you what that Scripture means. The child of you was still connected enough to that spirit of you to know how to pull in that spirit life and give it freedom . . . So with the freedom of the child in you, you brought in the very life of you, and you let it run free with all the joy and all the creativity with which you were created and with which the Father has ever endowed you . . . It is the Father saying to you, 'Go forth, and be whatever. Just don't track mud on the clouds'!"

This is a perfect example of Gabriel's humor. One day when he was given a glass of water with ice cubes in it, he took a drink and said, "There's a glacier in my glass!" We all laughed loudly. I guess it proves that everything is relative.

Earthly life vs. Eternity

When Gabriel told us that Heaven is our natural habitat it made a lot of sense to this writer. Whatever worldly pursuits we have and whatever dreams do come true for us; there is always a seeming emptiness. There is a belief that there must be something more. And Gabriel's teachings convince us that indeed there is something more. Life on earth is a short term visit that lasts only 80-100 years and is over. We have come many times to earth. We have incarnated so many times, in fact, that we have met every other person now living on the Earth. Gabriel told us so.

It is well past time to go back home to God and stop this never-ending karmic ride. We created it when we came to believe that we were separate from God, when we came to believe that physical form is all there is and all we are. We are so much more. Life is eternal and our spirit is eternal as God, for He created us in spirit form. Now is the only time eternity knows. Now is the time to awaken to our divinity and live it. Now is the time to forego all our error perceptions and ask the Holy Spirit to transform them all into true perception. God knows us as His beloved children. God is One, God is All, God is Love. There is one God, though we call Him by many names. Jesus knows us as his beloved siblings. As our elder brother, he came to show us the way he took and the way we must go, also. He said he would not leave us without comfort, and he never has, to those who call on him.

The Essential Lessons

The primary lessons that humankind must learn on earth are love and forgiveness. Jesus the Christ made it plain for us:

Thou shalt love the Lord thy God with all thy heart, and with all thy soul, and with all thy mind.
This is the first and great commandment.

And the second is like unto it, Thou shalt love thy neighbour as thyself. (Matt 22:37)

"Until forgiveness is complete, the world does have a purpose . . . a gentle Savior; born where sin was made and guilt seemed real . . . the world will end when all things in it have been rightly judged by His judgment. The world will end with the benediction of holiness upon it. When not one thought of sin remains, the world is over. It will not be destroyed nor attacked nor even touched. It will merely cease to seem to be. ACIM M 14:2:1-12

Epilogue

There is much wisdom in the words of the Master Jesus at the Last Supper. Some excerpts are presented here because they provide profound instructions for us all as we approach our own last supper before we ascend. Others are presented to remind us of what we already know but do not incorporate into our daily lives.

The first three books of the New Testament are the Gospels according to Matthew, Mark, and Luke. Each one of these books contains a few verses describing the Last Supper. When we turn to the Gospel according to John, we find several chapters on the subject.

The Last Supper was held on what we now call Maundy Thursday. It was just prior to this meal that Jesus washed the feet of the disciples. Peter rebelled at this gesture, probably because he saw Jesus as his Lord and Master and himself as unworthy of this action by Jesus. Then, when Jesus said, *If I wash thee not, thou hast no part with me.* (13:8) Relenting, Peter then says that Jesus ought to wash also Peter's hands and head. Jesus replied, *He that is washed needeth not save to wash his feet, but is clean every whit: and ye are clean, but not all.* (13:10)

In this Truth Age, we have come to understand that the feet represent understanding. It is therefore likely that the washing of the disciples' feet by Jesus signified the awakening of their understanding to his teachings. Most of them did not quite "get the message"; only John truly understood the Master's teachings, according to Archangel Gabriel. Jesus then said, *I have given you an example, that ye should do as I have done to you. Verily, verily, I say unto you, The servant is not greater than his lord; neither he that is sent greater than he that sent him.* (13:15-16)

Jesus then testified *one of you shall betray me.* 13:21 He knew it was Judas but only identified him as *He it is, to whom I shall give a sop, when I have dipped it.* (13:26) Even then, when Jesus told Judas *That thou doest, do quickly,* (13:27) the disciples thought Judas was on a financial errand, since he held the money for the group.

After Judas left, Jesus said *Whither I go, thou canst not follow me now; but thou shalt follow me afterwards.* (13:36) Again Peter protested and said that he would lay down his life for Jesus' sake. But the Master answered, *I say unto thee, the cock shall not crow, till thou has denied me thrice.* (13:38)

The prophecies in these words included the promise by Jesus that the disciples would follow him to Heaven 'afterwards,' and he foretold Peter's denial of knowing Jesus after Jesus was seized by the Roman soldiers.

In my Father's house are many mansions (14:2) relates metaphysically to the many states of consciousness in humankind. Such symbolism is throughout the Bible.

I go to prepare a place for you. And if I go and prepare a place for you, I will come again, and receive you unto myself; that where I am, there ye may be also (14:2-3) means that as Jesus was an example, a way-shower and a pattern for us to follow, he embodied the Light of the Christ which is embodied in all of us. Many have interpreted *I will come again* to mean that Jesus will manifest on earth some day in the future. What he meant was that each of us will, at some point in time, become aware of the Christ Light in us. Gabriel was asked once if Jesus would return and his answer was that what Jesus taught is eternally true, so there would be no need for him to come, and that if he did come, he would only be slain again.

I am the way, the truth, and the life: no man cometh unto the Father, but by me. (14:6) Again, many believe that one must accept Jesus 'as my personal savior,' but the way to salvation is acknowledging the Kingdom of Heaven within and thus awakening to the Light of Christ as a personal identification and a spiritual truth.

A Course in Miracles, by Foundation for Inner Peace explains:
'When I said, "I am with you always", I meant it literally. I am not absent to anyone in any situation. Because I am always with you, *you* are the way, the truth and the life.' ACIM T - 7: III: 1:7-9

It simply does not get any clearer than that! Only those who refuse to accept the teachings in *A Course in Miracles* will continue to insist on keeping Jesus on the Old Rugged Cross and worship him.

"Do not make the pathetic error of "clinging to the old rugged cross". The only message of the crucifixion is that you can overcome the cross. Until then you are free to crucify yourself as often as you choose. This is not the gospel I intended to offer you." ACIM T - 4: in: 3: 7-10

The Master went so far as to say that we could do all things that he did 2,000 years ago:

He that believeth on me, the works that I do shall he do also; and greater works than these shall he do; because I go unto my Father. (14:12) I once understood this to mean that we can accomplish anything Jesus did because he ascended to God in Heaven. More recently I saw this remark as indicating that all the works Jesus did were the direct result of meditating frequently throughout his life on earth.

The promise of life after what we call death is found in Jesus' words, *Yet a little while, and the world seeth me no more; but ye see me: because I live, ye shall live also.* (14:19) With some exceptions, the world cannot, with mortal eyes, see the 'dead,' but we do live on in another realm. Jesus demonstrated that when he materialized many times after his resurrection.

But the Comforter, which is the Holy Ghost, whom the Father will send in my name, he shall teach you all things, and bring all things to your remembrance, whatsoever I have said unto you. (14:26) In *A Course in Miracles* we find several definitions of Holy Spirit (Holy Ghost). One of them was given us by Gabriel: The transforming energy of God.

When we recall Jesus' teachings we desire to emulate him and we are then given the transforming energy of God to do so. The soul is a memory bank of all that we have experienced since the Beginning, in all lifetimes. A desire to step upon a spiritual path and continue on it will bring to mind, from our soul, all teachings we have ever heard or read to assist us on the path. *Getting to Know Your Soul* (see Bibliography) is beneficial to anyone seeking a conscious spiritual path. This reminds me of a time when a person dropped off to sleep during a Gabriel seminar. Gabriel took notice of it and remarked that the person would hear Gabriel's words 'on some level.'

Peace I leave with you, my peace I give unto you: not as the world giveth, give I unto you. Let not your heart be troubled, neither let it be afraid. (14:27) We often have a troubled heart, as life brings into our experience losses, discomforts, and tribulations. Here the Master is telling us that the peace that he gives to us makes us fearless and untroubled. Jesus was a man of joy, peace, and love. Only in knowing that he was the Son of God could he feel and express these attributes. To feel and express them in the darkness of fear and want that prevailed on earth then seems like a miracle. We think it would take a miracle for us to feel and express joy, peace, and love in our daily existence. The awareness of our God Self brings us to that joy, peace, and love. It is ours for the taking and Jesus promised it. We must decide.

I am the true vine, and my Father is the husbandman. Every branch in me that beareth not fruit he taketh away: and every branch that beareth fruit, he purgeth it, that it may bring forth more fruit . . . As the branch cannot ear fruit of itself, except it abide in the vine; no more can ye, except ye abide in me. (15:1-4) It is interesting to note that Jesus admitted that he had branches (traits) that did not bear fruit. This was the humanness of the man Jesus. The Christ Light is the message he brought via the man Jesus. Without that Light in us—which is always present—and our awareness of it, we can do nothing. Without that awareness we rely only on our ego to lead our lives. And the ego gives us all our error perceptions. Thus Jesus said, *without me ye can do nothing.* (15:5)

If I had not come and spoken unto them, they had not had sin: but now they have no cloak for their sin. (16:22) When we have no role model in our lives; no words of wisdom and truth to live by, we are unaware of our negative attitudes and behaviors. Once we hear Jesus' message of love, forgiveness, and joy we know there is a better way to live our lives. We can then choose to behave and believe differently. We can consciously choose a positive path, a spiritual journey.

They hated me without a cause. (15:25) Jesus had the foresight to know that in time the world would see clearly that he brought only truth and light to Earth. He knew then that he was hated by the rabbis who could not perform miracles as he did. He was hated by the Roman rulers because he spoke of a 'kingdom,' which they felt threatened by. He may have been hated by those he healed but to whom the illness returned. It did not signify that Jesus' healings sometimes failed (there is no such thing as a 'failed' healing) but rather the healed person brought back the illness because he felt unworthy to keep good health, or continued to tell others, in detail, how sick he had been, and thus restored the malady by focusing on it. How often do we, when misunderstood by others, feel that we are hated without a cause?

If I go not away, the Comforter will not come unto you; but if I depart, I will send him unto you. And when he is come, he will reprove the world of sin, and of righteousness, and of judgment. Of sin, because they believe not on me; Of righteousness, because I go to my Father, and ye see me no more; Of judgment, because the prince of this world is judged. (16:7-11)

The Comforter (Holy Spirit) will reprove—scold—the world of its sin because it did not believe the prince of peace, the man who told us to love one another and love God with all our heart, soul and mind. Where is the person who has lived by these precepts? The Holy Spirit will scold the world because 1) of its self-righteous attitude and independent actions, instead of seeking guidance from God, as directed by the Master, and 2) because humankind refuses to accept eternal life as demonstrated by the resurrection and insists on accepting death as the end of life. The Holy Spirit will scold the world because it continues to believe in a prince of the world (a devil) instead of realizing that the devil and his domain (hell) are only figments of our imagination, conjured up as a final condemnation for those we hate and judge. Jesus prophesied that the world would need scolding in generations to follow him. The scolding will not be an action against us but instead, when we turn toward Heaven and consciously step upon a spiritual path, our past misdeeds will torment us, and that is the 'scolding.' But we, as children of the Most High, can and must forgive ourselves, forgive others and dedicate ourselves to the age-old teachings Jesus gave us 2,000 years ago.

Howbeit, when he, the Spirit of truth, is come, he will guide you into all truth: for he shall not speak of himself; but whatsoever he shall hear, that shall he speak: and he will shew you things to come. (16:13) Truth is, truth needs no defense, truth is eternal. That is why the teachings of Archangel Gabriel are so profound and precious to us now. The eternal truth he brought may be denied or discounted, but our belief system does not determine truth.

We will bend to the truth of this Age of Spirituality or we will break. We will choose to abandon old beliefs and embrace truth or we will break under the weight of our ignorance and stubbornness. The Spirit of truth whispers in our ears, while meditating, what is for our highest good, and included in our highest good is prophecy ('things to come'), for when we can foresee the future we can readily prepare for it.

ye shall weep and lament, but the world shall rejoice: and ye shall be sorrowful, but your sorrow shall be turned into joy. (16:20) Jesus told his disciples that they would lament because he knew they would grieve when he was crucified. He also knew that the world that had crucified him would rejoice. Then he assured them that their sorrow would be turned to joy, which of course it was, on Resurrection Day.

I have glorified thee on the earth: I have finished the work which thou gavest me to do. And now, O Father, glorify thou me with thine own self with the glory which I had with thee before the world was. (17:5) As Jesus offered up his prayer to God, he asked God to glorify him with the blazing Light of God which Jesus remembered sharing with God before the Earth was formed. This same Light is ours to return to, as we follow the Christ back home.

That they all may be one; as thou, Father, art in me, and I in thee, that they also may be one in us: that the world may believe that thou hast sent me. (1:21) We find this same oneness noted in *A Course in Miracles*:

"God's Will is that His Son be one, and united with Him in His Oneness." ACIM T - 11: I: 11: 8

When the day arrives that each one of us will be enjoying our 'last supper' on Earth, we may have a conscious awareness that it is indeed our last supper. But surely, the Higher Self of us will know it to be true. And home we'll go, ascending unto the Father and finished with the karmic cycle that we have allowed to lock us in for so long.

NOTES

Chapter 1

1. Euripedes' Phrixus, 830.
2. J. Boss, *In Silence They Return,* 125.
3. Stemman, R., *Spirits and Spirit Worlds,* 26.
4. J. Greber, *Communication With the Spirit World of God,* 2.
5. R. R. Springer, *Intra Muros,* Preface.
6. Ibid., 64.
7. Ibid., epigraph by Rt. Rev. Phillips Brooks, D.D.
8. A. Borgia, *Life in the World Unseen,* 16.
9. Springer, *Intra Muros,* 58-59.
10. Ibid., 60.
11. Borgia, 95.
12. Ibid., 86-87.
13. Springer, *Intra Muros,* 6.
14. Ibid., 65.
15. Archangel Gabriel, *The Illusion of Time,* 3/24/90 (audiocassette)
16. Springer, *Intra Muros,* 44.
17. Borgia, *Life in the World Unseen,* 31.
18. Foundation for Inner Peace, *A Course in Miracles,* T 13: VII: 1:4-7.
19. Borgia, *Life in the World Unseen,* 123.
20. Ibid., 119.
21. Springer, *Intra Muros,* 14-15.
22. Borgia, *Life in the World Unseen,* 44.
23. E. Holmes and F. Holmes, *The Voice Celestial,* 26.
24. Borgia, *Life in the World Unseen,* 48.
25. G. G. Ritchie, *Return From Tomorrow,* 70.
26. Springer, *Intra Muros,* 12.
27. S. E. White, *The Unobstructed Universe,* 252.
28. Borgia, *Life in the World Unseen,* 50-51.
29. Ibid., 70.
30. Ibid., 62-63.
31. Springer, *Intra Muros,* 58.
32. Borgia, *Life in the World Unseen,* 175.
33. Ibid., 35.

34. Springer, *Intra Muros,* 7-8.
35. Ibid., 76.
36. Borgia, *Life in the World Unseen,* 118.
37. Springer, *Intra Muros,* 7.
38. Borgia, *Life in the World Unseen,* 14.
39. Archangel Gabriel, *The Crucifixion: It's True Meaning,* 35.
40. Borgia, 154.
41. Springer, 85.
42. Ibid., 12.
43. S. E. White, *The Unobstructed Universe,* 383.
44. J. Boss, *In Silence They Return,* 163.
45. ACIM, W pt. 1:200: 4: 1:3-4

Chapter 2

1. Archangel Gabriel, *Gabriel's Farewell Message,* 13.
2. Ibid.
3. Gabriel, *Why We Are Here Now,* 16.
4. Gabriel, *Desires of Personality,* 19.
5. Gabriel, *Why We Are Here Now,* 13.
6. Ibid., 16-17.
7. Gabriel, *Spirit, Form and Healing,* 14.
8. Gabriel, *Gabriel's Farewell Message,* 9.
9. Ibid., 10.
10. Ibid., 4-5.
11. Gabriel, *Giving and Receiving,* 13.
12. Gabriel, *A Time for Change,* 17-18.
13. Gabriel, *The Power of Thought,* 11.
14. Gabriel, *Your New Year, 1994,* 17.
15. Gabriel, *Gabriel's Farewell Message,* 4.
16. Ibid., 15.
17. Ibid., 14.
18. Ibid., 7-8.
19. Gabriel, *The Three Kings,* 34.
20. Gabriel, *Spirit, Form and Healing,* 15.
21. Gabriel, *Voice of God,* 7.
22. Gabriel, *Real Courage,* 13.
23. Gabriel, *Energy of Spring,* 18.

24. Gabriel, *The Easter Story,* 16.
25. Gabriel, *Why We Are Here Now,* 32.
26. Gabriel, *A Time For Change,* 12.
27. Gabriel, *Star of Bethlehem,* 15.

Chapter 3

1. Archangel Gabriel *Spirit, Form and Healing,* 4.
2. Stewart Edward White, *The Unobstructed Universe*, 305.
3. Ibid., 294.
4. Gabriel, *Trust Yourself,* 27.
5. Gabriel, *Why We are Here Now,* 4.
6. Gabriel, *A Time for Change,* 5-6.
7. Gabriel, *How Things come to Be,* 9.
8. ACIM T—25:7:4:3.
9. Gabriel, *Energy of Spring,* 16-17.
10. Ibid., 22.
11. Ibid., 22.
12. Gabriel, *The Easter Story,* 18.
13. Gabriel, *Vibrations,* 21.
14. Gabriel, *Spirit, Form and Healing,* 16.
15. Gabriel, *Your New Year 1994,* 26-27
16. Ibid., 6.
17. Ibid., 27.
18. Gabriel, *Spirit, Form and Healing,* 4.
19. Gabriel, *A Time For Change,* 20-21.
20. Ibid., 19.
21. Gabriel, *Your New Year 1994,* 7-8.
22. Gabriel, *Real Courage,* 14.
23. Gabriel, *The Three Kings,* 5.
24. Willis Barnstone, ed., *The Other Bible,* 125.
25. Gabriel, *At This Time,* 8.
26. Ibid., 5-6.
27. ACIM T 14: III: 17:4-8.
28. Gina Cerminara, *Many Mansions,* 41-42.
29. Dick Sutphen, *Past Lives, Future Loves,* 13.
30. Hugh Lynn Cayce, *Cayce on Reincarnation,* 257.
31. Gabriel, *Your New Year 1994,* 6.

32. Gabriel, *How Things* Come *to Be,* 32-33
33. Gabriel, *Resurrection, 3.*
34. P. Rodegast and J. Stanton, comp., *Emmanuel's Book, 40.*

Chapter 4

1. Matthew 10:26.
2. I Cor. 4:5.
3. Archangel Gabriel, *Vibrations,* 5.
4. A. E. Powell, *The Etheric Double,* 9.
5. Herbert B. Puryear, *The Edgar Cayce Primer,* 38.
6. Ibid., 44-45.
7. Ibid., 164-165.
8. Archangel Gabriel, *Real Courage,* 8.
9. Gabriel, *Star of Bethlehem,* 3-4.
10. Ibid., 8.
11. Exodus 25:11, 30:3, 37:2.
12. *The Brain, 1982.*
13. Gabriel, *The Reality of Our Fantasies,* 10/17/95
14. Herbert B. Puryear, *The Edgar Cayce Primer,* 145.
15. Gabriel, *Your New Year 1994,* 11-12.
16. Wing-Tsit Chan, trans., *Tao Te Ching,* 14.
17. ACIM T—25: II: 5: 1-8.
18. Gabriel, *The Power of Thought,* 12.
19. Luke 12:31.
20. Gabriel, *Gabriel's Farewell Message,* 5.
21. Gabriel, *Taking Care of Your Soul,* 9.
22. Gabriel, *Your Soul,* 9/5/93.
23. P. A. Donovan and M. Lee-Civalier, *Getting to Know Your Soul,* 23.
24. Gabriel, *Taking Care of Your Soul,* 10.
25. Ibid., 10.
26. Gabriel, *Your New Year 1994,* 12.
27. Gabriel, *The Three Kings,* 16.
28. Ibid., 20.
29. Gabriel, *The Power of Thought,* 9.
30. Gabriel, *How Things Come to Be,* 27.
31. Gabriel, *Voice of God,* 15.
32. Martin G. Larson, *New Thought,* 252

33. Ibid.
34. Gabriel, *Spirit, Form and Healing*, 4.
35. Gabriel, *Desires of Personality*, 13.
36. Gabriel, *Voice of God*, 3.
37. Gabriel, *Gabriel's Farewell Message*, 12.
38. Gabriel, *Spirit, Form and Healing*, 3.
39. Gabriel, *Gabriel's Farewell Message*, 17-18.
40. Gabriel, *Your New Year 1994*, 11.
41. Gabriel, *Gabriel's Farewell Message*, 27.
42. Gabriel, *Voice of God*, 5-6.
43. Gabriel, *The Power of Thought*, 25-26.
44. Gabriel, *Gabriel's Farewell Message*, 5.
45. Gabriel, *Trust Yourself*, 12.
46. Gabriel, *Desires of Personality*, 11.
47. Ibid.
48. Gabriel, *Energy of Spring*, 10.
49. Gabriel, *Giving and Receiving*, 17.
50. Emanuel Swedenborg, *Divine Providence*, 82.
51. Ibid., 101.
52. ACIM T 6: V: A: 6:1-4.
53. E. Dupont and M. Lewis, eds., *New Age Healing*, 79.
54. Gabriel, *The Three Kings*, 27.
55. Gabriel, *Your New Year 1994*, 8.
56. Gabriel, *Desires of Personality*, 7-8.
57. Ibid., 13.
58. Ibid., 4.
59. Jesus the Christ, *Questions and Answers*, 2/12/96, 15.

Chapter 5

1. Gabriel, *Trust Yourself*, 13.
2 Gabriel, *Why we Are Here Now*, 11.
3. *Divine Providence*, 55.
4. ACIM T - 1:11: 4:1.
5. Gabriel, *How Things Come to Be*, 34.
6. Gabriel, *Spirit, Form and Healing*, 12.
7. Gabriel, *Your New Year 1994*, 3.
8. *In Silence They Return*, 102.

9. Gabriel, *Trust Yourself,* 5.
10. Gabriel, *Spirit, Form and Healing,* 12.
11. Gabriel tape, *Illusion of Time.*
12. Ibid.
13. Jesus the Christ, *Questions and Answers, 2/12/96,*16.
14. M. S. Wright, *Behaving as if the God in all Life Mattered,* 107-109
15. H. Holzer, *The Psychic World of Plants,* 21.
16. Ibid., 29.
17. Ibid., 48.
18. B. Schull, *The Psychic Power of Animals,* 163-164.
19. Ibid., 31.
20. Ibid., 25.
21. Ibid., 187.
22. Wright, *Behaving as if the God in All Life Mattered,* 161.
23. Gabriel, *Vibrations,* 4.
24. ACIM T—10: III: 7:2.
25. Gabriel, *Spirit, Form and Healing,* 7.
26. Gabriel, *Why We Are Here Now,* 20.
27. Ibid., 21.
28. Gabriel, *Gabriel's Farewell Message,* 23-24.
29. Gabriel, *The Crucifixion—Its True Meaning,* 37-38.
30. Gabriel, *Communication With God,* 22.,
31. Ibid., 22-23.
32. Gabriel, *A Time For Change,* 23.
33. ACIM T—19: 1: 2:7.
34. Gabriel, *Desires of Personality,* 24.
35. Gabriel, *Spirit, Form and Healing,* 5.
36. Gabriel, *The Three Kings,* 22-23.
37. Gabriel, *Gabriel's Farewell Message,* 6-7.

Chapter 6

1. Gabriel, *Desires of Personality,* 4-5.
2. Gabriel, *Energy of Spring,* 18.
3. Gabriel, *A Time For Change,* 17.
4. Gabriel, *Trust Yourself,* 4.
5. Gabriel, *Real Courage,* 10.
6. M. Swedenborg, *Divine Providence,* 174.

7. Jesus the Christ, *Questions and Answers,* 2/12/96, 15.

8. Gabriel, *The Power of Thought,* 19.

9. Gabriel, *A Time For Change,* 38.

10. Gabriel, *Why We Are Here Now,* 4

11. Boss, *In Silence They Return,* 104.

12. Gabriel, *Trust Yourself,* 14.

13. Gabriel, *How Things Come To Be,* 17.

14. Gabriel, *The Power of Thought,* 4.

15. Swedenborg, *Divine Providence,* 89.

16. Gabriel, *Trust Yourself,* 7.

17. Ibid., 8.

18. Gabriel, *Why We Are Here Now,* 6.

19. Ibid., 5.

20. Gabriel, *How Things Come To Be,* 11.

21. Gabriel, *Trust Yourself,* 22.

22. Gabriel, *Voice of God,* 16.

23. Gabriel, *The Three Kings,* 21.

24. Gabriel, *Trust Yourself,* 17.

25. Gabriel, *Why We Are Here Now,* 21-22.

26. J. Morris, *The Dream Workbook,* 3.

27. Gabriel, *Why We Are Here Now,* 25.

28. Puryear, *The Edgar Cayce Primer,* 135.

29. ACIM T—8: IX: 3:7-8.

30. Puryear, *The Edgar Cayce Primer,* 135.

31. Gabriel, *Why We Are Here Now,* 24.

32. Puryear, *The Edgar Cayce Primer,* 135.

33. Ibid., 136.

34. Gabriel, *Trust Yourself,* 15.

35. Puryear, *The Edgar Cayce Primer,* 184.

36. Gabriel, *Energy of Spring,* 9.

37. Gabriel, *Trust Yourself,* 31.

38. Morris, *The Dream Workbook,* 249.

39. Jesus the Christ, *Questions and Answers,* 2/12/96, 13.

40. Bro, *Nothing So Strange,* 114.

41. Gabriel, *Why We Are Here Now,* 28.

42. Ibid., 17.

43. Bro, *Nothing So Strange,* 105.

44. Gabriel, *Why We Are Here Now,* 13-14.

45. ACIM M—25: 2: 1-5.

Chapter 7

1. ACIM W pt. 1-123:5:1-6.
2. Gabriel, *Oneness*, 83.
3. Matthew, 5:3-11.
4. John 14:12.
5. Levi, *Aquarian Gospel*, In., 15-17
6. *Metaphysical Bible Dictionary*, 200.
7. Sanderfur, 61.
8. Gabriel, *Master Jesus*, 1/18/97.
9. Ibid.
10. Ibid.
11. Sanderfur, 107.
12. Ibid.
13. *MBD*, 368.
14. Gabriel, *Master Jesus*, 1/18/97.
15. *Levi*, 34:4.
16. Harrell, *The Bible: Its Origin and Growth*, 10.
17. *Gabriel, Temptations of Jesus*, 3/5/95.
18. *The Bible: Its Origin and* Growth, 134.
19. *MBD*, 23.
20. Ibid., 211.
21. Ibid., 181.
22. Ibid., 183.
23. Ibid., 119-120.
24. Ibid., 472-473.
25. Ibid., 231.
26. Gabriel, *The Three Kings*, 34-35.
27. Bancroft, *Twentieth Century Mystics and Sages*, 22.
28. Ibid., 43.
29. Ibid., 44.
30. Ibid., 78-79.
31. Ibid., 93.
32. Ibid., 228.
33. Ibid., 16.
34. Ibid., 326.

Chapter 8

1. Levi, *Aquarian Gospel*, In., 9.
2. Ibid., 11.
3. Gabriel, *A Time for Change*, 13.
4. Ibid., 12.
5. Gabriel, *Your New Year—1994*, 7.
6. Gabriel, *How Things Come to Be*, 38.
7. Ibid., *Star of Bethlehem*, 4.
8. Ibid., *Your New Year—1994*, 8.
9. Ibid., *Star of Bethlehem*, 7.
10. Ibid., *Your New Year—1994*, 7.
11. Ibid., *A Time for Change*, 17.
12. Ibid., *Star of Bethlehem*, 3.
13. Ibid., *Why We Are Here Now*, 15.
14. Ibid., *The Easter Story*, 21.
15. Ibid., *The Three Kings*, 25.
16. Ibid., 26-27.
17. Ibid., *A Time for Change*, 36-37.
18. Ibid., *Your New Year—1994*, 3, 8.
19. Ibid., *Vibrations*, 19.
20. Ibid., *Star of Bethlehem*, 6.
21. Ibid., *How Things Come to Be*, 32.
22. Ibid., *Spirit, Form and Healing*, 12.
23. Ibid., *Vibrations*, 13.
24. Ibid., 15.
25. Ibid., 24.
26. Ibid., 27.
27. Gabriel, *A Time for Change*, 37.
28. Ibid., *Gabriel's Farewell Message*, 23.
29. Ibid., *Temptations of Jesus*, 13.
30. Ibid., *The Power of Thought*, 6.
31. Ibid., *The Desires of Personality*, XXXXp?
32. Ibid., *Trust Yourself*, 13-14.
33. Ibid., *A Time for Change*, 13.
34. Ibid., *The Easter Story*, 22.
35. Ibid., *Trust Yourself*, 8.
36. Ibid., 20.

37. Gabriel, *Spirit, Form and Healing,* 11.

38. Ibid., *A Time for Change,* 8.

39. Gabriel, *How Things Come to Be,* 25,

40. Ibid., *The Desires of Personality,* 21.

41. Ibid., *A Time for Change,* 9.

42. Ibid., *Your New Year—1994,* 18.

43. Ibid., *Communication with God,* 7.

44. Ibid., 8-9.

45. Gabriel, *The Power of Thought,* 10-11.

46. Ibid., *Communication with God,* 17.

47. Ibid., *At This Time,* 10-11.

48. Ibid., *The Voice of God,* 8.

49. Ibid., 7.

50. Gabriel, *Star of Bethlehem,* 5.

51. Ibid., *Vibrations,* 8.

52. Ibid., 6-7.

53. Ibid., *Your New Year—1994,* 5.

54. Ibid., 3.

55. Gabriel, *Gabriel's Farewell Message,* 22.

56. Ibid., *Communication with God,* 11.

57. Ibid., *Spirit, Form and Healing,* 7.

58. Ibid., 4.

59. Ibid., 5.

60. Matthew 18:1-4.

BIBLIOGRAPHY

Books

The Apocrypha According to the Authorized Version. New York: Oxford University Press, n.d.

The Apocryphal Books of the New Testament. Philadelphia: David McKay, 1901.

The Apocryphal New Testament. London: Oxford University Press, 1969.

Appleton, E. R*., An Outline of Religion.* New York:, HC Kinsey & Co., 1934.

Barnstone, W., ed., *The Other Bible.* New York: Harper Collins, 1984.

Borgia, *A., Life in The World Unseen.* London: Psychic Press, 1987(1954).

Boss, J, *In Silence They Return.* St. Paul, MN: Llewellyn Publications, 1972.

Bro, M. H., *Nothing So Strange.* New York: Harper & Row, 1958.

Cerminara, G., *Many Mansions.* New York: New American Library, 1967.

Chan, Wing-tsit, trans., *The Way of Lao Tzu.* New York: The Bobbs-Merrill Co. Inc., 1963.

The Christ., *New Teachings for an Awakening Humanity.* Santa Clara, CA: Spiritual Education Endeavors, 1986.

Clowes, J., trans., *Heavenly Secrets*, vol.1, by Emanual Swedenborg. West Chester, PA: Swedenborg Foundation, 1998.

Cooke, Ivan, ed., *The Return of Arthur Conan Doyle*. Hampshire, England: White Eagle, 1975.

DK Direct, Ltd., ed., *New Age Healing*. Pleasantville, NY: Reader's Digest, 1992.

Donovan, P. and Lee-Civalier, M., *Getting to Know Your Soul*. New York: iUniverse, Inc., 2004.

Ellison, J., *The Life Beyond Death*. New York: Berkley Publishing, 1972.

Ferm, V., ed., *Encyclopedia of Religion*. New York: Philosophical Library, 1945.

Fillmore, C., *Metaphysical Bible Dictionary*. Unity Village, MO: Unity School of Christianity, 1931.

Foundation for Inner Peace. *A Course in Miracles*. New York: Viking Penguin, 1996 (1975).

Freeman, J. D., *The Case for Reincarnation*. Unity Village, MO: Unity Books, 1986.

Greber, J., *Communication With the Spirit World of God*. Teaneck, NJ: Johannes Greber Memorial Foundation, 1974 (1932).

Harrell, C. J., *The Bible: Its Origin and Growth*. Nashville, TN: Cokesbury Press, 1926.

Harris, B., *Journey Into the Spirit World*. London: The Spiritualist Association of Great Britain, nd.

Holmes, E. H., *Science of Mind*. New York: GP Putnam's Sons, 1939.

Holmes, E.H. and F.L., *The Voice Celestial*. New York: Dodd, Mead & Co., 1960.

Holy Bible, AV.

Holzer, H., *The Psychic World of Plants*. New York: Pyramid Books, 1975.

Komroff, M., ed., *The Apocrypha*, or non-canonical books of the Bible, KJV. New York: Tudor Publishing Co., 1936.

Lamsa, G.M., *The Hidden Years of Jesus*. Lee Summit, MO: Unity Books, 1968.

Langley, N., *Edgar Cayce on Reincarnation*. New York: Paperback Library, Inc., 1967.

Larson, M. A., *New Thought*. New York: Philosophical Library, 1985.

Levi, *Aquarian Gospel of Jesus the Christ*. Marina del Rey, CA: De Vorss, 1907.

The Lost Books of the Bible and The Forgotten Books of Eden. New York: World Publishing Company, 1971. *The Lost Books of the Bible* originally printed 1926 and *Forgotten Books of Eden* originally published 1927, both by Alpha House, Inc.

Manas, J. H., *Divination, Ancient & Modern*. New York: Pythagorean Society, 1947.

McConnell, K., *Don't Call Them Ghosts*. St. Paul, MN: Llewellyn Publications, 2004.

Metaphysical Bible Dictionary. Unity Village, MO: Unity School of Christianity, 1931.

Meurois-Givaudan, A. and D., *The Way of the Essenes: Christ's Life Remembered*.
Rohester, VT, 1993. First published in French under the title *De Memoire d'Essenien, l'autre visage de Jesus* by Arista Editions, Plazac, 1989.

Montgomery, R., *A World Beyond*. New York: Fawcett Crest, 1972.

Moody, R., *Life After Life*. New York: Bantam Books, 1976.

Morris, J., *The Dream Workbook*. New York: Fawcett Crest, 1985.

Moses, J., *Oneness*: Great Principles Shared by all Religions. New York: Ballantine Books, 1989.

Myers, A., *Communicating with Animals*. Chicago: Contemporary books, 1997.

Neal, C.A., *Revelation: The Road to Overcoming*. Unity Village, MO: Unity Books, 1990.

Pagels, E., *The Gnostic Gospels*. New York: Vintage Books, 1979.

Pike, J.A., with Kennedy, D. *The Other Side*. Garden City, NY: Doubleday & Co., 1968

Potter, C. F., *The Lost Years of Jesus Revealed*. Greenwich, CT: Fawcett, 1958.

Powell, A. E., *The Etheric Double*. London: Quest Book, 1979.

Price, I., *Ancestry of Our English Bible*. New York: Harper Row, 1906.

Prophet, E. C., *The Lost Years of Jesus*. Livingston, MT: Summit University Press, 1984.

Puryear, H. B., *The Edgar Cayce Primer*. Toronto: Bantam Skylark, 1986.

Ritchie, G. G., with Sherrill, E. *Return from Tomorrow*. Carmel, NY: Guideposts, 1978.

Rodegast, P. and Stanton, J. comp., *Emmanuel's Book*. Toronto: Bantam, 1987.

Sanderfur, G., *Lives of The Master*. Virginia Beach, VA: A.R.E. Press, 1988.

Schull, B., *The Psychic Power of Animals*. Greenwich, CT: Fawcett Publications, 1977.

Sherman, H., *The Dead Are Alive*. New York: Ballantine Books, 1991.

Smart, N., *The Religious Experience of Mankind*. New York: Scribner, 1969.

Soares, T. G., *The Origin of the Bible*. New York: Stratford Press, 1945 (1913)

Springer, R.R. *Into The Light—My Dream of Heaven*. Shakopee, MN: Macelster Park Publishing, 1994. Originally published as *Intra Muros*. n.p.: David Cook, 1898.

Stemman, R. *Spirits and Spirit Worlds*. London: Aldus Books Ltd., 1975.

Sutphen, D., *Past lives, Future Loves*. New York: Pocket Books, 1978.

Swedenborg, E., *Heaven and Hell*. West Chester, PA: Swedenborg Foundation, 2000.

Swedenborg, E., *Divine Providence*. West Chestrer, PA: Swedenborg Foundation, 2003.

The Three Initiates., *The Kybalion*. Clayton, GA: Tri-State Press, 1988. (1908 Yogi Publication Society)

Troward, T., *Bible Mystery & Bible Meaning*. New York: Stratford Press, 1913.

Turner, E.S., *Your Hope of Glory*. Unity Village, MO: Unity School of Christianity, 1959.

Turner, E.S., *Let There be Light*. Unity Village, MO: Unity School of Christianity, 1954.

Turner, E.S., *Be Ye Transformed*, Lee's Summit, MO.: Unity Books, 1969.

Valentine, T., *Psychic Surgery*. Chicago: Henry Regnery Co., 1973 (1935).

Van Zandt, E., ed., *Spirits and Spirit Worlds*.

Warren, S., comp. *A Compendium of Swedenborg's Theological Writings*. New York: Swedenborg Foundation, 1977 (1875).

White, S. E., *The Unobstructed Universe*. New York: E. P. Dutton, 1940.

Wright, M. S., *Behaving as if the God in all Life Mattered*. Jeffersonton, VA: Perelandra, 1987.

Videos:
Secrets of Delphi, from A & E series Ancient Mysteries, 1996.
Jesus' Silent Years, from Encounters with the Unexplained, Grizzly Adams Productions, 2001.

Archangel Gabriel Teachings (Cassette/ CDs)
Illusion of Time 3/24/90
Beliefs and Immortality 4/13/96
Master Jesus, 1/18/97

Archangel Gabriel Evening Sessions (Booklets):
A Time for Change 8/4/96
At This Time 6/5/94
Christ and the Antichrist 5/26/96
Communication With God 7/4/93
The Crucifixion: Its True Meaning 4/2/99
The Desires of Personality 10/1/95
The Easter Story 4/11/93
The Energy of Spring 4/2/95

Gabriel's Farewell Message 12/3/99
Giving and Receiving 10/8/95
How Things Come to Be 6/4/99
The One: 2 lectures in one booklet*:
Question & Answer 11/20/95
The True Meaning of Christmas
The Power of Thought 2/18/97
Questions and Answers 2/12/96*
Questions and Answers 4/8/96
Real Courage 3/6/94
Resurrection 4/3/94
Spirit, Form and Healing 8/1/93
Star of Bethlehem 12/5/93
The Story of Judith 2/4/96
Taking Care of Your Soul 6/2/96
Temptations of Jesus 3/5/95
The Reality of Our Fantasies, 10/17/95
The Three Kings 12/6/97
Trust Yourself 1/9/96**
Vibrations 9/4/98
Voice of God 2/6/95
Why We are Here Now 8/4/96
Your New Year—1994 1/2/94
Your Soul 9/5/93

*Received from Jesus the Christ
** Received from Jesus the Christ and Archangel Gabriel

HOME TO
THE LIGHT

CONTENTS

Dedicated to an awakening humanity as it embarks upon this Truth Age.

Let your light so shine before men, that they may see your good works, and glorify your Father which is in heaven. Matt. 5:16

Every good gift and every perfect gift is from above, and cometh down from the Father of lights, with whom is no variableness, neither shadow of turning. James 1:17

PREFACE

When Jesus the Christ came to me October 13, 2004, he instructed me, through a dedicated and spiritual minister, the content, and format of a book of meditations. He told me to use *The Bible, A Course in Miracles* and my own words.

Delighted with this holy task, I wrote and published (2005) *Homeward Bound: Meditations for Your Journey.* As I Wrote the text, day by day, it occurred to me that I would write a trilogy of books of meditations. The purpose would be to show a continuity of ageless wisdom, from *The Bible,* to *The Course,* to Archangel Gabriel's teachings (1987 to 1999), to modern literature. Archangel Gabriel is the announcer of the ages. He announced to the Blessed Mother Mary the pending birth of Jesus and he announced to Elizabeth the pending birth of John the Baptist.

For twelve years Archangel Gabriel channeled through Rev. Penny Donovan, a dedicated spiritual teacher chosen by Spirit to bring to humanity ageless wisdom, at this beginning of the Age of Aquarius, or the Age of Truth, as Gabriel called it. All his teachings were recorded and are available. See Bibliography. This book contains only a fraction of Gabriel's teachings. Readers are urged to read/hear all his lessons for personal enlightenment.

The second book of meditations, entitled *Be Still and Know* was published in 2008. It also contains 365 meditations, drawing on *The* Course and Gabriel's teachings. Even as I wrote it, I began the third book *The Peaceful Silence.* It also consists of 365 meditations, drawn from Gabriel's teachings and current (past century) literature. There was the trilogy.

But I felt that one more book of meditations had to be written. I desired greatly to produce a book of meditations using Jesus the Christ as the focus and the only source of quotations. I wanted to tell of the Old Testament predictions of his coming and the stories from the apocryphal books about his birth and early childhood. Also, I believed it essential to bring forth current writings about Jesus' crucifixion, as told in *The Way of the Essenes.* I wanted to describe the poignant scene of Jesus' appearance at the Sanhedrin, immediately after his resurrection (as told in *The Aquarian Gospel of Jesus the Christ)*, to prove to the rabbis that although they could condemn him to death on the cross, still he lived in spirit.

I desired greatly to pass on some of the words that Jesus brought to our small group in Albany, N.Y. Although Archangel Gabriel came from October 1987 to December 1999, Jesus' first visitation came in November of 1995. Gabriel told Jesus that he had taught us what he could, but that he could not truly identify with earthlings because he had never lived in a physical form on Earth. Jesus said that since he had lived on earth, many times, he could teach us: The path he took is the same path we all must take. He is, therefore, our best teacher. And Gabriel was Jesus' teacher. At one time Jesus told us to listen to Gabriel, for "he is an excellent teacher." In addition, I desired to explain my personal relationship to Jesus through the centuries, which I do in the Introduction.

In the text *The Course* refers to *A Course in Miracles.*

Please note that *Conversations With JC* is not paginated. Therefore, to reference my quotations from it I refer to the day and date of the meditation in which the words appear.

In the Bibliography 'The One' refers to Jesus the Christ, as he identified himself before we knew his true identity.

All Bible quotes are italicized to show respect for Scripture, assist the reader to locate the passage in the Bible, and to set the words apart from the author's words. All Bible quotations from King James Version.

Grateful acknowledgment is given to Eleanor Morris for her patient and precise editing.

INTRODUCTION

I wrote this last book of meditations (my fourth) in order that I might provide the reader with my personal experiences that interface with Jesus the Christ and his teachings. My purpose in doing so is to explain why I have such a sense of love for and devotion to him. He led me then, leads me now, and by my choice, will lead me until I reach my own Christhood.

In one of Archangel Gabriel's seminars (which he presented from October 1987 to December 1999), he described the crucifixion scene. Some of those present wept, including me. At the question and answer session he was asked why that was so. He said that those who wept had been present at the crucifixion scene. He did not specify our status then, nor identify our participation in it. One person who regularly attended the seminars was later identified as having been one of the Roman soldiers on Calgary.

Much later, in the 17th century, when I was the daughter of a missionary and his wife, we came to America. I was two years old when we landed in Boston Harbor. As a teenager I would write down my father's sermons as he received them, pacing. Now I know that he had actually been channeling the information from spirit, but required someone as a scribe to write it down. I longed to be like him and preach Jesus' message, but women were not allowed into the ministry at that time, and channeling of any kind was considered an evil practice, hence the "witches" being burned in Salem, Massachusetts.

In March of 1984 I attended my first psychic circle, or séance, during which time Jesus the Christ appeared before me. I had never seen spirit form previously, nor have I since. He was tall, with shoulder length auburn hair. His eyes were a gentle blue. His arms were outstretched and across them lay a huge 'Jewish loaf.' He looked at me and said, "Lay down your life for me and I will give you the bread of life". I was stunned. I did not know what he meant until several weeks later. In July 1984 I gave up drinking alcohol as it occurred to me that I was an alcoholic. Surrendering the disease and seeking a sober way, I turned my life around and pursued the spiritual path to which I still hold. Then I knew what the Master had meant. I receive the 'bread of life' daily.

The next experience I had regarding Jesus and his teachings was in 1994, in a past life regression. I was a married man with no children. I was preaching Jesus' lessons until, in my 30s I was killed for heresy. It was about 500 AD

In the late 20th century I was exposed to the teachings of Archangel Gabriel (1987-1999) and Jesus the Christ (1995-1999). Rarely in those years did either heavenly being give us personal information. Not because we did not ask for it, but because Gabriel made it clear that mediums and psychics on Earth could provide such readings. Gabriel said he did not come to teach us anything new, but only to remind us of what we *already know, but forgot.* The Master came to straighten out the 'crooked places' in which Scripture omitted or altered his words.

One day as I limped to the microphone to ask a question, Master Jesus asked me why I limped. I told him I needed hip surgery but thought I could heal myself, given the lessons we were learning from Gabriel. He told me that I had some fear in moving forward on my spiritual path. In other lessons Gabriel had explained that our ego reminds us of past experiences that led to pain or death. It seems my ego was reminding me of the time in 500AD when I was killed for teaching Jesus' lessons of truth, and maybe I better watch out for an early demise again. (Later I had surgery for a total hip replacement).

In the summer of 2003, just prior to moving to western New York State to be near my adult children, I sought a reading from a friend and excellent medium. She told me that Master Jesus would come to me as I neared the end of writing my book (my memoirs). On October 13th, 2004, as I neared completion of my story, I asked my dedicated teacher and devoted friend, The Reverend Penny A. Donovan, to sit with me in meditation to see if Jesus would bring her a message for me. She agreed most willingly. Immediately she went into a trance and Jesus the Christ came, saying, in part, "I understand you expected me at this time. I always keep my promise." He then told me what my third book would be, its format, and that I should listen to my Higher Self for guidance. He also said that he would help me.

I know that Jesus the Christ is my elder brother, that he has been, is now, and forever will be, with me as I desire his assistance in my life. I am blessed to have this knowingness. Thank you, Master, for all your assistance then, now and forever!

All quotations are about our Master Teacher, Jesus the Christ, or from him. From him I mean his words as provided in the Bible, *The Apocryphal New Testament,* and *The Aquarian Gospel of Jesus the Christ,* and, of course. *A Course in Miracles.* Jesus is also quoted in *The Way of the Essenes* and *The Life and Teachings of the Masters of the Far East.*

CHAPTER ONE

The Promised One

#1

For unto us a child is born, unto us a son is given: and the government shall be upon his shoulder: and his name shall be called Wonderful, Counsellor, The mighty God, The everlasting Father, The Prince of Peace. Is. 9:6

The wolf also shall dwell with the lamb, and the leopard shall lie down with the kid, and the calf and the young lion and the fatling together; and a little child shall lead them. Is. 11:6

Hundreds of years before Christ was born Isaiah wrote these prophetic words. Whether from a vision or from a deep desire to have a Messiah appear we do not know. But later Luke provided us with the words of the angel who appeared to shepherds in the field, telling them not be fearful of the bright star in the sky. Although shepherds were common in those days, shepherding was not a designation of a wealthy person or a person of fame. It is significant, for this reason that angels came to them for the announcement. The shepherds had been sitting by their fireside, looking at and discussing the brilliant star, but they did not move. Gabriel told us that finally an angel was sent by God to nudge them to go into Bethlehem to behold the wondrous sight of the newborn Savior. John quotes the Master Jesus as he gave the reason for his coming to Earth at that time: to bear witness to the truth. Seekers of truth were promised they would recognize his voice.

For unto you is born this day in the city of David a Saviour, which is Christ the Lord. Luke 2:11

Pilate therefore said unto him, Art thou a king then? Jesus answered, Thou sayest that I am a king. To this end was I born, and for this cause came I into the world, that I should bear witness unto the truth. Every one that is of the truth heareth my voice. John 18:37

#2

But while he thought on these things, behold, the angel of the Lord appeared unto him in a dream, saying, Joseph, thou son of David, fear not to take unto thee Mary thy wife: for that which is conceived in her is of the Holy Ghost. Matt. 1:20

It would be impossible to imagine the stress felt by Joseph when he heard his betrothed was pregnant. It was an unspeakable event in those days and he struggled to understand until an angel appeared to assure him that it was acceptable by God that he should take Mary as his wife. Although I was not raised in a religious home, I recall discussions within my family about the impossibility of a virgin birth. Having heard it, I believed it. Later in life I came to understand that with God anything is possible. Wonderful events in my personal experiences proved that. Later still, I read *The Lost books of the Bible and the Forgotten Books of Eden.* How exciting it was to read this eye-witness account of the virgin birth. Gabriel once explained that there are other ways in which to reproduce offspring, but we chose sexual intercourse because we thought it so much fun! Gabriel also explained that Mary's mother was also born by a virgin birth. It is not important that the apocryphal books were deemed inappropriate for the official canon of the church. It is, however, significantly important that those 'hidden books' are available to us today.

"Then a bright cloud overshadowed the cave, and the midwife said, This day my soul is magnified, for mine eyes have seen surprising things, and salvation is brought forth to Israel. But on a sudden the cloud became a great light in the cave, so that their eyes could not bear it.

"But the light gradually decreased, until the infant appeared, and sucked the breast of his mother Mary.

"Then the midwife cried out, and said, How glorious a day is this, wherein my eyes have seen this extraordinary sight! . . . A virgin has brought forth, which is a thing contrary to nature." *The Lost Books of the Bible and the Forgotten Books of Eden,* Protevangelion, XIV:10-16

#3

And lo a voice from heaven, saying, This is my beloved Son, in whom I am well pleased. Matt. 3:17

And they that were in the ship came and worshipped him, saying, Of a truth thou art the Son of God. Matt. 14:33

As Gabriel explained in one of his seminars, every one of us plans our life before we come to earth at birth, although we do not have a conscious memory of the plan. Jesus did the same, but he knew *consciously* that he was the Son of God even at birth, and was given by God the ability to speak to his mother and confirm his Sonship with God. This was his first statement of a truth and surely must have brought to his mother a special comfort and joy. When he said that he was 'that word' he was also confirming to the phrase in John 1:14: *And the Word was made flesh, and dwelt among us, (and we beheld his glory, the glory as of the only begotten of the Father,) full of grace and truth.* It must have startled Mary to hear her newborn infant speak. Surely that had never been done before. An infant looks at its mother with a tenderness indescribable and its silence as it gazes is a mystery. Jesus spoke and unleashed the mystery to Mary.

"The following accounts we found in the book of Joseph, the high-priest, called by some Caiaphas: He relates, that Jesus spake even when he was in the cradle, and said to his mother: Mary, I am Jesus the Son of God, that word which thou didst bring forth according to the declaration of the angel Gabriel to thee, and my father hath sent me for the salvation of the world." *Lost Books, I Infancy* 1:1-3

#4

Then spake Jesus again unto them, saying, I am the light of the world: he that followeth me shall not walk in darkness, but shall have the light of life. John 8:12

There is continuity of truth from the Old Testament to the New Testament. Prophecies of the Old Testament manifest in the New Testament. The continuity extends from the New Testament to *A Course in Miracles*. Those who refuse to accept *The Course* because it is a channeled work will deny this connection. How else could the Master Jesus bring the "Good News" of this century by expounding on the "Good News" of 2,000 years ago? Has humanity not evolved in understanding so that now we can appreciate the symbolism used by Jesus in his parables? Are we to believe that God spoke only to the prophets of old, to Jesus, to his apostles, to the rabbis of the time, and then withdrew from the human race? Why would God stop speaking to His human family after 500 AD? Surely God did not turn His back on us, for He is everywhere at all times. He is all around us and inside us, where the Kingdom of God exists. When a person asks to be followed, are they asking to be worshipped? We cannot follow God, though we can worship Him. We cannot follow Him because we are one with Him, as His own creations. We can follow Jesus and emulate his life. This worldly darkness that we seem to "live" in is but a vagary of the mind, a grand illusion that physical form is all there is. We are so much more. We didn't get it 2,000 years ago, and so Jesus returns yet again, through dedicated seekers and spiritually evolved individuals, to awaken us to the truth of our being.

"I said that I am with you always, even unto the end of the world. That is why I am the light of the world." *ACIM T—8: IV: 2: 4-5*

#5

For whosoever shall do the will of my Father which is in heaven, the same is my brother, and sister, and mother. Matt. 12:50

There is not another place in Scripture that Jesus more clearly indicates that Jesus and all others are related. When we seek to align our will with the Will of God, then we acknowledge our familial relationship with Jesus and he acknowledges it also. There is only one will, and that is the Will of God. When we go against it and devise alternative thoughts and actions contrary to God's Will, we find ourselves in trouble. The trouble can be in the form of relationships, self-worth, communication with others, physical health, emotional health, mental health. Jesus knew he was the Son of God. He also knew that we are, too. He also knew that we had fallen asleep to our divinity, and his mission was to come and unite our will with the Will of God. But he cannot do this for us. He must do it *through* us. His teachings then and now are applicable to our daily lives and activities. He did not speak to intellectuals of his day, nor does he in *The Course.* The only way to align our wills with the Will of God is to surrender to His Love and His Power in us. Surrender here merely means giving up our worship of the ego. It is not easily done. If it were, Jesus would not have had to return this century to advise us about God's Will for us and how to align ourselves with it.

"My mission was simply to unite the will of the Sonship with the Will of the Father by being aware of the Father's Will myself." ACIM T—8: IV: 3:4-5

#6

And Jesus came and spake unto them, saying, All power is given unto me in heaven and in earth. Matt. 28:18

Jesus knew that God had given him all power in Heaven and Earth because he knew that he was the begotten Son of God. In *The Course* he seems to be passing on this power, yet he clearly explains that all the power of Heaven and Earth are already in us, because we are all created by God. I sought diligently to find Jesus' quotation above in Scripture, only to realize that he was quoting himself in an earlier page of *The Course*. This is an example of his lessons in *The Course*. He addresses a topic with supportive explanation, without veering off to other topics. Then, later, as he explains another topic, he clarifies an earlier statement of his. There can be no misinterpretation of Jesus' words in the quotation below. He is very explicit about our connection to God and the limitlessness of the Power and Glory of God. We have been told for centuries that we are born sinners and must strive with all diligence to seek God's pardon for our sins. How could we be born sinners when God created us? What motive prompted early church fathers to instill such a false notion in us? God's Will for us is health, peace, joy, and abundance. He does not expect us to beg for our birthright.

"When I said, 'All power and glory are yours because the Kingdom is His' [ACIM T 7: VII: 11:6], this is what I meant: The Will of God is without limit, and all power and glory lie within it is boundless in strength and in love and in peace. It has no boundaries because its extension is unlimited, and it encompasses all things because it created all things. By creating all things, it made them part of itself. You are the Will of God because that is how you were created. Because your Creator creates only like Himself, you are like Him. You are part of Him Who is all power and glory, and are therefore as unlimited as He is." ACIM T—8: II: 7:1-7

#7

Think not that I am come to destroy the law, or the prophets: I am not come to destroy, but to fulfill. Matt. 5:17

"The name 'Moses' means drawing out, i.e. from water; water-saved . . . In Luke 9:30 Moses represents the law, and Elijah the effect of the law; the association of the two means cause and effect." Metaphysical Bible Dictionary, 462. Moses, as a bringer of the law for men to live by, was guided to Mt. Sinai, where he received the tablets containing the Ten Commandments. The mount symbolizes a high place in our consciousness where we may come into a conscious communion with God. The Ten Commandments are all focused on what one should not *do. They are still true today, but many ignore their instruction. If we all honored father and mother there would be no parental abuse. We justify killing in every war, moral standards have become such that even the word adultery is rarely heard. Stealing is common; gossip is full of false witnessing. Who has not coveted another's spouse, home, car, or material possessions? Writing to the people of Corinth, Paul said,* But covet earnestly the best gifts; and yet shew I unto you a more excellent way, *(I Cor. 12:31), and in the following chapter he proceeds to describe explicitly what unconditional love truly is. In* The Course *Jesus notes that men made up the concept of hell-fire. Men who have not as yet changed their minds about their true selves have not awakened to the Christ within.*

"I came to fulfill the law by reinterpreting it. The law itself, if properly understood, offers only protection. It is those who have not yet changed their minds who brought the 'hell-fire' concept into it. I assure you that I will witness for anyone who lets me, and to whatever extent he permits it. Your witnessing demonstrates your belief, and thus strengthens it. Those who witness for me are expressing, through their miracles, that they have abandoned the belief in deprivation in favor of the abundance they have leaned belongs to them." ACIM T—1: IV: 4:3-8

CHAPTER TWO

One Life; Multiple Incarnations

#8

When Jesus came into the coasts of Caesarea Philippi, he asked his disciples, saying, Whom do men say that I the Son of man am? And they said, Some say that thou art John the Baptist: some, Elias; and others, Jeremias, or one of the prophets. Matt. 16:13-14

Because these verses in Matthew seem to refer to reincarnation, someone at a Gabriel seminar asked him about it. His response was that we have lived many times, and that Jesus lived many times. He described several of Jesus' past lives. He also reminded us that we all have been murderers, saints, and homosexuals in past incarnations. He told us that in this lifetime we are a product of all we have ever been and learned in the past. This is the only lifetime that is important. How we live this lifetime will determine our next incarnation. When we transition we review lessons learned or not learned here and now. Humanity is gripped in the idea of karma, and that idea brings us back again and again to resolve some seeming transgressions of the past. They are 'seeming' in the sense that we have never harmed anyone without their permission, nor has anyone ever harmed us without ours. Because, and this phrase from Gabriel still rings in my ears, God wouldn't allow it. In His love for us He Wills us perfect health, joy, and abundance. He loves us, protects us, and guides us. Any adversity we encounter is of our own making. When we finally learn to love all our human family unconditionally, and forgive everyone every transgression against us, the lessons will have been learned and karma will have no meaning for us.

"In the ultimate sense, reincarnation is impossible. There is no past or future, and the idea of birth into a body has no meaning either once or many times. Reincarnation cannot, then, be true in any real sense. Our real question should be, 'Is the concept helpful?' And that depends, of course, on what it is used for. If it is used to strengthen the recognition of the eternal nature of life, it is helpful indeed. Is any other question about it really useful in lighting up the way? Like many other beliefs, it can be bitterly misused." *ACIM M –24:1: 1-8*

#9

"The Eden story came about in a male-dominated society. There was no man named Adam. Adam represents a state of consciousness in which you decided that solid form was 'the cat's meow', and you concentrated on form." Archangel Gabriel 1/18/97

Gabriel was not into 'male-bashing' and he said so at a seminar entitled "Female Energy". He reminded us that humanity has lived for five thousand years in a male-dominated society, before which the Goddess was worshipped. Gabriel seldom used idioms ("cat's meow") but it fit perfectly. We have become so entranced with solid form that we have totally forgotten our eternal nature, which is spirit. The allegory of the Eden story refers to the 'fall of man,' when we came to believe that we were separate from God. We have believed it ever since. Religions are based on the idea that God is up there somewhere, all powerful, and we are insignificant little creatures who must beg for any good we receive, appease God in whatever way we can think of, and pray that life is eternal, as Jesus demonstrated. It was by our own choice that we drifted away—in consciousness—from our Creator. The story of the prodigal son is our story. We have come to this 'far country' (Earth) and believe it is all we can ever have. God patiently awaits our return to Him and our awakening from this earthly sleep. *The Course* is required for our evolution back home to Heaven and God. Our only choice is when we will study it, learn from it, grow from it, and awaken.

"This kind of error is responsible for a host of related errors, including the belief that God rejected Adam and forced him out of the Garden of Eden. It is also why you may believe from time to time that I am misdirecting you. I have made every effort to use words that are almost impossible to distort, but it is always possible to twist symbols around if you wish." *ACIM T*—3: I: 3:9-11

#10

"Enoch sought to find a connectedness to God. Part of you believes that you are connected to God. In the Enoch period people had grown from caves to upright, thinking individuals. This was most prominent in Egypt, where Ra, a mythical king, manifested the idea of one God." Archangel Gabriel 1/18/97

Our soul is the part of us that knows we are connected to God; that urges us to pray and meditate. We pray to a Higher Power that many people call God, but around the globe other names are used. God by any name is still the one God of all Creation. When Gabriel said we grew 'to upright', we knew he was referring to an earlier seminar in which he explained before we walked upright we walked on all fours. However, he denounced the idea of evolution, for apes have ever been apes and humans have always been humans. Darwin himself admitted there was a 'missing link.' There is no missing link. Gabriel, in other seminars, explained how we co-created with God all the creatures and finally created a physical form for ourselves. This explains why the physical makeup of the apes is so similar to ours, but Darwin's theory is only that. The belief in many gods was prevalent until Ra; a mythical king in Egypt brought forth the idea of only one God, and named the Sun as such. Enoch is dealt with only sparsely in both the Old and New Testaments.

"Again it [the soul who became Jesus] was manifested in Enoch, who oft sought to walk and talk with that divine influence; with the abilities latent and manifested in self to find self in the varied realms of awareness, yet using the office of relationships as a channel through which blessings might come, as well as recommendations and warnings might be indicated to others." *Lives of the Master,* 61

#11

"The One God idea manifested here [on earth] by a mythical Ra. Ra believed himself to be God but it bothered him that he was limited. He could not make the sun rise, or create rain. He sought out Hermes, who was an alchemist. He knew how to manipulate energy and change forms with it. Hermes affiliated with Ra because Ra was powerful and Hermes could help him. But Ra was so enthralled with himself that Hermes finally saw it was a 'lost cause.' Then Hermes got lost in his own creative ability and never reclaimed Christ Love." Archangel Gabriel 1/18/97

It was in this seminar that Archangel Gabriel described some of the past lives of Jesus, including Hermes. Most humans can relate to the problem of being enthralled with self. It happens when we listen to the ego that tells us how great we are—the greatest on earth and greater than anyone else on earth. We listen and we become so puffed up with ourselves that we become a legend in our own time. Everyone else is less than we are and we wonder why they don't acknowledge us as such. The ego is a great deceiver in this regard. But at some point another person or a circumstance takes us back down to size in our lives. We get right size again and perceive ourselves as no better than, nor less than, anyone else. Hermes was not above this self-elevated thought at the expense of reclaiming his Christ Love. Here Cayce explains the time of Hermes was the beginning of construction of the pyramid at Giza. It is essential that the reader understand the White Brotherhood referred to a religious group of spiritual seekers and had nothing to do with race. The hall of the initiates would become a place of study for new members of the Brotherhood.

"Then, with Hermes and Ra . . . there began the building of that now called Gizeh, with which those prophecies that had been in the Temple of Records and the Temple Beautiful were builded, in the building of this that was to be the hall of the initiates of that sometimes referred to as the White Brotherhood." *Lives of the Master*, 70

#12

"Melchizedek knew Abraham when he was Abram, He knew the consciousness of Abraham but could not reach it. Abram had faith in the unseen; Melchizedek had knowledge of the unseen." Archangel Gabriel 1/18/97

People in Abraham's time believed in sacrifice. Abraham was ready to sacrifice his own son. We don't obliterate ignorance by the external; something internal is needed. Bread was easily recognizable as a necessity of life and you could travel with it without it spoiling. Bread could be the substance of life from which all comes forth. Everyone drank wine, even children. It represented the blood; the continuing ness of life, so the substance of God of all plus eternalness equal what people could comprehend. Ritual was very important at that time. One ritual was to slaughter a lamb and watch the blood run out. In those days it was believed that you ate what you desired to be. If strength, you ate bull. For faith in God, you ate lamb. Thus, the bread had to be specific; the wine had to be the finest. Melchizedek lifted up the consciousness of man by introducing Holy Communion to Abraham who in turn gave it to the people. Melchizedek lifted up the consciousness of man, by bringing external to internal. Bread and wine represented the internal connectedness to God.

" . . . this entity [Jesus] was that one who had manifested to father Abraham as the prince, as the priest of Salem, without father and without mother, without days or years, but a living human being in flesh made manifest in the earth from the desire of Father-God to prepare an escape for man . . ."
Lives of the Master, 77

#13

And Joseph said unto his brethren, Come near to me, I pray you. And they came near. And he said, I am Joseph your brother, whom ye sold into Egypt. Now therefore be not grieved, nor angry with yourselves, that ye sold me hither: for God did send me before you to preserve life. Gen. 45:4-5

The story in Scripture about Joseph is an interesting one indeed. His father favored him and gave him a coat of many colors. We can easily identify with the jealousy of his brothers when this occurred. But it was an extreme retribution when they sold Joseph to the traveling Egyptians, then dipped the multi-colored coat in goat's blood to convince their father that Joseph was dead. Jacob was beside himself with grief and believed he would never see his son Joseph again. As the story unfolds Joseph becomes a favorite of the Egyptian king, who puts Joseph in charge of his household. It was Joseph who interpreted the king's dream of seven fat cows and seven lean cows. Joseph told the king it meant seven years of abundance followed by seven years of famine. So the king commanded that a portion of all harvests be saved against the lean years. Then it was that Jacob sent his sons to seek food from the king. They had to deal with Joseph, and he knew them but they did not recognize him. Joseph inquired about the youngest son, Benjamin, and their father. The brothers were told to fetch Benjamin in order to receive food. Reluctantly Jacob sent Benjamin to Joseph in Egypt. Then Joseph revealed himself to his brothers and, with the Pharaoh's permission, sent for his father to join them all in Egypt and live there in abundance.

"Now, Joseph had become a man since arriving in Egypt, and was not recognized by his brothers, but he knew them. Because he had the power, he could have said he would give them no food. Here is the first consciousness that you could give forgiveness. Joseph saw his brothers with eyes of love; so much love that he left the room to hide his tears. Behold, the transgressor is returned (similar to the prodigal son). His Father did not scold him, but called forth the fatted calf to celebrate." Archangel Gabriel 1/18/97

#14

"For without Moses and his leader Joshua (that was bodily Christ) there *is* no Christ. *CHRIST* is not a man! *Jesus* was the man; Christ the messenger; Christ in all ages, Jesus in one, Joshua in another . . ." *Lives of the Master,* 107

Moses knew what he wanted to do but not how to put it into action. So he asked Joshua to lead him. Gabriel explained that as Joshua led Moses' followers through the hill towns, sacking them all, he said, "Take no prisoners". In truth Joshua was misusing his power by this mass slaughter. From a metaphysical standpoint his remark about taking no prisoners means that we must give up all the error perceptions which imprison us. Joshua rid the human consciousness of its darkness (Egypt) and led them to the Promised Land (Christ consciousness) The symbolism of the walls of Jericho is old wounds, old belief systems that we have, but we feel safe there because we are familiar with them. Gabriel explained that when we read In Scripture: *Every knee shall bend,* (Is. 45:23, Romans 14:11, Phil 2:10) it means every illusion will bow to Almighty God. It is an allegory; it's about knowing the true Self that is part of God.

"Moses said to Joshua, 'Get these people to the promised land.' Joshua was a warrior. He was good at sacking a city. At Jericho the walls were very thick, and Joshua knew they were very old. He knew (from Hermes) the power of vibration, so he asked the God of his being, 'When is the next earthquake?' He got the people to march around Jericho, blowing horns for seven days and the vibration rattled things. He walked barefoot until he felt tremors and told the people to shout a mighty praise to God at his command. The walls fell." Archangel Gabriel 1/18/97

#15

"Buddha's teachings are almost identical with Jesus' teachings. After Jesus' incarnation as Buddha, he had a mental understanding of human needs, compassion, and forgiveness. He contemplated how he had brought these aspects of himself, and how to bring [them] to fullness, so for 500 years of your time he surrendered absolutely to the Will of God." Archangel Gabriel 1/18/97

Anyone who has consciously stepped upon a spiritual path can understand at least in part the zeal that Buddha felt upon realizing that the world was not the perfect place in which he had been raised. We always think that all other children share our childhood environment. Then we mature and meet many other people. We learn that there is a vast variety of experiences that children have in the home of their youth. What we experience leads us to the life we choose to live when we are on our own. Buddha studied the Vedas and the Upanishads of Hinduism. The Upanishads addressed the internalness of God, 'Do not unto others what you would not have done to you.' Sounds like the Christian Golden Rule. Gabriel explained that there were many other incarnations as well as the few he explained on January 18, 1997. He told us of those in which the soul had a shift in consciousness. No wonder the teachings of Jesus and Buddha are so similar. When Jesus began his travels at a young age he went to India and felt very comfortable there because he had lived there as Buddha.

"Buddha was the son of a wealthy Raja and lived in a protected environment. At the age of twenty-nine he went outside the walls and for the first time saw death, disease, poverty, hunger, decayed bodies, and could not understand how this could be. He realized there are two sides to life. He renounced his home with all its comforts and left his wife and child. He decided to 'go within,' and to meditate. Others took him for a guru and began to feed him. He learned one great truth: that compassion, respect, love for all life was the only way to leave behind one's karma; not to build any karma by negative thinking." Archangel Gabriel 1/18/97

#16

"The name of Jesus Christ as such is but a symbol. But it stands for love that is not of this world. It is a symbol that is safely used as a replacement for the many names of all the gods to which you pray. It becomes the shining symbol for the Word of God, so close to what it stands for that the little space between the two is lost, the moment that the name is called to mind. Remembering the name of Jesus Christ is to give thanks for all the gifts that God has given you." *ACIM M*—23: 4:1-5

When Gabriel came to the point in this seminar when he described the incarnation of Jesus the Christ, he told us many things about Jesus. He told us about the meeting between Jesus and Mary Magdalene, how he asked her to help make way for him and his followers as they traveled. Mary Magdalene was never a prostitute. She was wealthy in her own right and she agreed to help Jesus if he would take her as a student. Gabriel also told us about Judas' life as it interfaced with Jesus' life. He told us about Pilate being an Essene, as was Jesus. Pilate offered Jesus a way to escape before the crucifixion but Jesus told him it was his time. Gabriel spoke of the crucifixion. [In Gethsemane] Jesus reviewed his life. He recalled his baptism: under the water where there was no earth sound, no breath; only God's Spirit. Out of the murky water into the clarity of light and warmth of day power came into him, "I am the begotten Son of God". He called in that power and again it manifested in him. "The Father doeth the works." Thus Jesus grounded forever this consciousness as our reality.

"In Scripture a dove appeared [when John baptized Jesus at the Jordan River]. A Voice said, *This is my son in whom I am well pleased.* (Matt 3:17, Mark 1:11) The Christ energy was far beyond the realm of consciousness of Jesus, but went into the soul properties of Jesus. Your scattered thoughts of love, wisdom etc. are sheep called into the fold (baptism). It is a washing away of all past states of consciousness. Now there is a oneness that would never be gone—a divine connection was made. Jesus was transformed; all past was washed away." Archangel Gabriel 1/18/97

CHAPTER THREE

Jesus' Childhood

#17

"On the morrow the same woman brought perfumed water to wash the Lord Jesus; and when she had washed him, she preserved the water.
"And there was a girl there, whose body was white with a leprosy, who being sprinkled with this water, and washed, was instantly cleansed from her leprosy." *Lost Books, I. Infancy* VI: 16-17

There are other wonderful stories in the apocryphal books that the early religious leaders decided to omit from the official canon of the church. The swaddling clothes from the infant Jesus were given as a gift and in a ritual of the day they were thrown into a fire. The fire did not destroy it. Then the clothes were kissed in adoration. These miracles surrounding the master when he was an infant serve to indicate that his very presence on earth and all that touched him influenced others, always positively. He had learned so many lessons in previous lifetimes that he came finally to teach all peoples that love and forgiveness are the necessary building blocks for a spiritual path in life. Miraculous healings take place today in operating rooms and on evangelical stages. All healing represents a removing of an error perception. Illness, disease, and painful experiences are not ordained by God, but are the natural out—picturing of our own negative thoughts. They are the source of our self-created misery. We are God's beloved children and His Will for us is health, peace, joy, and abundance. We deny ourselves any or all of these when we entertain negative thoughts, hold on to old resentments, judge others, and remain fearful.

"Miracles are healing because they supply a lack; they are performed by those who temporarily have more for those who temporarily have less." *ACIM* T—1: I: 8

#18

"Then the Lord Jesus said to the boys, 'I will command these [mud] figures which I have made to walk'.
"And immediately they moved, and when he commanded them to return, they returned." *Lost Books*, I. Infancy XV: 4-5

How fascinating to read of the miracles Jesus performed as a boy! It explains why he was worshipped from the very beginning of his life. This is consistent with the belief that he should always be worshipped. Yet the Ten Commandments say that we should have no other gods before us. Acknowledging Jesus as the only Son of God we came to believe that worshipping Jesus is the same as worshipping God. What we worship we cannot emulate because what we worship is so far above what we are that imitation is impossible. That gets us 'off the hook,' so to speak. We can *try* to be like Jesus but, we say, 'we are only human,' and so we do not have the potential to *be as* Jesus. Now, in *The Course*, Jesus comes to remind us that he was not the only Son of God but rather that all of humanity is the only begotten Son of God. The human race is the Sonship of the Father. This is a shocking truth because it turns our beliefs upside down. It is also a burdensome truth because it means that we must take responsibility to *become* as Jesus was. Jesus did not ask for worship in Scripture and he does not ask for it now. He merely said then and tells us now to *follow him*.

"When the Atonement has been completed, all talents will be shared by all the Sons of God. God is not partial. All His children have His total Love, and all His gifts are freely given to everyone alike." *ACIM* T—1: V: 3:1-3

#19

"And as often as Joseph had anything in his work, to make longer or shorter, or wider, or narrower, the Lord Jesus would stretch his hand towards it. And presently it became as Joseph would have it." *Lost Books*, I Infancy XVI: 2-3

The reason that Jesus could altar the size of a piece of wood for his father Joseph was because *he knew he could*. When we believe that we can accomplish something—in the workplace or in the realm of education or elsewhere—we do accomplish it because belief turns into knowingness. Jesus knew that he had the power of God in him, just as we all have it within but are unaware of it. Jesus knew that he could do anything that he was asked to do. That knowingness, combined with God's power which he had manifested through previous lifetimes, made him a powerful man. His aura was extremely large which is probably why, when people were any where near him, they felt the power of his aura. Our thoughts determine our destiny. When they constantly and consistently remain in the lower or bodily level we block the flow of God's love to and through us. When we elevate our thoughts into the spiritual realm we have the realization of our potential. These ways of thinking are simple choices to make. Maintaining positive thoughts requires vigilance. The reason for this is that most people stay at the lower level. Surrounded by worldly things and worldly thinkers we must be careful. This does not mean that we spend our waking hours on our knees in prayer. It means living our daily lives from a foundation of love. It means loving ourselves as God's holy children, and then sharing, having compassion, forgiving, asking God for understanding of those things we cannot understand.

"Miracles are thoughts. Thoughts can represent the lower or bodily level of experience, or the higher or spiritual level of experience. One makes the physical, and the other creates the spiritual." *ACIM* T 1: I: 12

#20

"Then the Lord Jesus calling the serpent, it presently came forth and submitted to him; to whom he said, 'Go and suck out all the poison which thou hast infused into that boy'; So the serpent crept to the boy, and took away all its poison again." *Lost Books*, I Infancy XVIII: 14

This miraculous story about Jesus as a boy stuns the imagination. We can either see it as an aberration of the viewer or writer, or we can accept it is a possibility of a child of God, devoted to serving His Father, in the body of Jesus. Gabriel explained that as a youth Jesus was practicing the use of the Power of God in him. Coupling this story with what Jesus said later in his life (John 12:14) we have the option of believing this story. The difference is faith. Jesus knew, from infancy and even before that—through all his lifetimes—that he was the Son of God. When he came as Jesus the Christ he demonstrated what we readily call miracles and yet when we read *The Course* we find that miracles are natural (T –1: I: 6) We need only seek to deepen our faith if we are to command the waves of the sea, the serpent etc. Jesus had the conviction—the sureness—that what he commanded the serpent to do it would do. Subservient to Jesus, it obeyed his command. With this kind of power in us, why would we need any other? We put a certain amount of faith in traffic signals as we fly through a green light, *knowing* we are safe. Is it because we can *see* the light? Our journey is one of developing a faith in which we will see the Light of God, in us and in everyone else. Our eyes will not see it, but our spirit will recognize it.

"Miracles bear witness to truth. They are convincing because they arise from conviction. Without conviction they deteriorate into magic, which is mindless and therefore destructive; or rather, the uncreative use of mind." *ACIM T*—1: I: 14

#21

"When the Lady St. Mary saw the kindness which this robber did shew them, she said to him, 'the Lord God will receive thee to his right hand, and grant thee pardon of thy sins'.
"Then the Lord Jesus answered, and said to his mother, 'When thirty years are expired, O mother, the Jews will crucify me at Jerusalem;
"'And these two thieves shall be with me at the same time upon the cross,
"Titus on my right hand, and Dumachus on my left, and from that time Titus shall go before me into paradise'." *Lost Books*, I. Infancy VIII: 5-7

This story clearly indicates that Jesus, even as a boy, had the gift of prophecy. Unlike the Bible, this apocryphal story reveals the names of the two robbers who were hung on crosses next to Jesus. The synoptic gospels mention the two robbers but give no names. John does not even mention the robbers at the crucifixion scene. But Jesus recognized them when very young and predicted the parts they would play in his life. Gabriel explained that all the apostles of Jesus had agreed before coming to earth to follow him. This story also indicates that from the very beginning Jesus knew how his life would unfold and end. Here, too, we are so like Jesus in his lifetime. We, too, before we incarnate on earth, decide our lives and how they will end. But Jesus consciously remembered and we do not. At any point in our lives we can rewrite the script we put together before birth, and change any circumstance including our demise. Jesus practiced reading minds, which would, no doubt, prove beneficial later on, in dealing with the Romans and his apostles, as well as the public with whom he interacted throughout his life. These abilities are all ours for the learning. We have all the potential Jesus had. This is what we must awaken to if we are to obey his command, "Follow me".

"He [Jesus] did practice runs as a child: restored a dead bird which had been stoned by another. He practiced reading minds and told teachers, 'Today you will teach such and so', and they would say, 'How did you know?' and the teachers became upset." Archangel Gabriel 1/18/97

#22

"For certain days Ravanna was a guest in Joseph's home on Marmion Way; he sough to learn the secret of the wisdom of the son; but it was all too great for him.
"And then he asked that he might be the patron of the child; might take him to the East where he could learn the wisdom of the Brahms.
"And Jesus longed to go that he might learn; and after many days his parents gave consent." *Aquarian Gospel of Jesus the Christ* VI: 21: 14-16

For some unexplainable reason we do not read in the Bible about Jesus' travels. Gabriel explained that he did travel beginning at the age of six, then returned home and left again for travels that took him many years. He returned home when he was about thirty years of age to begin his ministry back home. At the time of Jesus' life, thirty was the age when one would be recognized as a teacher. This story indicates that as a young child he was eager to learn. He had also come to teach all his life. It must have been difficult indeed for Joseph and Mary to let him go to a far away land at an early age, but Ravanna, a royal prince of Orissa, in India, convinced them that Jesus would be well protected and cared for. His early travels were in familiar territory. As Buddha he had lived his life in India. As a child he had traveled through Egypt. To view Jesus' life as it was really lived would be exciting indeed. Nothing in Scripture was written by his own hand. We only have his quoted words, and some of them are not as spoken by him. Whatever we hear and tell another in turn is usually colored by our own experience and imagination.

"When six years old Jesus was taken from the Essenes to India, where he was quite comfortable, since he had been there as Buddha. He learned and taught there. Then he went to Egypt; also familiar territory, and he knew their thoughts and thinking patterns. He learned and taught there. Ever was he a teacher." Archangel Gabriel 1/18/97

CHAPTER FOUR

Jesus' Journeys

#23

"Jesus traveled everywhere, for 28 or 30 years, depending on what you read. He came to this country, also. Jesus ever had free will." Archangel Gabriel 1/18/97

Perhaps the Bible is silent about Jesus' travels because he did not tell the apostles about them. After all, he had enough to teach them without distracting them with tales about his earlier years. What he had learned in his travels he now was required to live day by day and teach day by day. Another reason for not telling about his journeys except to his mother and Aunt Miriam was because his own brothers refuted them. They refused to attend a feast held in Jesus' honor upon his return from journeying. They saw him as a ne'er-do-well who came home without gold or any other wealth. They called him indolent and vain, a worthless fortune hunter, and a searcher of the world for fame. But his mother knew, from the time of his birth, that Jesus had a great mission on earth, just as her great mission was to bring him forth and remain by his side to the end. Small wonder that Jesus' brothers made fun of him and his adventures on the road. From their perspective he should have brought a fortune home with him, or at least some fame. But he did not. They were unable to see, or did not know about his miraculous birth, the miracles he performed as a child etc. Would a mother hold up an older sibling as being someone special? This would only serve to make the siblings feel less significant in their parents' eyes.

"And Jesus called aside his mother and her sister Miriam, and told them of his journey to the East.

"He told them of the lessons he had learned, and of the works that he had done. To others he told not the story of his life." *Aquarian Gospel* IX: 43:21-22

#24

"With great reverence, the librarian unwrapped one of the books and presented the parchment to Mrs. Gasque:

"'These books say your Jesus was here!'

"One sentence.

"Madam Caspari looked at them in awe. In a few suspended seconds the last verse of the book of John swept through her mind like an endless river." *Lost Years of Jesus*, 317

From elegant Tibetan manuscripts the librarian read these words of Jesus' presence in the Himalayas. One cannot imagine the treacherous journey he took to visit the people in that isolated part of the world. Of course he was well protected. Of course he had friends who prepared the way and made safe his passage. We must know this because, as the Son of God, he was watched over closely throughout his life. As the two women mentioned above discussed the wonderment of what they had seen and heard, they must have wondered why the world did not know of Jesus' travels. The reader might be interested in knowing that no less than six parties ventured to the Himalayan Mountains and discovered the books referred to above. How much confirmation do we need to accept the fact that Jesus traveled to Tibet? His travels took him to the known world in order that he might learn and teach simultaneously. Wherever he went he was well received, listened to and admired for his countenance and the lessons he taught. It is clear that he did not rush through the towns he visited. Caravan travel was extremely slow and to stop for a time must have been a welcome break for the master. He knew his travels would be far and wide and that he would be away from home a very long time.

"Among the Ladaks Jesus tarried many days; he taught them how to heal; how sins are blotted out, and how to make on earth a heaven of joy. The people loved him for his words and works, and when he must depart they grieved as children grieve when mother goes away." *Aquarian Gospel*, VII: 36:22-23

#25

"And when he reached Lahore, Ajainin and some other Brahmic priests, received him with delight . . .
"He taught him how he could control the spirits of the air, the fire, the water and the earth; and he explained to him the secret doctrine of forgiveness, and the blotting out of sins." *Aquarian Gospel* VII: 37: 5-8

Wherever Jesus went he taught the same lessons. He taught about forgiveness, healing, and how to control the air, fire, and water. Gabriel told us that we teach what we need to learn. As Jesus taught many people in many lands he probably solidified his knowingness in all the subjects he taught. In that way he would, upon reaching the age of thirty, (when he could begin teaching) have a complete knowingness of his power and how to use it. Jesus never used the word ego, because it was not a known word at the time. *The Course* explains how we submit to the ego in every circumstance, listen to its raucous, though erroneous call, do what it commands, not realizing that we gave it all the power it exerts over us. Though unnamed, the ego probably ruled many people in Jesus' time. The fact that there was much fear indicates that. Rulers who became full of themselves were unable to listen to the Voice for God over the thundering shouts of their own self-will. It is a revelation to know that Jesus, directly or indirectly influenced all major religions and philosophies.

Question "What part did Jesus play in any of His incarnations in the development of the basic teachings of the following religions and philosophies: Buddhism, Mohammedanism, Confucianism, Shintoism, Brahmanism, Platonism, Judaism"?
Answer: "As has been indicated, the entity (Jesus)—as an entity—influenced either directly or indirectly all those forms of philosophy or religious thought that taught God is One." *Edgar Cayce's Story of Jesus, 233*

#26

Now when Jesus was born in Bethlehem of Judea in the days of Herod the king, behold, there came wise men from the East to Jerusalem, Saying, Where is he that is born King of the Jews? for we have seen his star in the east, and are come to worship him. Matt 2:1-2

It is so interesting to read Levi's descriptions of Jesus' life and travels. It is not difficult to imagine that Jesus would want to honor the very men who traveled so far to see him years before at his birth. They honored him yet again. It must have been a grand reunion for these now aged men. It seems clear enough that Mary and Joseph told Jesus about the arrival of these royal dignitaries who had come to worship the king foretold by the stars they studied. Jesus related the story of his life thus far, but of course he had not yet begun his ministry. At the reunion other wise men gathered from the North. They were Kaspar, Zara, and Melzone. Levi relates that these seven holy men did not speak. but sat in silence in the council hall for seven days, in close communion with the Silent Brotherhood. They prayed for revelation, for light and for power, knowing the laws and precepts of the coming age required all the wisdom of the masters of the world.

"In time he reached Persepolis, the city where the kings of Persia were entombed; the city of the learned magi, Hor, and Lun, and Mer, the three wise men.

"Who, four- and -twenty years before, had seen the star of promise rise above Jerusalem, and who had journeyed to the West to find the new-born king.

"And were the first to honour Jesus as the master of the age, and gave him gifts of gold, gum-thus and myrrh." *Aquarian Gospel* VIII: 38:6-8

#27

And he carried away Jehoiachin to Babylon, and the king's mother, and the king's wives, and his officers, and the mighty of the land, those carried he into captivity from Jerusalem to Babylon. 2 Kings 24:15
We hanged our harps upon the willows in the midst thereof.
For they that carried us away captive required of us a song; and they that wasted us required of us mirth, saying, Sing us one of the songs of Zion. Psalm 137:2-3

The captivity of Judea was complete. Every person, including the royal family, was abducted and taken captive by Nebuchadnezzar, King of Babylon. The musicians refused to sing and hung their harps on the nearby willow tree. How, they thought, could they sing when they were prisoners of a foreign king? Many years later Jesus and the greatest sage of Assyria, walked the streets of old Babylon and saw the ruination there. Jesus commented that retribution comes, and whatever men do to others it will return back to them. Babylon had fallen into ruins by now, and only creeping things found a home in the rubble there. This is the ancient lesson of the Golden Rule. When we do unto others as we would have them do unto us, where can the retribution be? Who can then be harmed? Why have we not learned this lesson yet? We have turned it on its head and believe that we should not treat others well until we find out if they are going to treat us well. As long as we think in such an upside down way, we will continue to suffer by our own hand, as we judge, condemn and criticize our spiritual brothers and sisters.

"The ruined Babylon was near, and Jesus and the sage [Ashbina, greatest sage of all Assyria] went through her gates and walked among her fallen places.
"They trod the streets where Israel once was held in base captivity.
"They saw where Judah's sons and daughters hung their harps upon the willows, and refused to sing". *Aquarian Gospel*, IX: 43: 1-3

#28

And some of them were men of Cyprus and Cyrene, which, when they were come to Antioch, spake unto the Grecians, preaching the Lord Jesus. Acts 11:20

As Jesus traveled throughout the known world to learn, to heal, to teach and preach, he said various kinds of farewell when he left. Greece impressed him greatly and he noted in his farewell speech there that, although she had strayed widely in focusing on flesh and intellect, she still had the potential of awakening. He prophesied that the day would come when "Greece will breathe the ethers of the Holy Breath, and be a mainspring of the spirit power of earth". It does not seem likely to me that he was singling out Greece as worthy of guidance from God, but rather he was suggesting that she had been guided by Holy Breath before and would be again. In his parting remarks, Jesus stated that in order for a country to be guided by Holy Breath, it must take God as its shield and buckler, and tower of strength. Nations and persons should take heed of this advice. With God as our shield and buckler (small shield) we need no shield made of metal. With God as our tower of strength, we need no defense. Do not assume that Jesus, as a defenseless person, was crucified against his will. He knew what he came to do and he could have disappeared one more time had he desired to do so. He told Pilate "It is time". He told his apostles the same.

"The breadth of Grecian thought; the depth of her philosophy; the height of her unselfish aspirations have well fitted her to be the champion of the cause of human liberty and right.

"The fates of war have subjugated Greece, because she trusted in the strength of flesh, and bone and intellect, forgetful of the spirit-life that binds a nation to its source of power.

"But Greece will not for ever sit within the darkness of the shadowland as vassal of a foreign king." *Aquarian Gospel,* X: 46:22-24

#29

Question: "Please describe Jesus' education in Egypt—in the Essene schools of Alexandria and Heliopolis—in more detail; naming some of His outstanding teachers and subjects studied".

Answer: "Not in Alexandria; rather in Heliopolis for the periods of attaining to the priesthood; in the taking of examinations there, as did John. One was in one class, one in the other. Not (with) teachers, but being examined by them. Passing the tests there." *Cayce's Story of Jesus,* 193

It is hard to discount stories about Jesus that we find in more than one place. When we read stories that are written decades apart by persons unknown to each other and unrelated to each other, there is a tendency to accept the information as truth. For many people, communication between earthlings and spirit entities is considered valid and valuable. Edgar Cayce was a channel for information that healed thousands and comforted millions through his readings. He had no axe to grind; he was a photographer by trade. A good Christian who read the Bible, he became uncomfortable with the idea that reincarnation could be true, but he did not stop seeking information from spirit. The last of Jesus' travels took him to Egypt, where, at Heliopolis, near today's Cairo, he entered into a series of tests. The topics of the tests that Jesus were given: Sincerity, Justice, Faith, Philanthropy, Heroism and Love Divine. Is it necessary to say that he passed them all? The seventh and final test, Love Divine, was passed and Jesus became THE CHRIST. Temple bells rang out and a pure white dove descended from above and sat on Jesus' head. A voice that shook the temple said, THIS IS THE CHRIST; and every living creature said, AMEN.

"And Jesus said, In every way of earth-life I would walk; in every hall of learning I would sit; the heights that any man has gained, these I would gain;
"What any man has suffered I would meet, that I may know the griefs, the disappointments and the sore temptations of my brother man; that I may know just how to succour those in need." *Aquarian Gospel*, XI: 47:12-13

CHAPTER FIVE

His Ministry: Then and Now, Part I

#30

But when the Comforter is come, whom I will send unto you from the Father, even the Spirit of truth, which proceedeth from the Father, he shall testify of me. And ye also shall bear witness, because ye have been with me from the beginning. John 15:26-27

There are many who will be incensed at the idea that Jesus' words in Scripture require interpretations. Yet for others there will be an understanding that what was beyond the thinking capacity of people 2,000 years ago is clear to us at this time. For example, Nicodemus was a learned rabbi at the time of Jesus. Yet when Jesus said we had to be born again, Nicodemus asked the master how one could be returned to its mother's womb. He was unable to comprehend the symbolic meaning of Jesus' words. The population of that time was involved in farming, animal husbandry, crops and harvesting. What they saw is what they believed. Few could read and fewer could write. Education as a formal institution for the masses was unheard of. Jesus promised a Comforter because he knew every other person was, and is, his beloved spiritual sibling, (*ye have been with me from the beginning.* John 15:27). Since we cannot see the Holy Spirit we may discount Jesus' words. But anyone who has felt and experienced the Comforter in his/her life understands the power of His Presence. Still there are those who will interpret the symbolism to suit their personal beliefs.

"I myself said, 'If I go I will send you another Comforter and he will abide with you'. His symbolic function makes the Holy Spirit difficult to understand, because symbolism is open to different interpretations."
ACIM T −5: I: 4:4-5

#31

I am come a light into the world, that whosoever believeth on me should not abide in darkness. John 12:46

For now we see through a glass, darkly; but then face to face: now I know in part; but then shall I know even as also I am known. I Cor. 13:12

John quoted the master; Paul paraphrased the master's lesson about seeing through dark glass and then clarity of vision. Jesus came as a light to the world to reveal to us the truth of ourselves as his brethren, as well as to light the path he made to show us how to follow him. Paul rightly said that he knew in part but would later see face to face—that the day would come when he would see himself as Jesus saw him, a holy brother; and as God saw him, His holy Son. Here, for the first time, we learn that the dark glass symbolizes the ego. We are familiar with how the ego deceives us. It tells us how important we are and how unimportant others are. It shouts at us to be fearful, to doubt, to hesitate, to question every decision. As our eyesight is blurred when we look through a dark glass, our inner vision is impaired from seeing the spirit of us, which mortal eyes cannot behold. This is why we are here to put the ego in its rightful place. The ego serves to warn us of possible dangers, but it does not deserve the power we give it over our lives. The light of truth will dawn on us when we turn our backs on the noisy ego and listen, often, to the still, small Voice of God. Then we shall all be known by ourselves as God knows us now.

"When I said, 'I am come as a light into the world', I meant that I came to share the light with you. Remember my reference to the ego's dark glass, and remember also that I said, 'Do not look there'. It is still true that where you look to find yourself is up to you." *ACIM* 5: VI: 11:1-3

#32

Think not that I am come to send peace on earth: I came not to send peace, but a sword. Matt. 10:34

Would the Prince of Peace utter such words as this? It seems to conflict with all his other teachings about peace, turning the other cheek, forgiving others, and loving your neighbor as yourself. Only now do we have some sane insight into the reason why Matthew would misquote the master. What is not made clear now is what made the apostles feel guilty. In this chapter of Matthew Jesus names all his disciples and then he gives them instructions about their ministry. Did they feel guilty because they felt unworthy to serve the master this way? Did they feel guilty because they were unsure if they could do all that Jesus instructed them to do? Did they, because of what Jesus said in Matt 10:26 feel guilty about things they had done in their personal lives that would be uncovered and revealed to others? Guilt is based on some remorse of the past. These men all had a past before they began following Jesus. Who knows what secrets they held that made them feel guilty? There would have been no need for Jesus to come and bring us *The Course* if his every word had been faithfully reported. We might wonder why Jesus wrote down nothing himself, but entrusted his teachings to be passed on in writing as well as in action by his followers. Surely he knew generations to come would read his teachings. One wonders if he knew that his words would be so distorted; his teachings so misunderstood.

"If the apostles had not felt guilty, they never could have quoted me as saying, 'I come not to bring peace but a sword'. This is clearly the opposite of everything I taught." *ACIM* T—6: I: 15:2-3

#33

But Jesus said unto him, Judas, betrayest thou the Son of man with a kiss?
Luke 22:48
But behold, the hand of him that betrayeth me is with me on the table.
And truly the Son of man goeth, as it was determined: but woe unto that man by whom he is betrayed! Luke 22:21-22

Jesus did not believe in torture. He was a peaceful, loving man. He did not suffer on the cross, due to the fact that he had an 'out of body" experience. Would a loving God send His beloved Son to be so abused, tormented and then hung on a cross to die? The message for humanity is from the first Easter morning, when Jesus the Christ demonstrated that life is in fact eternal. Not only is the spirit eternal by nature, but with the proper preparations the physical form can also be transformed and taken to Heaven. That is why Jesus could materialize in the flesh after the crucifixion and reveal the wounds in his side and hands to his disciples. On the cross, after all the physical abuse that Jesus had endured, he had no anger nor sought any retribution. He knew who he was and he knew that only ignorance had led the people to crucify him. Surely the ones he had healed did not participate in this unholy act. Rome feared him because he was spoken of as a king. The rabbis feared him because he could perform miracles they could not. From the cross, Gabriel explained, Jesus could see a vast sea of darkness below him. It was the darkness of ignorance. He knew then that we are all children of God, lights of the world; but we did not.

"Nor could they have described my reactions to Judas as they did, if they had really understood me. I could not have said, 'Betrayest thou the Son of man with a kiss?' unless I believed in betrayal. The whole message of the crucifixion was simply that I did not. The 'punishment' I was said to have called forth upon Judas was a similar mistake. Judas was my brother and a Son of God, as much a part of the Sonship as myself. Was it likely that I would condemn him when I was ready to demonstrate that condemnation is impossible?" *ACIM* T –6: I: 15:4-9

#34

Go ye therefore, and teach all nations, baptizing them in the name of the Father, and of the Son, and of the Holy Ghost.
Teaching them to observe all things whatsoever I have commanded you: and, lo, I am with you alway, even unto the end of the world. Matt. 28:19-20

Jesus commanded his disciples to go forth to all countries and baptize the inhabitants in the name of the Holy Trinity, and he promised them that he would be with them to the end of the world. In *The Course,* the master explains that anyone can be a teacher of God who chooses to be one. He then describes the characteristics of God's teachers. Now he also explains that because of his constant presence with us we also are the way, the truth, and the life. The power that provides these three qualities was not made by Jesus or by us. God created the power to be equally shared by all. Jesus knew he had the power and he came to tell us we also had the power and to instruct us as to how to use it. Few have seen Jesus on earth today, and only those with a highly developed ability to do so. Jesus has channeled through many faithful believers. Most of us have to be satisfied with the feeling we get sometimes when we know somehow the master is near. It is a warm, safe, comforting feeling that cannot be denied nor described. He never would have told us that he would be with us always unless he meant it. Jesus was honest and he always keeps his promise.

"When I said 'I am with you always', I meant it literally. I am not absent to anyone in any situation. Because I am always with you, you are the way, the truth and the life. You did not make this power, any more than I did. It was created to be shared, and therefore cannot be meaningfully perceived as belonging to anyone at the expense of another. Such a perception makes it meaningless by eliminating or overlooking its real and only meaning."
ACIM T—7: III: 1:7-12

#35

Peace I leave with you, my peace I give unto you: not as the world giveth, give I unto you. Let not your heart be troubled, neither let it be afraid. John 14:27

When Jesus spoke these words in Scripture he followed his promise of peace with admonishing that we should not be troubled or fearful. When we experience either of these emotions, we block the flow of God's peace through Jesus to us. How often do we *consciously* desire peace? We have turmoil and trouble in our personal lives. We watch movies that portray troubled characters and some people work with troubled patients or inmates. Trouble is all around. Fear also takes up much of our daily thinking. If we did not fear as much as we do we would save a great deal of money that we spend for protection, denying the power of God to protect us. We do not ask for peace on a regular basis or with any constant regularity. We pray for peace when we observe the horrors of war, or natural disasters or accidents of any kind. The peace Jesus speaks of is not intermittent but steady, reliable, permanent. The commonest example of our denial of peace is the sickness we bring to ourselves. One might ask why we would consciously do such a thing, but think about it, for a moment. Ask self what benefits you derive from being sick. Do others have to assume a responsibility you are willing to forgo? Do others care for you? Do you thereby dodge a job or a task that repels you? It is difficult, even painful; to admit that sickness is an illusion, but what else could it be when God created us to be whole, healthy, and prosperous?

"When I said, 'My peace I give unto you', I meant it. Peace comes from God through me to you. It is for you although you may not ask for it. "When a brother is sick it is because he is not asking for peace, and therefore does not know he has it. The acceptance of peace is the denial of illusion, and sickness is an illusion." *ACIM* T—10: III: 6:6-7:2

#36

Jesus saith unto him, Thomas, because thou hast seen me, thou hast believed: blessed are they that have not seen, and yet have believed. John 20:29

We have worldly experiences and derive perceptions from them. Then from our perceptions, which are usually erroneous, we build up our belief system. When our beliefs are fixed, perceptions stabilize. The reason our perceptions are erroneous is because they are based on what our senses convey to us, not on the truth behind what they convey to us. We see one side of an event or hear one side of an issue and draw conclusions, which are often faulty. Upon this foundation of sand we build a set of beliefs. Or we hear another's belief system and adopt it as our own because it seems to fit our present situation. When we base our belief system on truth, it is dependable, sure and does not fail us. Though we were not there to behold the resurrection, many believe it to be so even though we were not there to see it. Because we believe what Jesus taught we believe also what he did. The Christ that lives on through eternity rises above the ego when we have the courage to give up its power over us. Christ does not triumph through battle but through transcendence. We can and must transcend the ego and come to know the Christ within.

"Perceptions are built up on the basis of experience, and experience leads to beliefs. It is not until beliefs are fixed that perceptions stabilize. In effect, then, what you believe you do see. That is what I meant when I said, 'Blessed are ye who have not seen and still believe', for those who believe in the resurrection will see it. The resurrection is the complete triumph of Christ over the ego, not by attack but by transcendence. For Christ does rise above the ego and all its works, and ascends to the Father and His Kingdom." *ACIM* T—11: VI: 1:2-7

#37

Even so every good tree bringeth forth good fruit; but a corrupt tree bringeth forth evil fruit . . . .
Every tree that bringeth not forth good fruit is hewn down, and cast into the fire.
Wherefore by their fruits ye shall know them. Matt. 7:17-20

The tree is symbolic of the human person. A person who is grounded in love and peace will bring forth words and actions that reflect love and peace. We know that kind of person by his or her actions. When people express love and peace in their lives we feel comfortable and safe with them. A trust develops. Those who are not comfortable with such a person is in his ego consciousness that reminds him action is more important than peace, that constant activity is far more important and exciting than stillness. Jesus did not judge people; for he knew always that in spirit we are all good, because we are God's children. He also knew that our actions did not reflect our 'goodness,' but were sourced in our ego self. God created us from Himself, which is spirit, eternal and good. People who choose to speak and act in 'not good' ways are the ones who bring forth judgment, criticism, anger, sarcasm and all other manner of negativity. Their fruits are misery, illness, unhappiness, worry, stress, fear, and sometimes violence. Others know them by their words and actions. Those of like mind join them with the conviction that others agree with them; therefore their attitudes and behaviors are acceptable. The loving person attracts other loving persons. The angry, disruptive person will attract those of like mind. There is only one kind of person—we are all God's children. The differences lie in our attitudes and our beliefs. And both are matters of choice.

"You may have taught freedom, but you have not learned how to be free. I said earlier, 'By their fruits ye shall know them, and they shall know themselves'. For it is certain that you judge yourself according to your teaching. The ego's teaching produces immediate results, because its decisions are immediately accepted as your choice. And this acceptance means that you are willing to judge yourself accordingly." *ACIM* T –16: III: 2:1-5

CHAPTER 6

His Ministry Then and Now, Part II

#38

In my Father's house are many mansions: if it were not so, I would have told you. I go to prepare a place for you.
And if I go and prepare a place for you, I will come again, and receive you unto myself; that where I am, there ye may be also. John 14:2-3

The gospel according to John records a long monologue that Jesus had with his disciples at the Last Supper. It was then that he promised he would prepare a place for his followers. When he spoke to his disciples he spoke to humanity. That he would say different things to them than the rest of us makes no sense. The only difference between his words to his disciples and his words to the masses was that he always spoke to the masses in parables for his deepest lessons. In the event his disciples did not understand the symbolism, he expounded on the parable to them in private. Scripture includes some of these private explanations. Jesus always keeps his promise. When this writer was told in 2003 that Jesus would bring me a message when the current book was nearly done, I made a mental note of it. The next year another medium brought Jesus' words to me. He told me, "I always keep my promise." What an exhilarating moment! What joy I felt! What a confirmation that he would never leave us nor forsake us. Jesus the man came to demonstrate the Christ Love that is in all of us. At our peril we ignore it. The peril is not danger, but a prolonging of the darkness. The 'many mansions' are states of consciousness. When the Light of Truth is accepted and felt within, freedom is ours forever.

"I love you. I am with you. *I am you.* I have it all right here for you. I told you that *I go to prepare a place for you.* Well, I did, and I have. It is your place. Occupy it, fill it, enjoy it, love it, exult in it, share it." *Conversations with JC, 2/22/84*

#39

These things have I spoken unto you, that my joy might remain in you, and that your joy might be full. John 15:11
And now come I to thee; and these things I speak in the world, that they might have my joy fulfilled in themselves. John 17:13

One finds it difficult to imagine that Jesus was a man of joy, when we read about his life and its end. He himself said he was absolute joy. We have a tendency to focus on the last hours of Jesus' life when we perceive that he was brutalized and crucified in agony. It is this focus that leads many to still believe there is glory in suffering. Jesus did not suffer on the cross. As Gabriel explained he remained focused on his Higher Self, the spirit of him that was and is connected to God. We all have that same connection to our Maker. Even though Jesus knew from birth how his earthly life would end, he loved life while he walked and lived it. He loved God and was joyous that he could represent God-like qualities to the masses and teach his followers how to live their own lives. He loved children. He laughed a lot. He had a sense of humor. He was joyous indeed. It saddens me when I see a crucifix, for the glory of Jesus the Christ was not the crucified body but the resurrected spirit. Joy is part of our eternal spirit. We interrupt it when an old belief is uncovered and frightens us. Fright is not the answer; the lesson is the answer. Releasing negative emotions from all old beliefs disperses the clouds that hamper our vision of Christ in us.

"When an event frightens you and uncovers an old belief in lack, then that event has served its purpose. Of course, it is not there to frighten you, but to allow you to release that negative emotion from the old belief that clouds your vision of the Christ. I have told you that I am absolute joy, and the process of the practice is to observe when your joy is interrupted. Become alert to the negative that has surfaced, release it, and move back into absolute joy. That truly is practicing your perfection." *Conversations With JC,* 4/17/84

#40

"Let the Christ in you interpret for you, and do not try to limit what you see by narrow little beliefs that are unworthy of God's Son." *ACIM* T 31: VIII: 9:4-6

When we perceive Jesus the Christ as the only Son of God we not only disbelieve that we can imitate his life but we think it is blasphemous to consider it. Scripture does not reveal to us that Jesus asked for worship. He only asked, and many times, that we follow him. In John 14:12 he clearly states that there is nothing he did that we cannot do also. It took nearly 2,000 years for some to bring that passage forth and realize that we are on the same path that Jesus walked. He knew he was the Christ. Christ is Love and Jesus the man expressed Christ Love throughout his life. Where the Bible states that Jesus Christ was the only begotten Son of God, Gabriel clarified the mistranslation. Originally the words were, "Christ, begotten Son of the only God". What a difference it makes! How enlightening is truth! But with the enlightenment of truth comes the awareness of our personal responsibility. No longer can we say, sure, Jesus the Christ did it, but after all he was the Son of God, and we cannot hope to achieve what he achieved. Responsibility seems like a burden, but when we take responsibility for own lives and choose to emulate the Christ in Jesus we will awaken to the Christ in us.

"When you follow a path that does not lead you to where you want to be, your discomfort is only a signal saying, 'You have chosen this; do you wish to choose again?' Choosing my path for yourselves is a source of great joy for you and for me. Of course, my joy does not depend on your choosing, for I know, like me, your infinite choice is your true Christ-Self." *Conversations with JC,* 5/14/84

#41

Let not your heart be troubled: ye believe in God, believe also in me. John 14:1

Trouble seems to be the one thing that haunts us throughout life. Other people trouble us with their attitudes and behaviors. We trouble ourselves when we worry, fear, or doubt. We become comfortable in a world full of trouble, believing that joy can be ours only for brief moments at a time. We profess to believe in God, but many also believe that He is a judgmental and a punishing God. Would a God of love put us on earth to watch us be miserable? What kind of God would do that? If we fear God, like the ancients advised, where is the joy? Where is the love? Where is the peace? God is Love. When we acknowledge that as a truth we still think that in all the Power of God there is a desire for retribution. We blame God for 'natural disasters', not realizing that it is our very emotions that create the vibrations resulting in those disasters. We need not be troubled throughout our lives. God's Will for us is joy, or he would not have sent Jesus to demonstrate the Christ Love that brings with it infinite joy. Surrounded by those who are troubled we sometimes feel guilty that we are joyous! That is the ego telling us joy is not ours, because we are not part of God. The still, small Voice of God whispers that we are truly sons of God; one with Him. We are one with God and with each other. That was the glorious message of Jesus the Christ, in the Bible and in *The Course*. When we accept this truth joy will be fulfilled in us.

"Let not your heart be troubled. You are the light of the world. You are not on trial. There is not a case that could be built against you to separate you from my love. Rejoice in that! Trial and tribulations are illusions. They are created by your ego to separate you from me, or so it would seem in your perception. I say to you, there is no power, no law, no activity that can ever separate you from my love." *Conversations With JC*, 6/13/84

#42

Therefore take no thought, saying, What shall we eat? or, What shall we drink? or, Wherewithal shall we be clothed?
(For after all these things do the Gentiles seek) for your heavenly Father knoweth that ye have need of all these things.
But seek ye first the kingdom of God, and his righteousness; and all these things shall be added unto you. Matt 6:31-33

We can read the Bible daily; memorize the sequence of the books and memorize passages. These are mental exercises that may help us in studying the Bible or impressing others of our knowledge of Scripture. But until we internalize the messages we are only automatons. Jesus did not ask us to memorize his words. He did not say come to know what I taught cognitively. He said he came to show us the way, and he told us that he is the way, the truth, and the life. He also told us that all he did we, too, could do, when we believe in him. We are feeling creatures and we must feel the prayers we pray. We must feel the Presence of God when we meditate. It may take a few times or several times of meditating, but the one goal of all meditation is to feel at one with God. We are all one with God and with each other, but we have come to believe we are all separate from God and each other. Recently I saw a billboard by the roadside that said, "Don't make me come down there."—God. Do we really still believe that God is up there, somewhere? Jesus said, "I and the Father are one." He instructed us to follow him. 'Follow' means to listen and learn from, to observe and learn from, and to learn to speak and behave as.

"When you say, 'I AM,' you are stirring that into action to fulfill your conscious demand. One of the first and mightiest things that became clear in my consciousness was my ability, everyone's ability, to qualify this energy, consciously directed, with whatever the seeming need demanded. Thus, the energy may produce for your use, gold, silver, money, food, clothing, means of conveyance, or whatever the conscious demand is." *The "I AM" Discourses,* 269

#43

Be still, and know that I am God: I will be exalted among the heathen, I will be exalted in the earth. Psalm 46:10

It is unfortunate that the many churches of various denominations do not have classes in teaching meditation. The Prophets meditated. Jesus meditated. The psalmist exhorts us to be still and know the I AM, which is God. Some few denominations hold guided group meditations, which is a beginning of that practice. But true meditation is stilling the mind in a quiet setting without interruption. It is a solo flight, so to speak. In a group each person goes within to a quiet space of his own, of her own. Meditating alone can include mantras, candlelight, incense, music, certain physical postures, but these are all options. As one begins the practice of meditating—preferably every day or night at the same time—these options can be chosen. But later on they are abandoned as unnecessary. Others might want to begin the practice by listening to a voice guiding them through the relaxing, the breathing, and the focusing inward. Eventually one is able to meditate amid the noise of a city street. At first the feeling of at-one-ment is fleeting. But that fleeting moment confirms the possibility, and the moment grows into part of a minute, then a minute, then more than a minute. There is no wrong way to meditate. Nothing will happen to a person who does not meditate that would not have happened otherwise. But, oh, the benefits derived!

"The students should always understand that it is in the 'Great Silence' or stillness of the outer, that the Inner Power flows in its ever-increasing accomplishment; and soon they will come to know that even as they think of their 'Mighty Source, the I AM,' they will *feel* an increase of strength, vitality, and wisdom which will enable them to go forward with a *feeling* of Mastery, that will surely one day open wide the door through the limitations of their human creation, into the *Vastness of their True Freedom.*" The *"I AM" Discourses*, 312

#44

Peter seeing him sayeth to Jesus, Lord, and what shall this man do?
Jesus saith unto him, If I will that he tarry 'till I come, what is that to thee?
follow thou me. John 21:21-22

Gabriel observed that if we do not have a problem ourselves we find others who have problems. All of this involvement in solving problems for others takes time away from a positive attitude about improving ourselves. We all have bad habits of one form or another. We usually view them as part of our lives by saying 'That's just the way I am'. This attitude makes great excuses for negative personality traits, such as rudeness, impatience, a quick temper, criticism, judgment etc. At its extreme we act as though it is 'my way or the highway'. There are many ways we become aware of a need to improve ourselves. An embarrassing moment, a friend reminding us of a short-coming, a neighbor, or co-worker that attacks us verbally. Or self-review at some point in time, such as the age of 18 or 21, when new freedoms are granted by society's laws. Or maybe the age of 30, or when one marries; or when one enters into parenthood. Too often we look at all our bad habits at once and feel incapable of changing them all. One correction at a time, one day at a time is the best way to rid self of faults. Angelic help is always available. The Holy Spirit, when invited, will remind us when we regress. To follow Jesus, as he asked us to do, is truly beneficial. To be as patient, as forgiving, as loving as he was enhances our well-being. This is not an impossible task. Once upon a path of spiritual growth, we must remain vigilant to remain on it.

"The student should constantly look within his human self and see what habits or creations are there, that need to be plucked out and disposed of; for only by refusing to any longer allow habits of judgment, condemning and criticizing to exist, can he be free. The true activity of the student is only to perfect his own world and he cannot do it as long as he sees imperfection in the world of another of God's children." *The "I AM" Discourses*, 318

#45

Then said Jesus unto his disciples, if any man will come after me, let him deny himself, and take up his cross, and follow me. Matt. 16:24

It is interesting to note that Jesus said this long before he had to take up his own cross. Even today we think we must have a 'cross to bear' in life. It must have been an idiom of that time, also. Jesus advised his disciples, and all of us, to follow him. He knew he was God's Son and he knew we had lost sight of that Light in us. When he said 'deny himself,' he was not suggesting that we should deny the holy, God-connected Self, but rather the self we know as the ego self. Denying the ego self means that we live a life of peace and joy and harmony, by denying the ego with its fears, its doubts, its shouts of discounting our very being. Could this denial of the ego be 'the cross' he was talking about? It could very easily be, for when we listen to the ego we fail to take on new adventures, new challenges, new paths of learning and experiencing. The ego holds us back at every turn. It especially holds us back when we step upon a spiritual path, consciously. We are always on our way back home to God, but a conscious decision to tread that path makes us alert to the ego's subtle ways of stopping us. Most people who decide to seek and know their Higher Self are confronted with trivial things that seem to block the road. We must see them as trivial and not defocus our attention from our dedication to God. We *are* His children and he *will take* us back.

"Oh! That humanity who through church service after church service, are acknowledging my Ascension. Oh! Why can they not feel the True Reality and know that in my Ascended, Eternal, Light Body, I can and do reach all who will open their hearts to My Reception? Oh, children of earth! Learn to couple your *feeling* of the Truth with the acknowledgment of the Truth that you wish to have manifest in your Life. Then, you will be enabled to go forth to any height of achievement in your quest for Freedom." *The "I AM" Discourses*, 353

#46

And there are also many other things which Jesus did, the which, if they should be written every one, I suppose that even the world itself could not contain the books that should be written. Amen. John 21:25

Here Jesus speaks of his journeys in the known world and explains why they were not included in Scripture. Perhaps he thought the story of his travels would detract from the lessons of love and forgiveness he came to bring. It is unlikely that he would have wanted to distract his listeners from the messages he came to teach and demonstrate. The unusual nature of his travel to which he might have been referring was that he learned as well as taught. His disciples probably thought he should be seen only as a teacher. He is saying, however, that he told his disciples about his travels and what he learned and saw and experienced on them. They must have been impressed with his willingness to go on such long journeys at such a young age. His accounts of the countries he visited must also have enthralled these disciples who traveled only as Jesus' disciples and probably never went outside Israel until they became his disciples. Travel at that time was difficult at best, and through the Himalayan Mountains he traversed treacherous terrain. Of course he had a retinue with him, but that did not make the journey any easier or faster.

"In response to the earnest desire within the hearts of many, I wish to say that during the years in which the scriptures seem to have been unaware of my activity, I was going from place to place in search of the explanation of the *Light and Presence* which I *felt* within myself; and I assure you beloved students, not with the ease and speed with which you are able to seek to-day. Those of that day in my association were joyous to receive the knowledge of those unchronicled experiences; but, owing to the unusual nature of them, it was thought unwise to place them before the multitude."
The "I AM" Discourses, 315

#47

When the unclean spirit is gone out of the man, he walketh through dry places, seeking rest, and findeth none. Then he saith, I will return into my house from whence I came out; and when he is come, he findeth it empty, swept, and garnished. Then goeth he, and taketh with himself seven other spirits more wicked than himself, and they enter in and dwell there: and the last state of that man is worse than the first even so shall it be also unto this wicked generation. Matt. 12:43-45

There are those who think that a thought is okay as long as it is not put into action. Now it is spelled out very clearly about the thought process. A negative thought vibrates through the brain and the body before the thought leaves the brain to reach out into the entire universe. This is a very alarming description of negative thinking. This means that negative thoughts are far-reaching automatically from the brain and body that spawn them. The lesson, then, is to be aware vigilantly of our every negative thought and immediately replace it with a thought of peace. For negative thoughts lead to negative attitudes and behaviors and combined with others of like mind, disputes and arguments ensue. At the extreme, wars are begun. Where can peace be then? It is far easier to focus on peace and prevent war than to pray for peace after a war has begun. History proves this to be true. Be careful what you think. Think peaceful thoughts to bring peace on earth.

"When one wishes to give way to his own feeling of resistance, rather than still that feeling and replace it by Peace, he destroys himself, mind, body, and world; because the 'Law' is, that whatever discordant thought and feeling is sent forth by a human being, it must first vibrate through the brain and body of the sender, before it can reach into the rest of the Universe. After swinging out, it begins the return journey to its creator. While coming back, it gathers more of its kind, and that becomes the accretion of which the Individual's world is composed. This is the 'Law' and it is immutable." *The Magic Presence,* 117

#48

Ye have heard that it hath been said, An eye for an eye, and a tooth for a tooth: But I say unto you, That ye resist not evil: but whosoever shall smite thee on thy right cheek, turn to him the other also. Matt: 5:38-39

Today, the lion is not only in the streets but in many homes as well. The lion of vengeance, anger, hatred, vicious thought roams recklessly and it all begins in our thought system. We decry the constant violence in our cities. For relief we seek entertainment in the form of more violence. How can this be 'fun?' We chalk up domestic violence to the poor childhood of the parents, but is that all we want, excuses? The most important task on earth is to rear our offspring. Where is the teacher to show how best to do this? Instead we merely pass on what we learned as children. Does simply growing up qualify us to teach others how to grow up? All the prejudices, angers, and judgments that we learn from parents/teachers, we in turn teach them to our children. We can say it is up to them to unlearn those bad habits. Did we? Sometimes we did; sometimes we did not. We called the Native Americans 'savages,' but what was the murder rate among the indigenous people? How many domestic violence cases existed? I have no information on this, but I presume that tribal standards disallowed abuse of children, the future generation of the tribe. And elders were always respected.

"The outer world likes to flatter its vanity by the feeling, that it has the ability to accomplish great things; but, so far as the control and Perfection of the feeling is concerned, the outer world is still in a savage state. Human beings sting others, as well as themselves through vicious feelings, just as surely as does the scorpion. The predominant feeling in our modern world is terrifically vicious, when personalities are opposing and criticizing those who disagree with them. So-called civilized people commit murder every day of the week, through sending out angry and irritated feelings that kill the higher impulses in others." *The Magic Presence*, 360-361

CHAPTER SEVEN

Lessons of the Resurrection

#49

"The message of the crucifixion is perfectly clear: *Teach only love, for that is what you are.*" *ACIM T* 6: I: 13:1-2

The reason that love is the message of the crucifixion is that in spite of all the abuse Jesus received prior to the crucifixion, he did not judge or condemn any of his perpetrators. He did not fight back. He did not resist arrest. He surrendered to the Roman soldiers quietly. Even on the cross he prayed, and he prayed for his torturers. He did so because from the lofty spiritual heights of Truth he knew that they were in the dark about their intentions, their motives, and themselves. They followed orders as good soldiers, and so they had no personal intentions except to obey orders. Whether they liked the task of attacking Jesus physically or not, they had no personal motive but to please their officers in charge. They were in the dark about themselves because they could only see themselves as bodies in uniforms. They could not see the eternal spirit in them that Jesus could see. The master could see the light within them, but he knew their consciousness was dulled to the point where they were unaware of it. At this time we all are unaware of the light of God within us. But God sees us and knows us as His own. Jesus sees us and knows us for what we truly are, his holy siblings. This is the light we must come to acknowledge, feel and express. We need to make our children aware of this light within. Only then will they mature to be loving, forgiving, compassionate children of God.

"The message every child must learn is that God does not punish. God creates and shares love energy, and asks each of us to do our very best at living love on a daily basis. You punish *yourselves* by non-loving behavior, dear ones." *New Teachings for an Awakening Humanity,* 170

#50

The Lord will give strength unto his people; the Lord will bless his people with peace. Psalm 29:11

In the book of Proverbs (3:13-17) we find that all wisdom's paths are peace. There are also many wars and battles described in the Old Testament. When Jesus came he did so to show us the way of peace. When a famous writer was asked what he thought of Christianity, his reply was, "I think we ought to try it sometime." There are millions of self-proclaimed Christians, but the mentality of war remains prominent in the belief system of many people today. What is 'peace,' after all? Can it be defined? Gabriel defined it during his twelve years of visitations: "Peace is not the absence of war. It is the flow of life unfettered, in perfect balance. It is the presence of a consciousness in which war has no place—is not included in the consciousness". A world can hardly be imagined in which human consciousness did not include war. Yet Jesus prophesied that peace on earth was a possibility. Why else would the angels at his birth proclaim 'peace on earth,' if it were not a possibility for humankind? Could they have meant that peace on earth was possible just for Jesus—or just in Jesus' lifetime? He was a man of peace, but there was no peace on earth during his lifetime, except in the peace that prevailed in his mind and his aura.

"One person joined by another, in a growing decision for PEACE, will form an indestructible belief pattern of such magnitude that the broader body of power and execution of policy will reflect it. Nothing short of this will save the planet. So become the peace, teach peace, and join together in a mighty demand for peace at every level of local, national, and international government. There must not be any possibility of veto allowed on this issue if humanity is to be saved. Commit to peace, therefore, and settle for nothing less". *New Teachings*, 170-171

#51

"Consider, then, that in this joint will you are all united and in this only. There may be disagreement on anything else, but not on this. This, then, is where peace abides. And you abide in peace when you so decide." *ACIM T* 9: VII: 2: 1-4

We have the habit of glibly speaking of peace on earth, and we take the idea of peace on earth very seriously at Christmastime. Then we return to our daily tasks. "Peace is not the absence of war; it is a consciousness that does not take in the idea of war at all" (Archangel Gabriel). Perhaps there are reasons why we don't really want peace in our lives every day. We may think it would be very boring. After all, most excitement we know comes with such things as dissension, anger, and criminal intent. We are so fascinated by a serial killer or a mass murderer that, after the fact, we write books and make movies about them. How mentally healthy is that? I am reminded of a story Gabriel told once about a woman who came to earth many times with designed intent for the most horrific experiences for herself. One of them was that she was skinned alive. Angels went to her after that transition and told her that she didn't have to suffer like that. Her response was, "but it is so exciting!" Some people seem to live a life of one trauma after another, as though life is supposed to be that way, or that is what God intended for them. God's Will for us is health, peace, joy, harmony, and abundance. Can parents reading this think of anything else they desire for their worldly offspring?

"The golden Christ energy is at your disposal and a part of my message regards the necessity for everyone on the planet to meditate every day without fail.

"With peace as your only motive in living, you become peaceful on every occasion and through your example more of God's creations may be convinced of the emergency and join in our project for love and peace." *New Teachings,* 16.

#52

"The Atonement is therefore the perfect lesson. It is the final demonstration that all the other lessons I taught are true. If you can accept this one generalization now, there will be no need to learn from many smaller lessons. You are released from all errors if you believe this." *ACIM T*—3: I: 7:8-11

If the lessons Jesus the Christ taught 2,000 years ago were heeded, properly recorded and followed by generations since, there would be no need for him to return. Now he comes, through *The Course, New Teachings,* and other writings, to straighten out the crooked places of our understanding. Jesus was a healer. Have we come to believe that wholeness in mind and body are God's Will, or do we put more faith in a pill or an injection? Jesus demonstrated love. When we meet a new person is it our intent to see something about them we can love or do we wait for a point of disagreement? Jesus forgave others and told others to be forgiving. How many resentments do we hold, justifying our anger? The lesson of love that he taught has been re-defined by society. We have one kind of love for our pets, another kind of love for our children, another kind for a partner, another kind for friends. Unconditional love, the love Jesus taught, is not splintered, and divided. Unconditional love, agape love, is without reservation or condition; without judgment, without condemnation and without labeling. We are all one family of God. When only love guides us, we know joy. We know peace. We know God.

"I regret that the teachings I brought 2,000 years ago have not been understood or followed as they were intended. I will later speak of the necessity for the churches and institutions as you know them to analyze themselves and to take this last opportunity to divest themselves of the need for self-aggrandizement and power. They must cooperate with all teachers of light, including myself, who remind you that the only purpose of a minister or spiritual teacher is to model love. Thus they introduce the concept of turning within so the inner spark of God can blaze brighter in every person. All else follows this." *New Teachings*, 48

#53

"Do not make the pathetic error of 'clinging to the old rugged cross'. The only message of the crucifixion is that you can overcome the cross. Until then you are free to crucify yourself as often as you choose. This is not the gospel I intended to offer you. We have another journey to undertake, and if you will read these lessons carefully they will help prepare you to undertake it." *ACIM T 4*: in: 3:7-11

During those wondrous years that Gabriel made visitations to instruct us, he was asked one day if Jesus was coming for the Second Coming and when. He told us (paraphrased) that there would be nothing new to teach us, as Jesus said it all then. He also said it would do no good for him to come because he would only be killed again. It is not difficult to imagine that some would consider him blasphemous now as many considered him so at that time. Some cling ardently to the old rugged cross because they believe in 'tradition' or they continue to believe that it is good and worthy to suffer. Jesus chose the cross not to suffer (for he did not; he elevated his consciousness above the body and its pain), but to demonstrate to all of humanity that life is eternal. The life of the spirit never can die, for it is of God. The personality, on the other hand, is of our own making. It is based on all the experiences we had in our multiple lifetimes on earth. When we subjugate our personality to the Will of God then it will die to the soul.

Our personality is not us, for we are the individualized expressions of spirit. God is spirit. We are his blessed kids.

"Take me down from the old rugged cross if you yourself would be free! See me alive and beautiful and forget the story of the crucifixion and all its guilt and pain. Focus only on the resurrection if you are grateful for my coming . . . if you would call me elder brother to the human family. Your symbol of the crucified body on a cross must end unless you realize it is your human personality that must die to your soul. Then and only then does this symbol serve you at all." *New Teachings*, 80

#54

"It is extremely difficult to reach Atonement by fighting against sin. Enormous effort is expended in the attempt to make holy what is hated and despised. Nor is a lifetime of contemplation and long periods of meditation aimed at detachment from the body necessary." *ACIM T* 18: VII: 4:7-9

When we give this some serious thought, it makes sense that peace cannot be found by fighting against something. War does not bring peace; it usually leads to more wars—wars of retribution and vengeance. Raging against sin does not correct the person raged at, nor can it bring the raging person to a point of peace and quiet, where meditation must take place. The Atonement can be broken down into three words, and Gabriel told us about this: at-one-ment with God is the only true goal of any meditation. That is why it is done alone. A guided meditation to a group is fine and helps everyone to learn how to be still, how to go within and how to clear the mind of daily thoughts that crowd in upon us. Long periods are not required. A motive of desiring to know God's will is necessary and then a quiet, uninterrupted place facilitates the meditative state. People have meditated ever since the first human looked up at the night sky and wondered what the stars were all about, or gazed at the ocean in wonder, or stood atop a mountain and beheld the plain below. Peace of mind requires meditation, which in turn connects us to love, to light and to our spiritual Source.

"That which is called meditation, contemplation, or being still within, is as old an activity as human life itself. In fact, it began as a gift to those with individualized souls so they could stay in touch with the First Cause while they were living in the material world of physicalness. Meditation, therefore, is the primary way a human being can find peace of mind and connection to love, to light and to the spiritual sources which are always available to the individual seeking holy guidance . . . the true knowing of life's blueprint and direction." *New Teachings,* 90

#55

"I said before that what you project or extend is up to you, but you must do one or the other, for that is a law of mind, and you must look in before you can look out." *ACIM T*—12: VII: 7:1

Being still is contrary to the busy world we live in. The people who are considered most worthy are the working, productive ones. Value is placed on individuals who succeed at business, education, sports, the arts etc. Fame is not for the multitude. Those who are not famous are considered as 'the masses'. They are the ones who pay to hear, see, and be with the famous, the wealthy, the degreed. This is a worldly habit. God sees us all as the same—his beloved children. He sees us as lights in the world, walking around within a dark little cloud of our own making. The cloud represents our ego. Clouds are not solid, yet in our minds we listen to the ego as though it were our maker, our boss, and our guide. It is only a cloud and as such can be blown away with a strong exhale. This can only be done when we desire to put the ego in its place—relegating it to the sidelines while the Holy Spirit takes center stage in our life's choreography. Then and only then can we see ourselves as the lights of the world that we truly are. The first step is to be still. Being still is the first step in the practice of meditation. There is no wrong way to meditate; motive is essential. The motive is to be at one with God by *feeling* at one with God.

"Meditation begins with the simple act of stopping the everyday activities and sitting quietly, with a salutation or prayer of reverence and thoughtfulness to God in mind and heart. This, combined with the quieting of the mind by the natural act of deep breathing until a relaxed state is reached, brings one to the place where God can be known. For the nature of God cannot penetrate into the busy mind . . . it comes only to the peaceful mind, willing heart and relaxed body. All religions speak of this, the Christian Bible included."
New Teachings, 90

#56

"Your learning potential, properly understood, is limitless because it will lead you to God. You can teach the way to Him and learn it; if you follow the Teacher Who knows the way to Him and understands His curriculum for learning it. The curriculum is totally unambiguous, because the goal is not divided and the means and the end are in complete accord. You need offer only undivided attention. Everything else will be given you. For you really want to learn aright, and nothing can oppose the decision of God's Son. His learning is as unlimited as he is." *ACIM T*—12: V: 9:1-7

The soul's memory knows where we came from—God and His Heaven—and longs to return. Consciously we don't recall it. But every time we pray, meditate, attend a religious ceremony, it is that inner longing of the soul to return. We seek to find ways in which we can know and do God's Will. We identify a worldly teacher and listen ardently to the lessons taught. What we fail to understand is that all the answers are within us and the only true spiritual Teacher is the Holy Spirit. *The Course* provides the curriculum. God has no axe to grind and Master Jesus' only desire is to awaken us to the same light that was and is in him. We all have negative "baggage" in our subconscious. Sometimes we begin to shed light on it through counseling, a willingness to change, or a traumatic event that snaps us awake. Total surrender of all negativity is necessary to change our daily lives.

"Yes, each human being without a connection to God is chained by those hellish negative thoughts given by parents and all the society members who have placed their own opinions into the baby's memory banks. Even spiritual people have misinformation in their subconscious memories. And it is not until that memory in the subconscious . . . or hidden, emotional record beneath conscious awareness . . . is stirred and cleansed with light that healing takes place. You must be willing to give up those false beliefs, negative barriers and limitations . . . whatever they are . . . and *surrender* them in order to spiritually change your daily existence." *New Teachings, 96.*

#57

"When you combine with God through your soul, and with any teacher who has joined with our Creator's identity and energy, you begin a process of inner healing that frees you from the old ways which attract back to you undesirable life experiences. For what you think and feel are real things, with a life of their own. As they travel from your mind and body into the unseen ethers of space, they magnetically call an identical energy forth to join them. There, like attracts like, whether positive or negative." *The quality you send out is what you receive!" New Teachings,* 98

We draw to our experience what we expect. Fear attracts fearful situations, peace draws peaceful situations. The very thoughts we have start a vibration and the energy moves out away from us and attracts like energies. Negative thinking promotes, therefore, illness, pain, and suffering. These are not God's Will for us. We create our own misery. As Gabriel said, "All wounds are self-inflicted." We say that we are our own worst enemy, and that is true. When we give up the idea of 'enemies', and acknowledge all humanity as God's great family, we will be on our way to understanding the importance of love that Jesus demonstrated. We are here to learn love. God sends the Holy Spirit to guide us on this sacred path. The Holy Spirit is the transforming energy of God. He comes only when invited and as surely as the sunrise. Let us take time to see our thoughts for what they are. Positive thoughts bring us positive experiences. Negative thoughts bring us negative experiences, be they lost jobs, lost relationships, lost health.

"When you can tune in—and everybody can—to that God-Self of you, then miracles happen. *A miracle is your natural state of being.* When you are not having miracles in your life, you are out of your element. It is like teaching a fish to tap dance! But, when you are in your spiritual self, what you would call a miracle is a natural out-picturing of your divine good. And where do you think that would come from? . . . the God of you, because God loves you." *Getting to Know Your Soul,* 28

#58

"I can be entrusted with your body and your ego only because this enables you not to be concerned with them, and lets me teach you their unimportance. I could not understand their importance to you if I had not once been tempted to believe in them myself. Let us undertake to learn this lesson together so we can be free of them together. I need devoted teachers who share my aim of healing the mind. Spirit is far beyond the need of your protection or mine. Remember this:
"In this world you need not have tribulation because I have overcome the world. That is why you should be of good cheer." ACIM T—4: I: 13:4-11

Some of the phrases found in the Bible we find the master saying yet again 2000 years later. Skeptics could say that there is a false prophet speaking now. Some would say it cannot be that Jesus would come again to speak to us, and if he did, why would he not reveal himself at this time? Gabriel was asked about the Second Coming and he made it clear it is an individual awakening, that Jesus will not come again because if he did he would only be killed again. The lessons then and now are the same. We are slow learners or we would have done a better job of following Jesus as he asked us to do in his teachings. Jesus overcame the world so long ago, but we have resisted the lessons and in our resisting we have brought chaos to the world and to our own private worlds. Master Teachers are abroad among us and others channel through dedicated mediums. Others, unseen, direct us personally as we embark upon and travel our spiritual path.

"I, the Christ, am not the only channel of God's truth. There are many others. But for those who believe and have faith in me, I assure that I am no farther away, once you restore your communication system, than a mental phone call. One day soon many more will actually see me than do now, especially the children." *New Teachings*, 158

CHAPTER 8

Fulfilling Jesus' Promises

#59

And Jesus called a little child unto him, and set him in the midst of them, And said, Verily I say unto you, Except ye be converted, and become as little children, ye shall not enter into the kingdom of heaven. Matt. 18:2-3

It is common for a little child, in the face of all obstacles, to say "I can too". They have a confidence that defies our senses because they have no sense of limitations—for themselves or others. When we tell them we can't do something they wonder why we see ourselves as having limitations. I'm reminded of the story about a kindergarten child who drew a picture that the teacher, try as she may, could not interpret. Giving up, she asked the child what it was a picture of. The child replied, with great confidence, "It's a picture of God". The teacher reminded the child that no one knows what God looks like. Immediately came the response, "They do now!" There is a tendency in children, even when parents mistreat them, to hope each day the parent will be different; thinking "Maybe today s/he will feel better, accept me, love me." There is the constant hope that the parents will accept them and express the same love toward them that they feel toward the parents. Some people grow up to adulthood still hoping for an expression of love that never comes their way from parents. Children at play accept one another; they do not 'naturally' judge their playmates. Neighborhood children accept one another unless the parents impose sanctions on them because of their own prejudices.

"You were told in the Bible that you needed to become like a little child. I meant by this that you must have no limitations in your thinking. No barriers that say, 'Oh, that's not possible.' And like a child, you must be accepting of a loving Father/Mother's role in your life. Not a Parent who would be unworthy of trust or would abuse you, but one whose affection and concern are eternal and assured. THIS IS THE BASIS OF LOVE." *New Teachings,* 158

#60

For where two or three are gathered in my name, there am I in the midst of them. Matt. 18:20

Time after time we find Jesus' words repeated in recent writings. It is as though he wants us to know what he said then was true and when he repeats it at this time it remains true. His life on earth so long ago was consistent; why should not his words remain so? Each of us, each of God's children, has the power to heal self and others. We are totally asleep to that and other powers within us. We substitute force for power. God is love and love is the greatest power in all the cosmos. We think force is essential against our perceived 'enemies' and against each other. From a fist in another's face to weapons of war, humanity has become engrossed in conflict. I wonder what we are so afraid of? A soft answer, as the Bible says, turneth away wrath. It must be the ego self of us, trying to defend itself, that makes us react like a pulled rubber band suddenly released. The ego is not worth defending. It has no eternal substance. It is of our own making and yet we allow it to rule us. Instead of the ego's raucous call to arms, we have the option of listening to the still small Voice for God. He whispers in our ear constantly—it is the intuitive thought, the gut hunch—but we fail to respond. Then comes that gentle but sure reminder and we think, "I had a hunch I should have done thus and so, but I did not pay attention to it." We must be vigilant to the Voice and respond.

"At last one of the three men who had escorted us managed to utter a ""Remember this' said the Master, 'It takes only one man to make a request of my father and he will be answered; it takes only three men to ask in my name, with a single impulse and their wish will be fulfilled. This I can assure you'." *The Way of the Essenes, 204*

#61

"Remember this well. It is not the person of Jesus who has addressed you for the past three years, but a truth without age, expressed through him. You will tell people that you have known the meeting point of the forces of renewal and that these forces are theirs. I have called you here to prevent you from establishing dogmas in my name or in the name of my Father. Dogma is human, and we are not human. Teach our works and our harmony, but not a law." *Way of the Essenes, 273*

All the great religions of humankind share the same basic moral tenets. Could this not be the basis of finding common ground among all the religions? When religions become separated by various dogmas, the idea of unity is lost. We design a set of rules that fit us at the time and decide to begin a new religion. Christianity has splintered in so many different directions that one is hard put to define a true Christian. In fact, there may not be any true Christians in the sense of followers of Jesus. He was the Prince of Peace. Does this mean that today's Christians are unfaithful to their religion because they sanction war? It is not for me to say, but when Jesus lived and taught what love, unconditional love, looks like and how it behaves, he was full of hope that we would emulate him. We only love those we choose to love. Others are suspect, or hated, or feared. Fear is a disabling emotion that prevents us from growing on our spiritual path. We are all going home to God, but that does not mean death. It means awakening to the God within, for that is where His Kingdom is. The Bible tells us so.

"Many people today seek their own laws. Yet in so doing, they often find only partial values of these universal principles. In actuality, the full value of these universal principles has been recorded similarly in all major religions since time immemorial. The principles of inner development are basically no different now than they were in the days of Jesus, Buddha, Mohammad, Shankara, or Confucius." *Oneness*, 2

#62

"Later the talk led to God and one of our party said, 'I would like to know who or what God really is.' Then Jesus spoke and said, 'I believe that I understand the motive of the question you would like to clear up in your own mind. It is the many conflicting thoughts and ideas that are puzzling or disturbing the world today without reference to the origin of the word. God is the principle behind everything that exists today. The principle behind a thing is Spirit and Spirit is Omnipotent, Omnipresent, Omniscient. God is the one Mind that is both the direct and the directing cause of all the good that we see about us. God is the source of all the true Love that holds or binds all forms together. God is impersonal principle'."
Life and Teachings of the Masters of the Far East, Vol. 2, 51-52

As children we are (hopefully) taught about God, and we picture him as an old, wise man, sitting on a cloud watching us. That is an anthropomorphic God, made in man's image. When we mature to a point where we can better understand the magnitude of a Creator, we begin to believe in a Higher Power that is in control of the world and everything in it. But wait, where then is our free choice? God gave us free choice and with it we worshipped Him for a very long time. Then we decided to create things other than the perfection we enjoyed in Heaven. We created on and on, using the various vibrations we could control, with our God-given power. Finally we created physical form, the lowest possible rate of vibration in the cosmos. Here we settled down and came to believe that form in the physical was all there really is. We lost sight and memory of the Paradise we shared with God and each other. We are stuck here in this darkling place. But there is salvation, for although we have forgotten God, He has not forgotten us. Do we human parents ever forget our children?

God is love; and he that dwelleth in love dwelleth in God, and God in him. I John 4:16

#63

Ye are the salt of the earth: but if the salt have lost his savour, wherewith shall it be salted? it is henceforth good for nothing, but to be cast out, and to be trodden under foot of men. Ye are the light of the world. **A city that is set on an hill cannot be hid.** Matt: 5:13-14

Salt is one of the four basic taste sensations. It has been a preservative for centuries and without it, spoilage occurs. Good food becomes inedible. In his definition of salt, Webster's dictionary state: 'scattered elite, as in salt of the earth.' Perhaps Jesus saw a few people as being salt of the earth, such as his disciples and other followers. More likely, since his next statement refers to us as lights, the scattered elite can mingle with the others and bring to them the light that makes them elite. Now we know that the light in us has been there since Creation. We have simply lost an awareness of it. There is nothing we can 'become' that we are not already. Many people think if they act, think, and behave in a certain way they will 'become' spiritual beings. We were created spiritual beings by God, our Eternal Spirit. Our task is to *awaken* to what we already are. The days must end when we think that God is up there somewhere and we are down here on earth. The Kingdom of God is within—true 2,000 years ago; true now. Adam fell asleep in Eden, but nowhere in Scripture does it say he woke up. Jesus, Archangel Gabriel, and all Master Teachers, come to awaken us to our God-given divinity.

"When I said, 'I am the Christ, the only begotten of God', I did not declare this for myself alone, for had I done this I could not have become the Christ. I say definitely that, in order to bring forth the Christ, I, as well as all others, must declare it; then must live the life, and the Christ must appear. You may declare the Christ all you will and, if you do not live the life, the Christ will never appear. Just think, dear friends, if all would declare the Christ then live the life for one year or five years, what an awakening there would be. The possibilities cannot be imagined. That was the vision that I saw." *Life and Teachings,* 53-54

#64

That which is born of the flesh is flesh; and that which is born of the Spirit is spirit. Marvel not that I said unto thee, ye must be born again.
The wind bloweth where it listeth, and thou hearest the sound thereof, but canst not tell whence it cometh, and whither it goeth: so is every one that is born of the Spirit.
John 3:6-8

God is present in all people. We are prone to see others as separate from us simply because they *seem* separate. As spirit entities, we are all one with each other. It is the spirit in another that we must seek to find. Before that, we must seek to find it in ourselves. We know flesh when we see it, and we judge others by what they do in the flesh. Jesus told us not to judge but to love others. He knew that, regardless of one's behavior, attitude, or words, there was inside of him/her an eternal spirit. When we awaken to the Spirit in us, we become aware of the closeness of God. We do not believe he will answer our prayers; we **know** he will answer our prayers. We know, too, that He speaks to us constantly. He speaks to us through others. He speaks to us through words we read. He speaks to us through intuitive thoughts. Intuition is a communication gift of God. It is His method of talking to us. We cannot ever tell where a thought came from, like the wind whose source we cannot name. But we know wind when we *feel* it and we know God when we *feel* His presence.

"You can see and talk with God at any time, just as you can with father, mother, brother, or friend. Indeed, He is far closer than any mortal can be. God is far dearer and truer than any friend. God is never wrought up, nor angry, nor cast down. God never destroys, nor hurts, nor hinders one of His children or creatures or creations. If God did these things, He would not be God. The god that judges, destroys, or withholds any good thing from his children or creatures or creations is but a god that is conjured up by man's ignorant thinking; and you need not fear that god unless you wish to do so. For the true God stretches for the His hand and says, 'All that I have is yours'." *Life and Teachings,* 53

#65

"For more than fifty years after that day on the cross I taught and lived with my disciples and many of those I loved dearly. In those days we gathered at a quiet place outside Judea. There we were free from the prying eyes of superstition. There many acquired the great gifts and they accomplished a great work. Then, seeing that, by withdrawing for a time, I would be able to reach and help all, I withdrew. Besides, they were depending upon me instead of upon themselves; and, in order to make them self-reliant, it was necessary for me to withdraw from them." *Life and Teachings,* 55-56

Here, in two different books, published 66 years apart, mention is made of Jesus' presence and continuing existence in flesh to teach his disciples and other followers. We know that he materialized to many people on Resurrection Day and some days thereafter. It ought not to be difficult to accept the idea he would stay for years so that he would desire to teach in a quiet setting, to students eager to learn. Then he left the monastery at Mount Carmel. One time, at a seminar given by Archangel Gabriel, someone asked why Gabriel would not come longer than twelve years. Gabriel told us in the beginning of his visitations that he would come for twelve years, which he did. Gabriel's response was much like Jesus' reason for leaving Krmel (Carmel) when he did. He said (paraphrased) when the teacher is present students do not work, they listen. When the teacher leaves, then the students get busy and pass on the teachings they have heard.

"Master Jesus went on teaching in secret at the Krmel into his old age. "When the time came, he left his body of his own free will. His resplendent form of light, whose density was such that it seemed to be his physical body, was seen rising slowly over the Krmel." *The Way of the Essenes, 364*

#66

"Perhaps it was the chief triumph of Christianity that it transformed the Cross into the symbol of all that is grandest and most sacred." Encyclopedia of Religion, *209*

Before I consciously started upon a spiritual path in my life, I viewed a movie entitled *Brother Sun, Sister Moon*. Perhaps because it had such an impact on my life I still consider it the best movie I ever saw. I have viewed it numerous times since. At the end the protagonist, St. Francis of Assisi, disrobes in the town square and walks to the edge of town, uplifts his hands and his body forms a cross. It inspired me. Now, as I read the origin of the cross' symbolism as told by Master Jesus, I know why I was so stricken. It was a defining moment for me. I cannot recall the year this occurred, but it signaled a new beginning for a conscious spiritual path. From the ancient symbol of joy the cross came to represent for some the glory of suffering and dying for God's sake. Now we know God does not require suffering nor any kind of sacrifice for His sake. The only sacrifice we can make for God is to sacrifice our negative thoughts, words, attitudes, and behaviors. Then and only then can we know God as God is, and know that we are His alone.

"The cross was, in the beginning, the symbol of the greatest joy the world ever knew. The foundation of the cross is the place where man first trod the earth, therefore the mark that symbolizes the dawn of a

celestial day here on earth. If you will trace it back, you will find that the cross disappears entirely and that it is the man standing in the attitude of devotion, standing in space with arms upraised in blessing, sending out his gifts to humanity, pouring all his gifts forth freely in every direction."
Life and Teachings, 56

#67

"You must know that you are truly divine and, being divine, you must see that all men are as you are. You will know that there are dark places you must pass with the light that you are to carry to the highest and your soul will ring out in praise that you can be of service to all men. Then, with a glad free shout, you mount to your very highest in your union with God."
Life and Teachings, 58

We all pass through dark places in our lives—those dark spots of pain, confusion, and doubt. Through it all the light that is within continues on, whether we are aware of it or not. And we usually are not. If we were consciously aware of that light of divinity within we would not perceive the dark places as dark places but rather as opportunities to learn new lessons. As we mature physically we learn to deal with life on life's terms, but as we grow spiritually we learn to live a life of honesty, openness, and willingness to change. That spiritual growth brings us to a point where any situation—any situation—can be faced head-on with the first thought being, "What is the lesson in this for me?" God's world—the world He created—is eternal and perfect. Note the planets and their cyclic action. There is harmony in Heaven. Note the migrating birds. The largest flock wings this way and that with never a collision. Yet we collide with each other at every turn. This is because we have not consciously begun our spiritual path. We serve God best when we love ourselves and all others. Then there can be harmony on earth as well as in Heaven.

" . . . Now you must understand that the worlds shining before you and of which you can only perceive the coarsest, outermost shells, are the organs of my Father's body.

The perfect Human Being is no other than my Father, and you are his children, as you are the particles of his body. He calls you to Him so that you may grow incommensurably in consciousness, so that you, too, may become perfect men, creators of worlds." *Way of the Essenes, 267*

#68

And as Moses lifted up the serpent in the wilderness, even so must the Son of man be lifted up. John 3:14
And I, if I be lifted up from the earth, will draw all men unto me. John 12:32

In his recent words, Jesus often quotes his own words, from Scripture, and then explains them. Today is not a time for new lessons, but rather Jesus' explanation of what he said then and the meanings we missed then, or were incapable of understanding then. My favorite example is when Jesus told Nicodemus that one had to be born again and Nicodemus asked how one could be put back in the mother's womb. He was a learned rabbi of the day, and yet his thinking was as concrete as the mass consciousness, or race mind. He was unable to comprehend the deeper meaning, the symbolism of what Jesus meant. Humanity has evolved a little bit more to the point where symbolism is accepted, esoteric meanings are understood and the parables make sense in today's world as they did then. As we evolve more and more in understanding, Jesus comes to explain his original intent 2,000 years ago. Jesus, with his holy vision, could see an earth like heaven, where all would see eye to eye instead of the idea of 'an eye for an eye.' When we reach that point we will not only believe but *know* there is one shepherd, one fold, one family of God who will one day be lifted up and know the Oneness in which we were created.

"When I said, 'I am lifted up', and that by being so lifted up I would draw all men to me, I knew that, in the light of that experience, some day all would see eye to eye and know full well when they could be lifted up as I am lifted. I saw heaven right here on earth among men. This is the Truth that I perceived and the Truth will make all men free. Then they will find that there is but one fold and one shepherd; and if one strays, it is safe to leave all the ninety and nine, to seek the one that he may return." *Life and Teachings,* 156

#69

In the way of righteousness is life; and in the pathway thereof there is no death.
Prov. 12:28

Many believe that being "righteous" means being holier than others in every way we can imagine, such as attending church daily, praying hourly and thanking God constantly for blessings bestowed upon us. Faith without works is dead; therefore we need to put into action the Love of God we represent. Sometimes loving others means being a good listener, honoring their presence, offering a quick smile to a stranger, offering a helping hand when one is obviously needed. We have no trouble loving others, but we balk at others loving us. We suspect a price must be paid. This is based on past experiences. But if we live our lives based on past experience, what new adventures dare we take? In what direction will God guide us if He knows we are fearful to even *try?* Gabriel used to admonish us for using the word 'try', because it implies the possibility of failure. Going fearlessly ahead, confident in Self and trusting implicitly in God, we cannot fail. Fear and forgiveness do come to mind simultaneously. Yet fear of others prevents us absolutely from forgiving others. Fear is always based on the past and the past must be foregone if we are to live in the *now, the precious present.* For yesterday is history and tomorrow is being designed by us today.

"The emptiness engendered by fear must be replaced by forgiveness. That is what the Bible means by 'There is no death', and why I could demonstrate that death does not exist." *ACIM T*—1: IV: 4:1-2

CHAPTER 9

The Accepted Time

#70

And the peace of God, which passeth all understanding, shall keep your hearts and minds through Christ Jesus. Phil. 4:7

The peace that is beyond our understanding is the peace we seek but have not yet found. In this peace we fear nothing and can be shaken by nothing because we have a knowingness that nothing can affect us but God. And only good can come to us or through us from God. This peace denies all negativity to invade it. This kind of denial is useful because it is not about 'hiding' anything. We ordinarily refer to denial as hiding something from self. This kind of peace hides nothing but rather corrects all our error perceptions. Our error perceptions are based largely on our five senses, which deceive us in their limitations. When all error is brought into the light of truth we can know this peace. The light of truth corrects error and at the same time dispels the darkness, which accompanies error. In this peace we are truly free, for nothing engenders fear in us. If we could not attain this peace, Jesus would not say so, and Paul would not have written it to the Philippians.

"That is why the Bible speaks of 'the peace of God which passeth understanding.' This peace is totally incapable of being shaken by errors of any kind. It denies the ability of anything not of God to affect you. This is the proper use of denial. It is not used to hide anything, but to correct error. It brings all error into the light, and since error and darkness are the same, it corrects error automatically." *ACIM T* 2: II: 1:9-14

#71

Behold, what manner of love the Father hath bestowed upon us, that we should be called the sons of God: Therefore the world knoweth us not, because it knew him not.
Beloved, now are we the sons of God, and it doth not yet appear what we shall be: but we know that, when he shall appear, we shall be like him, for we shall see him as he is. I John 3:1-2

The manner of love the Father has bestowed on us is unconditional love, and His Son came to demonstrate that kind of love to us. Unconditional love does not make conditions, does not 'keep score', and does not wait for love to come before returning it. It does not brag itself, it does not behave in obnoxious ways. Paul said it all right in the thirteenth chapter of his first letter to the people of Corinth. The world did not understand Jesus when he came and lived a life of unconditional love, full of compassion and forgiveness. The world didn't know him because his words and actions were so contrary to the world's thinking then. We think we know him better now, yet we have fallen far short of emulating the love he lived and taught. Jesus told us that we were his brothers and sisters and could do all he had done. He told us to follow him as innocent children. When we achieve a state of innocence we will see him as he is—eternal spirit. Innocence is infinite trust, open willingness to learn and change, acceptance of all people and situations just as they are. In this state we see truly instead of through error perceptions. We have no desire to attack for we love all of our spiritual siblings on earth. When the Christ Love appears in us we shall see Him instead of the man Jesus, and we will be seen by the world as Sons of God.

"Yet this vision can be perceived only by the truly innocent. Because their hearts are pure, the innocent defend true perception instead of defending themselves against it. Understanding the lesson of the Atonement they are without the wish to attack, and therefore they see truly. This is what the Bible means when it says, 'When he shall appear (or be perceived) we shall be like him, for we shall see him as he is'." *ACIM T*—3: II: 5: 7-10

#72

We then, as workers together with him, beseech you also that ye receive not the grace of God in vain.
(For he saith, I have heard thee in a time accepted, and in the day of salvation have I succoured thee: behold, now is the accepted time; behold, now is the day of salvation.) II Cor. 6:1-2

These words were written centuries ago, yet, like most of the Bible, the words were promises of things to come. Sometimes, upon seeing a person handicapped, we say, 'There, but for the grace of God, go I.' The grace of God is not selective. God graces us all with His Love at all times. The fault is ours. We have lost sight of God in our lives. We have lost sight of God altogether. God patiently waits for our recognition of Him in us. When we step upon a spiritual path and consciously, ardently desire to know God, the path is clear before us. Words we read, ideas we think, words other people say to us or in our presence, all seem to point the way along the proper path. At some point on our journey we become more patient, more accepting of others, more understanding of self and others, more willing to be still and know God. It is at that point that we know God's grace is in us and it brings to us only good. God does not choose those who receive His grace and those who do not. It is there for our taking, as we become aware of it. By the grace of God we are lifted in our consciousness and by the grace of God we return unto Him.

"They will know that the Holy Spirit, the whole of the Divine Spirit in them, says today just as it did long ago that, if they hear its voice and harden not their hearts, they will find they are the light of the world and they that follow that light shall not walk in darkness. They will know that they are the door by which all enter into the light of life and those who will go in and out by that door will find eternal peace and great joy and will discover that now is the accepted time." *Life and Teachings,* 159

#73

"No one can ask another to be healed. But he can let himself be healed, and thus offer the other what he has received. Who can bestow upon another what he does not have? And who can share what he denies himself? The Holy Spirit speaks to you. He does not speak to someone else. Yet by your listening His Voice extends, because you have accepted what He says." *ACIM T* 27: V: 1:6-12

It was clearly explained by Archangel Gabriel that when a person is healed it is because that person has accepted the healing. Jesus healed ten lepers, but only one held to the healing and thanked Jesus for it. The other nine lepers did not hold to the healing and therefore the leprosy revisited them. It revisited them not because God struck them with the disease again; not because they did not go back to thank the master for the healing. The reason they did not hold to the healing and remain healthy is because they believed they did not *deserve* to be healed. Possibly they chose a karmic ride, which included leprosy for the rest of their lives. Or perhaps they insisted on telling others how bad the leprosy *had been when they were diseased.* A healing must be accepted and the disease, illness, wound, must not be revisited for any reason to anyone else. To daily thank God for good health is an excellent way to keep it. We admire healers the world over, but if the patient chooses not to be healed he will not be healed. It is an example of our free choice. God ordains us perfect health and anyone who does not enjoy it has planned a dis-ease for a lesson to be learned, or to help others learn a lesson. Sickness is one of the many bushels under which we choose to hide our light. It provides a convenient escape from responsibility and it seeks a care-taker, sometimes for life.

"To understand the inner teaching concerning that nature of SIN and the part it plays in healing or lack of it, we must consider three code words for 'sin'. One general word means *to hurt another,* with act or thought or word. This is the only sin that counts in the secret lore." *What Jesus Taught in Secret*, 39

#74

The Spirit of the Lord is upon me, because he hath anointed me to preach the gospel to the poor; he hath sent me to heal the brokenhearted, to preach deliverance to the captives, and recovering of sight to the blind, to set at liberty them that are bruised, To preach the acceptable year of the Lord. *Luke 4:18-19*

When Jesus read these words from Isaiah 61:1 in the Old Testament, he then said *This day is this scripture fulfilled in your ears.* Jesus knew that he was sent by God to heal and help the suffering and imprisoned. He knew that God's Will for all His children is perfect health—physical and mental. He understood that each person had to give self permission to be well and whole. Before giving a healing, Gabriel explained, Jesus would mentally ask the patient if s/he truly desired to be healed. With permission he helped the person comprehend that he had the power to make self ill and also had the power to heal self. Jesus came to preach in 'the acceptable year of the Lord.' It must have been *that year*, or in the scheme of eternity *that time when he walked the earth.* If that was the acceptable time of the Lord, would not all ensuing years be acceptable time of the Lord for us all? Would anyone suspect that God would only send a healer for three years out of eternity? What kind of capricious god would that be? God is Love, unconditional love. It is never capricious. It is enduring, eternal, all-accepting, endlessly patient, and all-forgiving.

"'The broken-hearted' gives us the root meaning of those who have *breaks in their low selves* . . . It means that their line of contact with their High Selves has been broken or blocked by convictions of guilt or by fixations . . ." *What Jesus Taught in Secret*, 27

#75

But as for me, my prayer is unto thee, O Lord, in an acceptable time: O God, in the multitude of thy mercy hear me, in the truth of thy salvation. Ps. 69:13

When we ask God in prayer for anything it is because that is the acceptable time to receive it. When the prayer is answered is the acceptable time for God to answer it. In His Infinite Wisdom He knows every facet of our lives and every thought we think. He also is constantly aware of all those around us, and how they impact on our thinking. He has our highest good always in mind for us, because we *are* our highest good. We have simply lost track of it over time. In place of His divine guidance we have put our own self-will at work in our lives. We base our decisions on the past, and therefore continue to make the same mistakes repeatedly. We base our concepts on what our five senses reveal to us, and therefore we build our world based on illusions. Far and above all that the senses reveal is the eternal wisdom known by God. As His beloved children, made in His Image, we have constant access to that eternal wisdom. Self-will run riot rules our lives and only when we hit a terrible bottom of despair or feel overwhelmed by life's slings and arrows do we turn to God in prayer. Then comes relief. Then comes guidance. Then comes assurance of God's love for us. Each day, each hour, offers an opportunity for a new beginning.

"The learning that the world can offer but one choice, no matter what its form may be, is the beginning of acceptance that there is a real alternative instead. To fight against this step is to defeat your purpose here. You did not come to learn to find a road the world does not contain. The search for different pathways in the world is but the search for different forms of truth. And this would keep the truth from being reached." *ACIM T* 31: IV: 6:1-5

#76

"All your difficulties stem from the fact that you do not recognize yourself, your brother, or God. To recognize means to 'know again,' implying that you knew before." *ACIM T* 3: III: 2:1-2

The soul of us contains the memories of all past experiences, thoughts, and beliefs. This was explained by Archangel Gabriel. The soul remembers its beginning, when we were one with God and knew it. In the process of devolution we came, in our consciousness, away from God to the point where we do not recognize our original selves, or any of our brothers/sisters who were once holy siblings. All humanity is connected to each other and to God. This is still the case, but we have forgotten that connection and instead focus on our own tiny world of experience, shutting out all others who do not interact with us on a regular basis. Some we do not care about, some we detest. Some we love and some we like. We humans sort out the relationships we have and choose who we will care about, who we will care for and who we will discount. This kind of sorting out love has nothing whatsoever to do with the agape love that Jesus expressed, lived, and taught. We are unable to love those we are unable to forgive. That is why the master said to Peter, *I say not unto thee, Until seven times: but, Until seventy times seven.* (Matt 18:22). Hanging on to old resentments (re-feelings) blocks us from accepting the agape, the unconditional love that Jesus demonstrated and of which he said God is made.

"'Why is it that the teachings of Christ no longer seem to exert any influence upon the people of today?' and . . . in reply . . . 'that we no longer possess Christ's precepts in their pristine purity and clearness, but that in the course of time, many human errors had crept into the Christian religion'." *Communication With the Spirit World of God,* 353

#77

"This beautiful ancient Song of the Soul [The Magnificat] was attributed to the Mother of Jesus. In that respect it is quite true, for it is a song of joy begotten in the Soul through the new consciousness of life conceived within its womb to be born into manifestation in Christhood. But it is far older than the days of the Master, having been known in the times of ancient Israel." The Logia, 97

When we began to feel ourselves separate from God, our consciousness was based on our perceptions. Our perceptions are based on our five senses. The 'new consciousness' that awaits us on our spiritual path is the result of giving up the idea of separation, and turning within to the Kingdom of God. Jesus' mother Mary conceived in her mind a perfect human being. The birth of Jesus was a miracle of conception without human intercourse. The Infancy gospel of the apocryphal New Testament attests to this fact. Jesus came forth from her as that perfect example of what man can be. He taught us the truth of us. He taught us that forgiveness and love are paramount goals in life. Instead, we have each chosen another path and it has only brought us fear, doubt, remorse, anger, and frustration. This need not be. We can choose again, and choose rightly this time, to read the words of Jesus and consider how he lived his life; we are not destined to die on the Cross. Jesus' aim was to save humanity, but only on the Cross did he realize he could only save himself, Gabriel told us. Jesus then ascended and continues to comfort us throughout time, until we all accept the new consciousness that is ours even now. We must awaken to an awareness of Self, and we must willingly *choose* to do so.

"Consciousness, the level of perception, was the first split introduced into the mind after the separation, making the mind a perceiver rather than a creator. Consciousness is correctly identified as the domain of the ego. The ego is a wrong-minded attempt to perceive yourself as you wish to be, rather than as you are. Yet you can know yourself only as you are, because that is all you can be sure of. Everything else is open to question." *ACIM T* 3:IV: 2:1-5

#78

He hath filled the hungry with good things; and the rich he hath sent empty away. Luke 1:53

There is a perpetual hunger among humans, regardless of the riches, the possessions, the accomplishments that we attain. All our seeking and finding in this world leaves us empty, devoid of something we cannot name. That original connection, that eternal connection with God, brings a longing to be something more. In fact, we *are* something more. And as we come into a knowingness of what we truly are—children of God, eternally alive in Him—the empty space fills up. We no longer feel an unidentified lack in our lives. We have not suddenly become saints, but we have come to know that God loves us grandly and always will. There is a surety in our minds that God's Love has never left us and we have never left Him. Prayers and meditations enforce this deep and abiding faith. We do not become braggarts or egotists. We become humble in the truth of us. Our holiness is real and we know it. This is the time when we come to realize that everyone on earth is our brother/sister. What happens to one happens to all. We take turns helping each other out. We accept all people as God accepts them—just the way they are. For those who remain in the darkness we once knew, we pray for them. We lift them, in our minds, into the pure white light of the Christ and leave them in love. This is our service to God. This will take us back home to Him.

"The Rulers of this world who have always oppressed the lowly, with special reference to those rulers who oppressed all who sought to follow the true path in life and worship and serve only the Living God as One whose Life was within them. For this thing has happened in all ages, that those who have sought the pure and lowly way have been oppressed by the rulers in the religious, social and national realms." *The Logia or Sayings of the Master*, Notes, 97

#79

For he hath regarded the low estate of his handmaiden: for, behold, from henceforth all generations shall call me blessed. Luke 1:48

The blessed Mary, mother of Jesus, perceived herself as a woman of low estate. How interesting to note that from her perception of 'low estate' she was elevated to the position of bearing the Prince of Peace, the way-shower of humanity, the example to follow for the human race for all time. We, too, must realize that although we perceive ourselves as of low estate, we have the potential within us to attain great heights of accomplishment. We raise our children to believe that they can do anything to which they aspire. Were we taught the same, or is this a new directive for this generation? I do not recall hearing it when I was young. As children of the Most High we have within us potential to do whatever our heart desires. The secret is to *know* this. Words are empty without actions. Faith is empty without actions. To set a goal and go forward to achieve it undoubting, unquestioning, we can achieve whatever we choose. God knows our dreams and aspirations. When we convince ourselves that we are capable of reaching them, all kinds of unseen help comes to our awareness and many people offer their help freely and willingly because they agreed to do this even before their birth or ours. From this perspective we can see that not only do we have the potential to achieve but also others have the potential to assist us. And we, in turn, to assist others. This penetrating idea of cooperation will bring us to Oneness, as God intended.

"Not simply the generations of man understood historically, but the individual Soul as it passes through its various generations of lives upon the world. Throughout these, though they cover untold ages, the Divine Love has known no change, whatever the changing conditions may have been." *The Logia*, 97

CHAPTER 10

Jesus' Materializations

═══════════════════════════════════════

#80

And after six days Jesus taketh Peter, James, and John his brother, and bringeth them up into an high mountain apart, And was transfigured before them: and his face did shine as the sun, and his raiment was white as the light. Matt. 17:1-2

It is extremely significant that Jesus took three of his disciples with him to the mountain for his transfiguration. He did not choose them randomly. Peter represents faith. James represents will, and John represents love. It is not too difficult to understand why the Master would choose these attributes for viewing such a highly significant moment in his life's journey. Faith must have a firm foundation for belief. What more of a firm foundation could be provided than an eye-witness account of the transfiguration? When we seek to know God's Will for us we listen attentively at all times for His divine instruction and guidance. From the moment of the sight of the transfiguration, the Will of God is made known to those who have faith. God is Love, and John represents the Love of God made flesh. John was the only one of the disciples who truly understood Jesus' message, Gabriel explained. On this mountain top Faith, Will, and Love observed the transfiguration of Jesus the man to Christ the love energy. It is this Christ Love that Jesus came to reveal to humankind for all time. He grounded the Light of Truth to the Earth for his and all future generations. As we choose the time to follow him on that God-guided path we journey back to our Source.

"The symbol of the High Self is 'light' and it is sometimes seen in the physical sense as an intense white light which comes from no known source and which has in it no heat." *What Jesus Taught in Secret*, 86.

#81

Now when Jesus was risen the first day of the week, he appeared first to Mary Magdalene, out of whom he had cast seven devils. Mark 16:9

The first person to whom Jesus appeared was Mary Magdalene. One might wonder why he chose her to be the first, when the lives of his apostles were so entwined with his own life. Or why his mother would not have been the first one there. Mary Magdalene was the first one to reach the sepulcher where Jesus had been laid, and she went, with Miriam, to anoint the body with oil, as was the custom of the times. The truth of the matter, as explained by Gabriel, is that Mary Magdalene was Jesus' wife. She never was the prostitute Scripture tells of. Jesus met Mary at the Essene community at Qumran and secretly married her. The marriage was kept secret in order to protect Mary, for Jesus knew that when he was crucified her life also would be in danger. Only those close to the Master knew of the marriage. After the crucifixion she was helped by friends to escape to another country. She traveled to France where she taught until she passed into spirit. Gabriel also explained that the wedding in Cana, where Jesus turned water into wine, was Jesus' marriage feast. It was the custom in those days to have a wedding feast followed months later with the wedding vows. It was by Jesus' choice that they had no children, since they too would have been in jeopardy after his transition.

"Now, Mary Magdalene was sitting not a great way off, and Jesus went to her and said,

"'Why seek the living among the dead? Your Lord has risen as he said, Now, Mary, look! behold my face!'

"Then Mary knew it was the Lord; that he had risen from the dead."
Aquarian Gospel, 173:21-23

#82

And they talked together of all these things which had happened . . . . while they communed together . . . Jesus himself drew near and went with them [but they knew him not] . . . . And it came to pass, as he sat at meat with them, he took bread, and blessed it, and brake, and gave to them. And their eyes were opened, and they knew him; and he vanished out of their sight. Luke 24:14-31

On that first Easter Sunday, two of Jesus' disciples turned for home in Emmaus. They were despondent and discouraged as they shared their memories of what had transpired at Golgotha. This lovely story in Scripture shows that Jesus not only knew that two of his disciples were traveling back home after the crucifixion, but he also knew that they believed that Jesus' ministry was over and they were going back home discouraged and disappointed. The Bible dos not reveal the names of these two disciples, but Levi reveals their identity, in his *Aquarian Gospel of Jesus the Christ*. Jesus had the power to prevent them from knowing who he was until he wanted them to know. And so he played 'dumb' about the crucifixion, choosing to hear their version of what had happened. He also quoted the Old Testament, which he had so ardently taught to his followers and the multitudes. When the trio arrived at their destination in Emmaus, Jesus was invited by Zachus and Cleophas to join them in a meal, since night was drawing nigh. He accepted. As he broke the bread at the evening meal, he revealed himself to them and then disappeared. With this news, they went back to Jerusalem to tell their fellow disciples.

"Towards the evening of the resurrection day, two friends of Jesus, Zachus and Cleophas of Emmaus, seven miles away, were going to their home. And as they walked and talked about the things that had occurred a stranger joined their company . . . And now the men had reached their home . . . And instantly their eyes were opened up, and they perceived that he, the stranger, was the Lord, the man from Galilee; that he had risen from the dead; and then the form of Jesus disappeared." *Aquarian Gospel,* 174: 1-23

#83

Afterward he appeared unto the eleven as they sat at meat, and upbraided them with their unbelief and hardness of heart, because they believed not them which had seen him after he was risen. Mark 16:14

Although the disciples had gone to the sepulcher and saw that it was empty they could not believe that Jesus was not dead. If they remembered Jesus saying that he would rise from the dead they probably did not believe that he could do it. Did they not recall that he had raised Lazarus from the dead (John 11:43-44)? Or that he had raised a child from the dead (Mark 5:41-42)? Apparently he told his disciples *often* about his resurrection. They still did not believe or believed at one time and then forgot when he was crucified. Jesus found it necessary to appear in flesh form to convince his disciples that he truly had resurrected from the dead and could even transmute his spirit form back into flesh form. What he had done was ascend from flesh to spirit and then transformed back into flesh to prove his existence to his dearest followers. Gabriel explained that all humankind will likewise ascend, each in our own time. The first step is to love our body—not to worship it—as a means of communication. If we do not love our bodies, why, Gabriel asked us, would we want to take them with us?

"I often said, I will arise; but you believed me not; and now come here and see. A phantom has not flesh and bones and brawn, like I possess.

"Come now, and clasp my hands, and touch my feet, and lay your hands upon my head'.

"And every one came up and clasped his hands, and touched his feet, and laid his hands upon his head." *Aquarian Gospel*, 175: 6-8

#84

"The wise men sat about the table talking . . . The door unto the banquet hall was in the east; a vacant chair was at the table to the east . . . And Jesus [came in] and sat down in the vacant chair; and then the wise men knew it was the Hebrew prophet . . . And Jesus said, Behold, for I am risen from the dead. Look at my hands, my feet, my side." *Aquarian Gospel*, 176: 5-11

The Bible does not mention the visitation of Jesus to the Wise Men. Perhaps it did originally, but we know now that much that was in the Bible was purged by the early church leaders. But centuries later Jesus appeared to a party traveling to the Himalayas. He himself had traveled there, teaching and learning as he went. He traveled to many countries from the age of 12 to the age of 30, when he went to the Jordan River to be baptized by John. His message of love and hope never varies. He preached love and forgiveness 2,000 years ago and whenever he appears to earthlings he repeats the same lesson. We are very slow learners. Some of us are too stubborn to accept that anything or anyone outside ourselves can properly direct us. Only when one turns the will and life over to the God of one's own understanding, can one begin to comprehend the magnitude of God, the vastness of His power, and His unfailing willingness to help us. But we must ask. We must take the responsibility of asking. We must admit that alone we can do nothing, but with God's help there is nothing we cannot do.

" . . . God is a loving, all-giving Father-Mother, who, when you approach, puts out His arms and enfolds you. It does not matter who or what you are or what you have been. You are His child just the same as when you seek Him with a true heart and purpose. If you are the Prodigal Son who has turned his face from the Father's house and you are weary of the husks of life that you are feeding to the swine, you can again turn your face to the Father's house and be certain of a loving welcome. The feast ever awaits you there." *Life and Teachings*, 52

#85

Command therefore that the sepulcher be made sure until the third day, lest his disciples come by night, and steal him away, and say unto the people, He is risen from the dead: so the last error shall be worse than the first.
Pilate said unto them, Ye have a watch: go your way, make it as sure as ye can.
So they went, and made the sepulcher sure, sealing the stone, and setting a watch.
Matt: 27:64-66

It would have been easy for Jesus to appear in the temple to the Jewish leaders and say Nyah, nyah, nyah, nyah; you didn't kill me after all. But he did not. He appeared as a fisherman to them and quizzed them about the moving of the stone from the sepulcher, the so-called 'disappearance' of his body and the validity of the soldiers' testimony that they saw the body stolen. Jesus knew better. He knew the truth of the matter and he knew the Jewish leaders had paid the soldiers to falsely testify. When he revealed to the Jews that he knew the truth, he then revealed to them his true identity, and they tried to seize him, but he disappeared before their faces. He had to prove to those who sentenced him to be crucified that they could, in fact, never kill the spirit of him. He had to reveal himself to them after the resurrection in order that they might come to believe that there is no death. Whether he succeeded in convincing them we do not know. We do know that we ourselves do not behave as though we are convinced.

"It was the Sabbath day and many priests and scribes and Pharisees were in the temple in Jerusalem. Caiaphas, Annas and some other ruling Jews were there. A stranger came in garb of fisherman and asked, 'What has become of Jesus who is called the Christ? Is he not teaching in the temple now?' The Jews replied, 'That man from Galilee was crucified a week ago, because he was a dangerous man, a vile, seditious man . . . ' But instantly the fisherman became a radiant form of light, and priests and scribes and Pharisees fell back in deadly fear; they saw the man from Galilee." *Aquarian Gospel*, 177:1-14

#86

"God speaks to man, not by an oracle of wood and gold, but by the voice of man.
"The gods have spoken to the Greeks, and kindred tongues, through images made by man, but God, the One, now speaks to man through Christ the only son, who was, and is and evermore will be.
"This Oracle shall fail; the Living Oracle of God, the One, will never fail. Apollo knew the man who spoke; he knew it was the Nazarene who once had taught the wise men in the Acropolis and had rebuked the idol worshippers upon the Athens beach." *Aquarian Gospel*, 178:5-8

Many individuals seeking to know their future visited the Delphic Oracle in Greece. Rulers from many countries brought riches in jewels, coins, and statues that adorned Mount Parnassus. It was believed that the god Apollo gave to the Delphic oracle the wisdom of the gods and thus the Delphic Oracle provided them with information that would enable them to remain in power. Untold treasures covered the mountain, as seekers of information tried to buy the right to a hearing at the pedestal where the pythia of the time stood to hear the Oracle. Some seekers were heard; all were not. For hundreds of years this practice continued. One day, as Jesus the Christ visited the location, the Oracle became a blaze of light. When it subsided, Jesus uttered the words above. He was, in essence, saying that for generations people had believed in the words of prophecy from the oracle.

But henceforth, beginning with the arrival of Jesus the Christ on Earth, God would speak through Him and others, to bring the wisdom of the ages. He came to reveal to humans the truth of us. He came to live the Christ Love he taught, that He might be an example to follow, a pattern for all.

If any man speak, let him speak as the oracles of God; if any man minister, let him do it as of the ability which God giveth: that God in all things may be glorified through Jesus Christ, to whom be praise and dominion for ever and ever. Amen. I Peter 4:11

#87

"What can the body's eyes perceive, with power to correct? Its eyes adjust to sin, unable to overlook it in any form and seeing it everywhere, in everything. Look through its eyes, and everything will stand condemned before you. All that could save you, you will never see. Your holy relationship, the source of your salvation, will be deprived of meaning, and it's most holy purpose bereft of means for its accomplishment." ACIM T—20: VIII: 6: 5-9

When we rely on what we see to determine what is true, we deceive ourselves. All we see around us is condemnation, judgment, separation between everyone, and separation from God. The only thing that is real is what we cannot see. Only spirit is real. And that we cannot see. What we can see we embrace as reality. We are seriously deluded. What God sees in us is light. We are the light of the world, and God is the Father of lights (James 1:17). We are His children and to know truth we must go within, center ourselves in peace, and listen to the still small Voice of God speaking to us. We may call it intuition, a gut hunch, a revelatory thought, an inner urge, or something else. But it is the Voice of God that speaks to us, and speaks to us every time we ask to know truth. At night before sleep we can ask the angels to take us to a place of enlightenment and truth. Turning a problem over to God before sleep guarantees an answer the next day, or soon thereafter. Sometimes upon arising we know the answer, or we have a new, objective outlook about the problem that enables us to make an appropriate decision for our highest good.

"Claudas and Juliet, his wife, lived on the Palatine in Rome and they were servants of Tiberius; but they had been in Galilee; had walked with Jesus by the sea, had heard his word and seen his power; and they believed that he was Christ made manifest. Now Claudas and his wife were on the Tiber in a little boat; a storm swept from the sea, the boat was wrecked and Claudas and his wife were sinking down to death. And Jesus came and took them by the hands and said, Claudas and Juliet, arise and walk with me upon the waves. And they arose and walked with him upon the waves." *Aquarian Gospel,* 178:16-20

#88

And when the day of Pentecost was fully come, they were all with one accord in one place. And suddenly there came a sound from heaven as of a rushing mighty wind, and it filled all the house where they were sitting. Acts 2:1

The last the disciples saw of Jesus was on the day of Pentecost. He had taught them all he could. Now he would call on Father God to endow them with powers that Jesus himself had demonstrated on earth. Now he commissioned them all to go forth to people everywhere and heal and teach, to pass on the lessons he had taught everywhere he went. When a teacher is present students do not go forth on their own. Having taught the lessons, the teacher leaves and the students go forth to sow the words of truth to others. Anyone who chooses can be a teacher of God. *A Course in Miracles* explains this. It also provides many lessons by which one may learn the wisdom of the ages in order to qualify to pass them on. Definitions are provided and the characteristics of teachers of God revealed. We all are potential teachers of God. As we learn this truth, we will realize that no intermediary is required. For centuries we thought we needed a clergy person to intercede for us, to tell God what it was we desired and to ask God's forgiveness. There is nothing for God to forgive us for. God provides all our needs. God created us in health and abundance and joy. Lacking these we lack the faith in God we need to manifest and nurture them.

"The eleven apostles of the Lord were in Jerusalem and in a spacious room that they had chosen by the Lord's command. And as they prayed the Lord appeared to them and said, 'Peace be to all; good will to every living thing.' And then he talked with them a long, long time . . . . 'Behold, upon the day of Pentecost you all shall be endowed with power from on high. But here you shall remain till then in holy thought and prayer'." *Aquarian Gospel*, 180: 1-18

CHAPTER 11

Christic in Us

=====

#89

Verily, verily, I say unto you, He that believeth on me, the works that I do shall he do also; and greater works than these shall he do; because I go unto my Father. John 14:12

The dictionary tells us that 'truly' is a synonym for verily, which appears so frequently in the bible. Jesus says it often, confirming his words are only truth. When we seem to have a 'mind of our own,' we often go down a dangerous path in life; a negative path in life, an unstable path in life. Depending on our own thinking we lead ourselves seriously astray. It takes a long time to realize our error in choosing that particular path. The realization that it is the wrong path may come in form of a traumatic awakening, an imprisonment or an addiction, a confrontation from another, especially a friend. The other choice we all have is to choose a path guided by our Creator. I do not speak of religion. I speak of spirituality. Spirit means breath and our very breath is God-created. This is not unusual since we are His begotten children. How could we not have the breath of life in us from Him? How could we think that this holy, beloved Father of ours could direct us down a path of negativity and disaster? Too early in life we assume we have all the answers we need. The truth is we have not even met all the questions as yet. God knows all the answers. God knows what we came to do on Earth. When we ask the Holy Spirit, the transforming energy of God, to guide us, we cannot fail. We cannot fail.

"The Bible says, 'May the mind be in you that was also in Christ Jesus', and uses this as a blessing. It is the blessing of miracle-mindedness. It asks that you may think as I thought, joining with me in Christ thinking." *ACIM T* 5: I: 3:4-6

#90

"You cannot distort reality and know what it is. And if you do distort reality, you will experience anxiety, depression and ultimately panic, because you are trying to make yourself unreal. When you feel these things, do not try to look beyond yourself for truth, for truth can only be within you. Say, therefore:
***"Christ is in me, and where He is God must be,
for Christ is part of Him."*** *ACIM T* 9: 1:14:3-7

We create our own reality based on what we see, hear, and feel. It is not reality; it is illusion, for all that we see is illusion. The only 'real' is outside the world of sense, higher than the illusions we believe in and accept as the only reality. There is a higher sphere of inner thought that escapes us as we focus on illusion. We may liken it to visiting a motion picture theater. We become engrossed in the story line. We identify with the actors. Feelings are evoked in sympathy of the players. Sometimes we weep for them. As we leave the theater we brush off the tears and return to the 'reality' of our lives. Life on the Earth plane is very much like the movie house. We create, by our own choice, our lives, and our experiences. We *feel* them therefore we believe them to be the only reality. As we come to understand that reality *is* the higher sphere of inner thoughts we find we can disengage ourselves from the illusions we have created. Next we learn to accept the inner thoughts as the new reality. Finally, we must *feel* the truth of reality. It is a knowingness that can not be denied. When we know and we know that we know, only reality comes into our consciousness and only the higher realms can teach us as we choose to remain there.

"The neophyte, who by some inner urge
Is set to find infinity will first
Of all be overwhelmed, like you, with loss
Acute of all that once seemed real. The mind
is hung above a deep abyss between
The solid world of sense material
And that high sphere of inner thought in which,
Though real, the soul feels not at home."
The Voice Celestial, 17

#91

"You will awaken to your own call, for the Call to awake is within you. If I live in you, you are awake. Yet you must see the works I do through you, or you will not perceive that I have done them unto you. Do not set limits on what you believe I can do through you, or you will not accept what I can do for you." ACIM T-11: VI: 0: 1-4

God can do nothing for us that He cannot do *through* us. That is a lesson to be learned before we can become aware of Christ in us. Jesus could do only so much for his followers and the multitudes. He could only heal if they chose to be healed. He could only raise the dead if they chose to be raised from the dead. He could only give sight to the blind if they chose to receive physical light. God and the Master, our example to follow, can only awaken us to our truth if we choose to be awakened to our truth. We have been given free choice as God's beloveds. Every moment of every day we make choices. Poor choices lead to more poor choices. Choices based on love, peace, joy and harmony lead to more such choices. In our very hands is our personal destiny. There is no capricious 'fate' that chooses who shall suffer and who shall enjoy good health. God ordained us to have perfect health. We go against His will when we choose poverty of any kind. We blame it on karma, but we make our own karma. We have made many poor choices and we can wallow in guilt or rise above the muddle in which we have put ourselves, by seeking guidance from the Holy Spirit and following it.

"This is a planet of choosing/ where you can see both the darkness and light/ and you have the freedom of choice./Heightened awareness /is very much an integral part/ of your planet's healing./Your world is in physical crisis/ but what is crisis? A learning process." *Emmanuel's Book*, 9

#92

"Much of what I taught on the earth has been greatly misconstrued. It has troubled me all this time that so much of the truth of it was left behind and was made into what mankind thought should be said. I have come in so many forms to so many people in so many ways to try to make right what was a wrong. My desire this day is to straighten the crooked places that the truth of what I brought might be fully understood and lived and not bound by the old ways." Jesus the Christ 1/17/98

When Jesus the Christ said he would not leave us comfortless he meant what he said, for he always keeps his promise. He has come to many psychic and mediumistic people to bring messages to earthlings. Some have seen him, some have heard him; all have been helped by him. I was told in 2003, by a medium, that he would come to bring me an important message when a book I was writing neared completion. In 2004, as I wrote the last chapter of my memoirs, he came to me through another dedicated medium, saying "I understand you were expecting me at this time. I always keep my promise." As a comforter he sends another in his name to help us in a myriad of ways: Someone to change a tire, someone to say words that comfort our grief, someone who says the very word we need to hear to bring us comfort in our sadness or encourage us. He guides us to people who can assist us on our path, support us in our efforts, whatever they may be. Sometimes we listen and respond. Sometimes we do not. He cannot comfort us if we refuse to accept the person, the words, and the deeds that bring us to our desired goal. Those before us left behind the words of truth he spoke that we sorely need to hear. Others distorted or omitted events of his life or altered his words. Because of this, he found it necessary to come again 2,000 years later to straighten the crooked places in our understanding.

I will not leave you comfortless. I will come to you. I John 4:18

#93

"He [Moses] did a symbolic thing: he smashed the tablets. Outwardly that was the manifestation of what was going on within Moses. To smash his rigid, unyielding, unmoving, unallowing attitude . . . There is nothing more limiting and binding than 'Thou shalt not'." Jesus the Christ 1/17/98

Whenever we succumb to the temptation to accept an attitude or a belief that is rigid we disallow a growth in our understanding. The 'shalt nots' were cast in stone. When we cast something in stone it cannot ever be changed. A rigid line of belief can be comforting to a seeking soul, but learning is change and change we must if we are to find peace in our lives. Rigid attitudes of prejudice, judgment, and condemnation keep us locked in and unable to expand our consciousness and our thinking. To be open to new ideas does not mean that we must accept them all. We are intelligent beings and have the capacity to discern, without judgment, what truth is, and what is not. The best way to prove a truth to ourselves is to put the teachings into practice. Practicing truthful things brings only good feelings, beneficial outcomes, and comforting results. When we are troubled, distressed and unhappy it is only because we have denied a truth, become unwilling to seek truth or have distorted truth to fit our rigid beliefs. The unyielding attitude refuses to even listen to a new idea, for the attitude has become 'cast in stone.' Rigidity is not compatible with Jesus' teachings. To become as little children, he taught us, is best. Children are open, trusting, and curious. These attributes help us mature as humans and awaken as God's children.

Let not sin therefore reign in your mortal body, that ye should obey it in the lusts thereof. Neither yield ye your members as instruments of unrighteousness unto sin: but yield yourselves unto God, as those that are alive from the dead, and your members as instruments of righteousness unto God. Romans 6:12-13

#94

"It is in the present moment that truth abides; not in yesterday, and tomorrow hasn't come. You only have the now of it." Jesus the Christ 1/17/98

The concept of staying in the now does not come easily to us. We find ourselves recalling past moments of yesterday, last month, or twenty years ago. We are tempted to focus on tomorrow or next year or retirement age. In all this defocusing from the present we miss the gift of it. What is past is past and what is to come is determined by our now. Denying now means that we are unwilling to participate in the now of time. It is a precious gift, to be employed in any way we choose. We have the choice every single moment to be aware of where we are, what we are doing, and whom we are with. We can make the most of it by being aware that we are exactly where we are supposed to be. We can make the most of it by being aware that we are doing exactly what we ought to do, and we are with those we choose to be with at this moment. If the moment is at 'work' we have chosen it, for whatever reason. Choosing to relish the job makes it more enjoyable, makes the time go faster, nurtures our sense of self-worth, I have seen janitors singing on the job; have seen policemen direct traffic as though they were dancing. They get the most out of the moment of now. A chosen occupation ought to bring constant joy, and it does when we focus on the task at hand and give it our best. Too often we defocus on what others around us are doing or fail to do. Enjoying every mile of scenery, every word of conversation, and every note of music heard on the radio enriches the vacation trip. Family interactions are best when the needs of all are considered.

"So break the old pattern of present-moment denial and present-moment resistance. Make it your practice to withdraw attention from past and future whenever they are not needed. Step out of the time dimension as much as possible in everyday life." *The Power of Now,* 45

#95

"And even when I came I was not accepted; not accepted. Why? Because I broke every rule. I broke every rule. I loved openly. I loved freely. I cared about people. I didn't care if it was the Sabbath; if someone needed healing so be it; be healed. I didn't follow the rules of the synagogue. I didn't follow the rules of Moses. I didn't follow any rule except the internal rule of the Voice of my Father within me." Jesus the Christ 1/17/98

When Jesus came to teach us the way he had to break all the rules because the rules were so rigid and restrictive. He came to teach love and love is not rigid and restrictive. If it is, it is not love. What Jesus is telling us here is that the rules of humans are of no significance at all when we listen to the Voice of God. The Voice of God may come to us in a gut hunch or sudden urge. If these feelings are positive we can be assured that they are the Voice of God speaking to us. Negative urges come from the ego and direct us down a path of destruction. The Jews hated Jesus because they had in mind a more powerful savior who would destroy Rome with force. Instead he came to teach love, and to demonstrate it. He was borne by a mother who was blessed to give birth miraculously because she could *mentally* conceive of a perfect man. Jesus came to awaken all humanity, to a place on earth where the population believed in one God, in contrast to much of humanity who then believed in several gods. Gabriel made it clear that Jesus came not to start a new religion, but rather to awaken humanity to its inner divinity. Gabriel reminded us that Adam slept in Eden, but nowhere n Scripture does it say that he woke up. It is our task to awaken now.

And therefore did the Jews persecute Jesus, and sought to slay him, because he had done these things on the sabbath day. John 5:16

#96

"People think that if you follow God you have to restrict yourself and be narrow, and not allow, and not be. God, to be expressed from within, is a freedom that you have yet to come to know. It is a freedom of love; not a freedom to go forth and hurt, but a freedom to go forth and love whoever you will. Whether they love you back or not has absolutely nothing to do with it. Most of the people that I loved didn't like me; not at all." Jesus the Christ 1/17/98

Be careful not to misinterpret 'love whoever you will' to mean *make love* to whomever you will. Jesus is speaking of unconditional love, agape love. Some of us tend to love only those who are of the same culture, language, color, or nationality. We watch our parents pick and choose who they will love and adopt the same method. The freedom that God gave each of us is the freedom to choose whom we will love. When Jesus said, 'follow me,' he meant to love as he loved, without discrimination. He traveled everywhere and loved everyone. We cling to groups and families and do not let anyone else in to our 'circle' of friends. We do not reach out to share and learn from others who speak differently, eat differently, or look different from us. Perhaps this comes from fear, or perhaps it comes from lack of self-confidence. Material wealth does not determine a person's worth, nor does the love of material things equate with love of God. Jesus knew that when we own possessions we place a high value on them. He advised the man to give up all his possessions and take up the cross and follow him. He did *not* say 'take up *my* cross.' (the crucifixion was years away). Interpreted as a sacrificial symbol, one could believe Jesus meant for us to suffer. That hardly fits with his teachings. The Cross symbolizes eternal life. Jesus proved that. And he said 'follow me' to instruct us to live in freedom. Freedom to grow, to be, and to love.

Then Jesus beholding him loved him, and said unto him, One thing thou lackest: go thy way, sell whatsoever thou hast, and give to the poor, and thou shalt have treasure in heaven: and come, take up the cross, and follow me. Mark 10:21

#97

"Now, within you is the same spirit that is within me. Lying asleep, curled up in the boat of your consciousness, is the Christ." Jesus the Christ 1/17/98

We find it easy to see ourselves as tiny, helpless individuals in the scheme of eternity, on a tiny planet in the suburbs of the Milky Way. Compared to the cosmos we are very small. The life span is approximately one hundred years. We cannot make the rain fall or the sun rise. We disbelieve in a Creator because we attribute the chaos around us to be His doing. We forget that in our free choice we have made exactly what we have on earth at this time. By free choice we can change it. One unaccepted factor is that we have the power to change it as we allow our guidance to come from God. Another factor we discount is that we have the power of God in us, since He created us in His Image, which is Spirit. We are blind to the concept that all change must come from within. How we long to change others, a situation, an attitude. Within us is the answer to all the conundrums of life. The Kingdom of God within is the Source of all answers. We belabor ourselves with questions which we deem to be unanswerable. The key is as close as our consciousness will allow. Prayer and meditation will bring all answers to us. As we practice prayer and meditation on a regular basis, we find not only all answers, but also that fewer questions arise. God is in charge and we are at peace.

At that day ye shall know that I am in my Father, and ye in me, and I in you.
John 14:20

#98

"Do you believe that God would send you anything that is not a blessing?"
Jesus the Christ 1/17/98

The God of love would not send anything but blessings to His beloved children. As someone once said, 'If we are not children of God, who are we?' The complex human form, the scope of our imagination, the potential of our intelligence all point to a Creator of indefinable and indescribable character. In its perfection the body provides us with a communication vehicle throughout our lives on earth. Our brain is capable of processing all thoughts we receive from God and all misguided directions we receive from the ego. Unlike all other creatures we have the ability to create *outside* ourselves. Gabriel came to explain the answers to the questions of the ages: Why are we here? How did we get here? Where are we going, and how? The wisdom received by our small group in Albany, NY was given to us because we were seekers after truth. And we believed in spirit communication. He told us that twelve other teachers—all ascended masters—also came to Earth to teach other groups. He described them as being 'centers of light.' The lesson brought to us was the same; only the words were different. The message is the same as that taught by Jesus, but now in modern language. The lesson is: Wake up and live from the Lord God of Your Being, for you are holy children of God. These heavenly teachers brought us the truth. When we accept it we will know the truth, live the truth, and it will set us free.

Ye are the children of the prophets, and of the covenant which God made with our fathers, saying unto Abraham, And in thy seed shall all the kindreds of the earth be blessed. Unto you first God, having raised up his Son Jesus, sent him to bless you, in turning away every one of you from his iniquities. Acts 3:25-26

#99

"Oh, absolutely! [Jesus' response to a question regarding his authorship of *A Course in Miracles*]. She was a tough customer, you know. She didn't believe in me. That's what made her so good, because she never got into the emotional part of it. She never thought, 'Oh, Jesus is coming to me; this is so wonderful. Wait until I tell my neighbors'. It was like, 'You're **who?**' And that was wonderful; that was wonderful." Jesus the Christ 1/17/98

In 1975 the modern words of Jesus the Christ were published. He gave them to a person who had no investment in his teachings. This objectivism was exactly what Jesus sought. The message was the same as the lessons he taught so long ago, though the words are different. Couched in modern English it is presented in such a way as to awaken us from the illusions we have come to accept as reality. The truth of us is that we are children of the Most High. When Jesus came 2,000 years ago he told us 'The Kingdom of God is within.' Where else would the Kingdom be, for a child of God? He came to teach *and demonstrate* love and forgiveness. Today we still need the lesson. He said we should judge not. Forgiveness follows judgment; lack of judgment allows us freedom so that forgiveness is not required. Love is the stuff of which we are made; not something we can learn. and expressing that love is the most natural thing in the world. Blocking that flow of love is what the ego does best. We have accepted so many blocks to our innate love that Jesus comes once more to teach us about the blocks and how to remove them from our consciousness. Love is the lesson now. Love was the lesson then. Centuries have layered the denial of that love that is our very essence. This Course is required to return us unto God, our Creator.

"This is a course in miracles. It is a required course . . . [It] does not aim at teaching the meaning of love, for that is beyond what can be taught. It does aim, however, at removing the blocks to the awareness of love's presence, which is your natural inheritance." *ACIM In*: 1:7

#100

[Jesus was asked if women followed him]. "There were a lot of women who followed, a lot of women who learned, a lot of women who went forth and taught. Many of them as powerfully and influentially as the men, but they were written out of your scriptures by a male-dominant world. There was Mary Magdalene, who went forth throughout Europe. There was Joanna, who looked faithfully after my mother until her time of transition; and also taught." Jesus the Christ 1/17/98

Gabriel explained that in the cosmos there are two energies in creation: action and repose. The terms 'male' and 'female' are terms invented by humans to express these two energies on the earth plane. God is androgynous, and his creations are androgynous. The idea of separation of the two energies came about when we devolved to the earth from our natural habitat, Heaven. When we identify the stereotypes applied to male and female we find that Jesus demonstrated both. He had the strength to endure the wilderness for forty days, the extensive traveling that he did, and the torturous treatment of the Romans before the crucifixion, as well as the crucifixion itself. He had the gentleness of a healer, the warmth of a human father, the tenderness of an animal rescuer, the patience of a saint. Perhaps it was this combination of qualities which endeared him to all his followers, men and women alike. Everyone could relate to a quality within self. It comes as no surprise that there were many women followers. Nor is it surprising that women were written out of Scripture, because at that time on earth females were considered chattels rather than partners. It would have been impossible to write the Bible without including the women found there. They played a significant role. Mary, Jesus' mother, Elizabeth who bore John the Baptist, and a multitude of others.

"Time after time we are brought back to the "Golden Chord" of all religions: that man and woman are expressions of God through their spirit, the Christ that dwells within each of them." *Women of the Bible Speak to Women of To*day, Preface, xv

CHAPTER 12

The Truth of Our Oneness

#101

"When asked what we should do in our daily lives, the Master replied: Love God, love yourselves, love each other, and be joyful." Jesus the Christ 1/17/98

These words were spoken by Jesus the Christ to us on that January day, when the question was put to him, "If you could summarize in one sentence your best advice to us in physical form, what would it be?" How familiar the words sounded. How ancient and how true they are. For 2,000 years we have quoted this verse in the Bible, cherished Jesus' words about love, read, and re-read them. But we have not put them into practice. How could we be so dense for 2,000 years and still running? There is only one answer. We have put the loud shouting of the ego above the still, small Voice of God in our consciousness. We listen to it berate us; make us feel guilty, small and unimportant. God speaks to us in positive whispers. We do not listen; we refuse to believe we are truly His. The ego reminds us that we once left God and He will never take us back. Master Jesus knows that some day we will accept his commandment and live it. When we love ourselves just the way we are we will have made a start. When we begin to practice unconditional love—accepting everyone exactly as they are instead of judging them—we will have begun the journey. Jesus loved his disciples, though they must have tried his patience. Three times Jesus asked Peter if Peter loved him. Why three times? Thomas would not believe Jesus had resurrected until he physically put his hand in the wound. We remain steadfast in our unwillingness to *believe*.

Jesus said unto him, Thou shalt love the Lord thy God with all thy heart, and with all thy soul. and with all thy mind. This is the first and great commandment. And the second is like unto it, Thou shalt love thy neighbour as thyself. Matt 22: 37-39

#102

"The true atonement is when you recognize that there is nothing to be forgiven for. Nor is there any ill that has been done to you. It's when you recognize that all of it was just an illusion and that in truth you never left home to begin with, and nobody has ever done anything to you or them that requires forgiveness. That is the ultimate forgiveness: when you realize there is nothing to forgive." Jesus the Christ 1/17/98

We seem to live a life that is filled with guilt. We find so many things to make us feel guilty. Guilt is demeaning, negative, and counter-productive to a child of God. We are all children of God. *The Course* explains that guiltlessness is invulnerable. What a concept! When we have not guilt—can we imagine such a thing? –we are invulnerable because we then know of our divinity and we know that no one can harm us *because God would not allow it.* Would a human parent allow a child to be harmed? Of course not. We protect them until they leave the nest, and sometimes long afterward. But God did not create us to put us through tests and trials. We come up with the tests and trials all by ourselves. Wakening to the Christ within, and then expressing it fearlessly and confidently, we know we are invulnerable, loved, loving, and lovable. God sees us this way; we do not. In the final analysis, and when we accept and learn the precepts of *The Course*, we will be free to be who we are, without guilt, without judgment, without any idea of separation. We will *know* that all humanity is the begotten Sonship of God, that we are one with God, and that we are on our way back home where we belong. Heaven is our natural habitat.

"There is nothing to forgive. No one can hurt the Son of God."
ACIM T 14: III: 7: 5

#103

"At the risk of offending ministers and pastors here, you don't have to go to church to know God. In fact, very few churches have God there. They have committees for the committees and they have rules and regulations that are sometimes impossible to keep. They are extremely critical and judgmental. Behind all of this is their idea of what God is." Jesus the Christ 1/17/98

The lessons brought to us from Gabriel and Jesus the Christ were full of hope and encouragement. These words seemed at first to shock some of us. The Master would not have said this if it were not true. He always—then and now—spoke truth. When we consider the churches we have belonged to we can testify to some of what he said. There was a time that I attended, with a friend, a church near my residence. We seated ourselves in a convenient pew and waited for the service to begin. An usher approached us and asked us to move to another pew, since this one was reserved for a certain member. Of course we complied. Committees are the mainstay of most churches. I myself appointed several during the time I was a pastor. Rules and regulations permeate most organized religious groups. Recently I attended a church that is blessed with a gifted singer. It was thrilling to hear his voice. I longed to applaud him when he finished; desired greatly to express my gratitude for his extraordinary talent. The singer received no applause. It wasn't done there. But one day a man broke the rule and began the applause; others, including self, joined him. Very few churches encourage the practice of meditation or offer meditation times in their service. Guided meditations are sometimes fostered but classes in meditation are rare. Given that the Kingdom of God is within, how better can we find it than in meditation?

"The secret of existence is unbarred
And even now the temple bell is heard
Inviting all to worship at the shrine
Of the Eternal Truth—this is the sign
That he will find the Father Spirit hid
Within himself and do what He has bid."
The *Voice Celestial*, 311

#104

"The true Self of you is God in you. The God in you does not see your perception of evil, nor looks on another as lesser than you. There is no point in it, for all are holy and pure." Jesus the Christ 9/21/96

We must read often and speak often these words that are found in Scripture, in *The Course* and in every inspired book that reminds us of our divinity. The human family is the holy Sonship of God. We have assumed the role of victim for so long that we find it incredible that we are God's holy children. This victim role has been assumed not only in this lifetime on earth, but in many, many lifetimes on earth prior to this one. Gabriel told us that we have lived so many lifetimes on earth that we have *met* every other person now living. This, too, seems incredible. Gabriel is an eye-witness to this repeating karmic ride. That is why he came as the announcer of the Age of Aquarius; the Age of Spirituality. Our real self, our true Self is God in us. Because the denial of this divinity is so pervasive in the human family, we must awaken to our own individual divinity one at a time. Through prayer and meditation we can so awaken. We cannot awaken by seeing a show on television. We cannot awaken by reading a book or conversing with another. The God Self of us must be realized *as* we connect to it, in our consciousness, with the help of the Holy Spirit. We must ask the Holy Spirit for this assistance, for He does not come uninvited. The student must be ready. The decision is a singular one, as is the path back home.

Then Peter opened his mouth, and said, Of a truth I perceive that God is no respecter of persons. Acts 10:34

#105

"This world is *not* your home. You are less than a visitor. You touch momently into the shadow (earth). Your vastness embraces all things, but doesn't *hold* to all things. You take from the earth and give back to the earth and return with the lesson learned. It is only the fleshy feet that are on the earth." Jesus the Christ 9/21/96

Heaven is our natural habitat because God created us there and there we existed, in spirit form, for a very long time, in earth terms. There is no time in Heaven; we had to create the idea to keep track of our experiences on earth. How can we readily understand spirit, our essence, when we cannot even see it with our mortal eyes? That is where faith enters in. Perhaps it would help if we think of our conscience as spirit. That nagging feeling that we are wrong; when we begin down a negative, destructive path. That feeling of remorse after we say an unkind word, the distress we feel when another sorrows and we cannot help them. But of course spirit is so much more than that. It is a vastness that embraces all things. Can we conceive of such a vastness? Can we encompass in our minds this vastness of God? Not in our mortal brain, for it is too limited to comprehend the pleroma of the cosmos. We are blest by God in ways we do not always comprehend. We can only say "Thank you, God, for thy abundant blessings on us." That is enough for God, for it indicates that we acknowledge Him in our lives, and desire to live a life of joy and abundance. God knows us as His children; as spirit, and he knows the ego's limitations we have put on ourselves. Faith will lead to knowingness and knowingness will bring us the freedom that our spirit already knows.

"Space is the *form* which MAN
Conceives to understand his universe.
He thinks in terms of form and so invents
What he calls matter, conceiving it as real."
Voice Celestial, 137

#106

"The ego perceives what is not divine. The spirit of you never touches the earth; but floats above it. The spirit of you is not pulled in and held by the earth's vibration. The spirit of you is ever free. How can you be rid of pain/ discomfort? Affirm, 'My Father-Mother God, I thank You for expressing through me'." Jesus the Christ 9/21/96

When some people consciously step upon a spiritual path they believe that the old concepts and the new–found wisdom can be reconciled. It is impossible. The result of trying to reconcile the old and new only results in frustration. It is a task that cannot be completed; a goal that is unattainable. To forego old beliefs is difficult to do. One must be convinced at the very deepest level of one's being that the new is the preferred way. When Archangel Gabriel came to teach, he reminded us that he was not bringing us something new. He came to remind us of what we already know. We have simply forgotten what we know. One day he explained that a mother bird does not teach her fledgling to fly, she teaches him to *remember* how to fly. Gabriel came to teach us to remember who we are: holy children of God. It was good to hear that the spirit of us never touches the earth. As we tread a spiritual path, earthly things become less and less important. As we tread our spiritual path the earthly things appear terribly distorted compared to the smooth, rhythmic, cyclical things of the ethereal plane. Accepting new ideas requires that we give up all the old concepts of limitation and separateness that bring us down into the gutter of judgment, ridicule, and prejudice.

"Nothing can reach spirit from the ego, and nothing can reach the ego from spirit. Spirit can neither strengthen the ego nor reduce the conflict within it. The ego is a contradiction. Your self and God's Self are in opposition. They are opposed in source, in direction and in outcome. They are fundamentally irreconcilable, because spirit cannot perceive and the ego cannot know." ACIM T 4: I: 2:6-11

#107

"Look not with earthly eyes. You have a purpose which has nothing to do with earthly life." Jesus the Christ 9/21/96

In this world of frenetic busyness we think that we constantly must be *doing* something. We use our 'down time' from work to busy ourselves traveling, playing sports, watching sports, and many other activities that require physical exertion. Fishing seems to be one activity that combines action and repose. The lone fisherman gathers his tackle, seeks a body of water, prepares the pole, line, sinker, bait, and lofts the line out into the water. Then it is a waiting game. I often wonder what fishermen are thinking about while they wait for the pull on the line from an unseen creature below the surface. Perhaps it is worldly thoughts; perhaps meditation. God has a divine plan for us. What a perfect time for mediation! Meditation is the plan of salvation. It is the plan that leads us all back to Him and His Heaven, our natural habitat, where we began our spirit's journey and where we find the only true peace that we can know. There is nothing we need to do; nothing we can do, to facilitate the journey. We need do nothing. Our only task to assist God in bringing us back to Him is to allow Him to remove our error perceptions and not interfere with His plan of Atonement.

Ellen Wallace Douglas

"I who am host to God am worthy of Him.
He who established His dwelling place in me created it as
He would have it be.
It is not needful that I make it ready for Him, but only
that I do not interfere with His plan to restore to me my
own awareness of my readiness, which is eternal.
I need add nothing to His plan."
ACIM T—18: IV: 5:10-11

#108

"I am the one to follow, for a while. I will help you release you on the earth. Your only commitment is to be at one with God; without it no journey has meaning." Jesus the Christ 5/18/96

The first time that Jesus came to visit and teach us was November 20, 1995. The small audience expected a Question and Answer Session by Archangel Gabriel. Instead, a softer, gentler voice emanated from Rev. Penny's vocal cords. He said he had come in Gabriel's place to answer our questions. When asked who he was he responded, Call me The One. Gabriel had mentioned a few times that one would follow him to teach us. As time went on, we realized that The One was none other than Jesus the Christ himself. In Scripture he told us to follow him. He said it many times. We could assume that he was speaking only to his disciples, but all his teachings were directed to the multitudes. Why would we believe that this repeated phrase was only to a small group of men who followed him? They did not need to be reminded of what they willingly chose to do. This time Jesus spoke in terms that modern humans could understand. He spoke of releasing us. He reminded us that we came from the 'known' to the 'unknown.' We came from the knowingness that we were one with God to the disbelieving of that truth. Jesus explained that our only commitment is to be at one with God.—consciously. We have come to believe that Earth is our home. We are strangers here and Heaven is our natural habitat. The journey without distance is the road back, in our consciousness, to God, to be aware of our oneness with Him.

"I once asked you to sell all you have and give to the poor and follow me. This is what I meant: If you have no investment in anything in this world, you can teach the poor where their treasure is. The poor are merely those who have invested wrongly, and they are poor indeed!" ACIM T 12: III: 1:1-3

#109

"I have walked in your shoes and am qualified to tell you. Allow the light to be. Reason it not away, or say 'I cannot'. God within you does all things." Jesus the Christ 5/18/96

There is no better teacher than the one who has experienced what she is teaching. The wounded healer is the effective healer, for the healing has taken place in her. Jesus walked the walk that we are walking now. He came to earth many times and learned many lessons. When all his lessons were learned, he returned wholly unto the Father and knew his oneness with Him. He told us that he would never leave us comfortless. He has come many times to many people to teach. He will do so until all have ascended to God—the Mother-Father Creator of us all. Whenever we say we cannot do something we are slamming the door of acceptance, and not even God can get into our consciousness. He gave us free choice and our unwillingness to listen keeps us from learning. Learning is change and many people fear change. Fear itself cannot be seen; it can only be *felt*. And feelings can lead us astray. Feelings are natural for us sentient beings, but they need not rule us. Fear stops us in our tracks and forward movement, growth, cannot take place. We are the lights of the world but every time we say 'I cannot,' or 'I don't know' we are putting a bushel basket over ourselves. When we acknowledge the Christ Light within us and express ourselves from it, God will call us home.

"If reality is recognized by its extension, what leads to nothing cannot be real. Do not be afraid, then, to look upon fear, for it cannot be seen. Clarity undoes confusion by definition, and to look upon darkness through light must dispel it." *ACIM T* 11: V: 2.7-9

#110

"Some of you are not sure what love feels like. All of you have had moments of great ecstasy—power, sex, etc. Envision that moment of absolute ecstasy and that is being loved. Say, 'I accept the love of God'. Learn to become *familiar* with feelings of being loved." Jesus the Christ 5/18/96

When we deny the existence of God we are denying something we have known, in order to identify and then deny it. We cannot deny what we have not known. This is a profound lesson found in *The Course*. God knows that we have all known a moment of ecstasy. To become familiar with that feeling means to feel like that for more than one moment in time. The oneness with God brings that ecstatic feeling constantly. Can we imagine that? Not with all our feelings of guilt, anger, resentment and fear. For fear and love do not sleep in the same bed. They are mutually exclusive by definition. Abandoning our negative thoughts, words, and actions and becoming familiar with feelings of being loved we have a glimpse of what Paradise is like. We can speak of God, pray to God, ask the Holy Spirit for guidance. But we must *feel* that we are loved. Moments of ecstasy bring us into the Love of God. We think we can only experience them in a split second of time. God's love for us is constant and eternal.

We have the task of bringing ourselves back to God consciously, and He will take the last step in our at—one-ment with Him.

"Son of God, you have not sinned, but you have been much mistaken. Yet this can be corrected and God will help you, knowing that you could not sin against Him. You denied Him because you loved Him, knowing that if you recognized your love for Him, you could deny Him. Your denial of Him therefore means that you love Him, and that you know He loves you. Remember that what you deny you must have once known. And if you accept denial, you can accept its undoing." ACIM T 10: V: 6:1-6

CHAPTER 13

Journey to the Higher Self

#111

"If you had no guilt you would be the full-blown Christ. In Scripture it says, *Harden not your heart, as in the provocation, and as in the day of temptation in the wilderness* (Psalm 95:8). Your heart is hardened when you block it with fear. Say, with *feeling*, 'From the heart of me I accept the love of God'. Say it a thousand times a day, if necessary." Jesus the Christ 5/18/96

This is a very strong statement; to think that it is only guilt that keeps us from knowing our Higher Self, our Christ Self. Any idea we entertain that we are separate from each other and separate from God keeps us from awakening to the true Self of us. Temptations are everywhere to entice us to negative thinking and negative behavior. The ego is tempted; not our spirit. The ego has no agenda except to keep us from a spiritual path which leads to a realization we do not need the ego. The ego fights very hard to keep its life, which has no value in the scheme of God's love or in the scheme of God's eternalness. Guilt seems to cling to us like a suction cup, and we must pull it off our consciousness if we are to allow our light to shine. We are not separate from each other, but we persistently believe that we are. Jesus did not teach separation; he taught love, forgiveness, sharing, and acceptance. He told us to be as little children. Not vulnerable and ignorant as we perceive children to be, but open, accepting, loving, curious, and sharing. These are the attributes of children, of true innocence. These are the attributes Jesus demonstrated. Isaiah (11:6) prophesied: '*a little child shall lead them.*'

"Guilt is always disruptive. Anything that engenders fear is divisive because it obeys the law of division. If the ego is the symbol of the separation, it is also the symbol of guilt. Guilt is more than merely not God. It is the symbol of attack on God. This is a totally meaningless concept except to the ego, but do not underestimate the power of the ego's belief in it. This is the belief from which all guilt really stems." *ACIM T*—5: V: 2:6-12

#112

"Say in the morning, and during the day, 'The love of God goes before me and transforms all things to the honor and glory of the God within'."
Jesus the Christ 5/18/96

In the Gospel according to Matthew we find, *The light of the body is the eye: if therefore thine eye be single, thy whole body shall be full of light,* Matt 6:22. Luke 11:34 also mentions this singleness of sight. When we focus our mortal eyes on a single thing it occupies our minds totally, to the exclusion of all else. For example, when we fall in love we have eyes for only one person. When we 'see' with spiritual eyes—visioning only good—our whole body is full of the Light of God. It is then that we know only light. We do not participate in any negative thinking. We do not assume a negative attitude. It is anathema to us. That inner knowingness radiates outward from us and extends to others. As they acknowledge that light in them they, too, are transformed into majesty. It is the majesty of God. Jesus knew he had the light in him. He radiated it outwards. Those around him felt it and acknowledged it. Perhaps this was what made people go to him for healing: they *knew* they were worthy of healing because they acknowledged the light in them, as received from Jesus the Christ. We were told long ago, and the Master has come yet again to teach us the same lesson: when we focus on good and know the goodness, the Godness in us, we are whole and we are joyous.

"When a mind has only light, it knows only light. Its own radiance shines all around it, and extends out into the darkness of other minds, transforming them into majesty. The Majesty of God is there, for you to recognize and appreciate and know. Recognizing the Majesty of God as your brother is to accept your own inheritance." *ACIM T*—7: XI: 5: 1-4

#113

"To reach into self as I did, [know that] you are engulfed in God. God surrounds you like a flame, and when you turn your consciousness to the flame it will burn away anything you are ready to surrender." Jesus the Christ 11/15/97

As I wrote this meditation, I sought in the concordance of *A Course in Miracles* for the word 'surrender.' At first I was surprised to find it does not appear in the book. Then I recalled a Gabriel seminar in which Gabriel used the term 'surrender,' and then he said he could 'see' us all pulling in, unwilling to consider the word. He asked his angel helper, Tinkerbell, why that was so. We could not hear her voice but she said to Gabriel (paraphrased), Americans do not like the word surrender, for they have never surrendered in a battle, and they see it as a sign of weakness. Perhaps that is why the Master did not use the word in *The Course*. When surrender is interpreted to mean giving up something of value, like freedom, we do not desire to surrender it. To surrender a negative attitude, negative behavior, or negative emotions is beneficial for one who is on a spiritual path. Gabriel reminded us that we cherish our prejudices and judgmental attitudes to the point we do not want to surrender them. We burrow in, so to speak, to these negative attitudes because others feel the same, we have not been taught otherwise, or we have not learned otherwise. When we pick up and read and accept *The Course*, we have in effect begun a search for truth. Immediately, or soon thereafter, we will yield to its compelling attraction. We know truth when we hear it. Accepting it in our lives is another step, and a difficult one for many of us. God calls us home to Him and we have turned toward home at last.

"For you have come too near to truth to renounce it now, and you will yield to its compelling attraction. You can delay this now, but only a little while. The Host of God has called to you, and you have heard. Never again will you be wholly willing not to listen." *ACIM T*—16: II: 6: 9-12

#114

"When you feel you must suffer you will. Take it from one who knows. Each time you surrender [a negative] the flame of God removes another layer of [negativity]." Jesus the Christ 11/15/97

Jesus indicates here that he went to the cross because he felt he must suffer to teach us a lesson about anger and assault. His perception that he must suffer has been replaced by the truth—that the Holy Spirit teaches only truth and does not perceive any judgment as justifiable. We often find ourselves tempted to give in to anger and assault—with our thoughts, words, or actions. The Holy Spirit teaches only peace and love. Focusing on peace and love we are never tempted to yield to anger, and would not think of hurting anyone verbally or physically. All judgment is out of accord with the Holy Spirit. Anger is never justified. It stems from judgment and judgment stems from the idea of separateness. Therefore, when we accept fully our oneness with God, we seek guidance from the Holy Spirit and are completely guided by the Holy Spirit. In order to feel the oneness with God we must surrender the resentments we hold so dear, the 'justified' anger that we have harbored so long. When we do that, we find a new freedom. We have retaken our power to live life one day at a time from the Lord God of our Being. We are free from concern about what others expect or demand of us. We each are our own holy person, child of God, and guided by Him.

"My one lesson, which I must teach as I learned it, is that no perception that is out of accord with the judgment of the Holy Spirit can be justified. I undertook to show that this was true in an extreme case, merely because it would serve as a good teaching aid to those whose temptation to give in to anger and assault would not be so extreme. I will with God that none of His Sons should suffer." *ACIM T*—6: I: 11: 5-7

#115

"When you say 'I am Son of God' and curse self or others, you neutralize the 'I am'. Say, 'I am the Son of God' from the *spirit* of you. Know it and live it, and do not allow the mind to [dissuade] you." Jesus the Christ 11/15/97

The spiritual path is an individual one insofar as one must make a conscious decision to return to the Father as Creator. The spiritual path is a shared one in that we must see self and others as equals in the eyes of God. God sees humanity as his one Sonship. He does not discriminate in any way. He blesses us all with health, peace, joy, and abundance. Lacking any of these in our lives we have *chosen* that lack in order to learn a lesson. The lesson, too, is self-chosen. When we accept the idea of one brotherhood of humankind, and some already have, then we will be on our way to world peace. As long as we believe in separateness we will judge, condemn, hate, and go to war with others. Gabriel revealed to us at one time that all wars on earth (against other races), have been incited by the white and yellow races. Interracial fighting has existed in the black and red races, but they have never attacked another race. Therefore, we can learn from them, if we are willing. We can repeat the words 'I am Son of God' a million times, but it must be said with *feeling* to be effective. And we must be vigilant in this effort to know ourselves as His children. When we allow the mind to judge another—and we are so good at it—we neutralize the power of the spoken phrase 'I am Son of God.' To believe and then live the truth of it and to remain vigilant for it, we can know with every fiber of our being that we are His beloved children. Gabriel explained that for females who have a problem with 'son' of God, consider the word 'sun' instead. We are all shining lights of the world, and *God is the Father of lights* (James 1:17).

"Say, then, to everyone:

"Because I will to know myself, I see you as God's Son and my brother." ACIM T—9: II: 12: 5-6

#116

"I was not crucified because others hated me. I was crucified because I thought I could save the world, and went to utter despair, [then] lifted my eyes to reclaim who I am—and you are." Jesus the Christ 11/15/97

The Bible tells us that Jesus came to save the world. That was his holy intent, based on what he believed at the time. He truly believed that if he came to teach humanity that it is holy, (and he died to prove it), everyone would be saved from the erroneous perceptions we held, and come to love and forgive. He chose the crucifixion to this end. Many times in his short ministry he disappeared from the crowd when Roman soldiers sought to seize him. Surely, he could have done so at the garden of Gethsemane. But he desired to be captured, and he told his disciples that he would be, that it was meant to be. He also told them he would rise again in three days. Gabriel told us that Jesus' intent was to save humanity, but only on the cross did Jesus realize he could only save himself. Salvation must be sought and accepted as an individual decision. There on the cross, he was the only light. He looked over the dark sea of anger, hatred, fear, and revenge and knew that he had not saved anyone. He also told us that he would not leave us comfortless and he never has. He always keeps his promise.

Turning to him, and knowing he is our elder brother, we can find our way back home to God. We each are our own savior.

"This world is a picture of the crucifixion of God's Son. And until you realize that God's Son cannot be crucified, this is the world you will see. Yet you will not realize this until you accept the eternal fact that God's Son is not guilty." *ACIM T*-13: In: 4:1-3

#117

"The greatest lesson I learned was that I cannot save the world. [Salvation comes to] only one person at a time. Our teachers are the experiences we create. Heal yourself." Jesus the Christ 11/15/97

Gabriel told us about Jesus' coming to earth. He said Jesus went to Gabriel and told Gabriel that he was coming to earth to save humanity. Gabriel responded, 'Go for it,' or words to that effect. But in his eternal wisdom, Gabriel probably already knew what Jesus had to learn: that salvation must come to each person in that person's chosen time. When we clash with another we chalk it up to 'personality conflict,' when in fact it is a conflict of egos. We need to learn to put the ego in its proper place, as a protector but not as a ruler over us. Giving up the ego's battles we can relate more closely to and follow more closely, the teachings of the Holy Spirit. He must be sought for help, but when we ask for help, the Holy Spirit guides us unerringly home. We each must seek to save ourselves and allow self to be awakened to the Kingdom within. This lesson of Jesus' is a perfect example of the truth of what Jesus said. He told us that what he did, we can do, *because* he learned. By the crucifixion he learned the hard way. Now he can teach us. Have we not all 'learned the hard way'? God made us all perfect, but we must accept that perfection in our own mind and consciousness. When we give up all our guilt, we will fully know self as the Christ Self.

"Egos can clash in any situation, but spirit cannot clash at all. If you perceive a teacher as merely 'larger ego' you will be afraid, because to enlarge an ego would be to increase anxiety about separation. I will teach with you and live with you if you will think with me, but my goal will always be to absolve you finally from the need for a teacher." *ACIM T—*4: I: 6: 1-3

#118

"The Voice of God is an internal thing. You can invite God to talk to you. God is no respecter of persons. God comes when your soul is open. God deals not with earthly things, but rather with the spirit, soul, and mind of you." Jesus the Christ 1/16/99

We are unable to hear the Voice of God in the midst of traffic, the workplace, or a busy household. We must be still to hear God. God will not compete with anything. God does not chase us. God's Will is love, peace, happiness, brotherhood, love of self and others. Because we are one with God His Voice is always with us. We don't hear because we choose not to listen. We have a tendency to ask God for earthly things, but earthly things are none of his concern. As co-creators with God, we created the earth and everything in it. God's concerns relate to the soul, the spirit, and the mind of us. We believe what we see around us is reality. It is not. It is illusion. The real world is spirit and spirit is eternal, therefore the real world is eternal. The Earth is full of temporal things because the Earth is temporal. The Bible reminds us that Heaven and Earth will pass away. This does not mean that a time will come when we will no longer exist as God's children. It means we will no longer need this school of learning called Earth, where we come to learn the lessons that take us back home to God. *The Course* explains this and provides a roadmap for our learning. Taking *The Course* is a personal choice, but the roadmap must be used by every human being—when we choose to accept it and walk it.

"Why should you listen to the endless insane calls you think are made upon you, when you can know the Voice for God is in you? God commended His Spirit to you, and asks that you commend yours to Him. He wills to keep It in perfect peace, because you are of one mind and spirit with Him."
ACIM T-5: VII: 3:1-3

#119

"When you come to Earth God never interferes. ' Thy will not mine be done'. God says it right back. When you turn your thoughts to God, you go up to a waiting God. God has immutable laws. When you are not cooperating with them you are in trouble. The first law is Love. The Voice of God is always feeding you information, at times in your dreams. Trust it."
Jesus the Christ 1/16/99

The only way for us to have peace, complete and constant, is to obey God's laws, which are immutable. We do not have the choice or the power to change God's laws. The first of God's laws is love. Jesus came to teach us love. He taught us the best way that anything can be taught, by demonstrating it in the way he lived. He loved everyone. He did not say that he hated Pilate, or the Scribes or the Pharisees. He never said he hated anyone or anything. He loved everyone because he understood—he *knew* that everyone was his sibling, brothers and sisters in God's grand family of humankind, the holy Sonship of God. He came to awaken us to the Kingdom of God within, and in that awakening we would come to love everyone also. How did we manage to misinterpret his life and his teachings? How did we come to think that this good Jewish boy would want to turn his back on the religion of his beloved parents, one of them divinely blessed with his birth? He came to awaken humanity. He has now made it very clear that whereas Adam fell asleep in the allegorical story of Eden, he never woke up in all the ensuing pages of Scripture. We, as a human family, are still asleep to our own divinity. The age now dawning is the age when we will awaken. This is the Age of Aquarius, the Age of Spirituality, the Truth Age.

"When you are not at peace it can only be because you do not believe you are in Him. Yet He is All in All. His peace is complete, and you must be included in it. His laws govern you because they govern everything. You cannot exempt yourself from His laws, although you can disobey them. Yet if you do, and only if you do, you will feel lonely and helpless, because you are denying yourself everything." *ACIM T–* 8: IV: 1:3-8

#120

"Never let the voice of fear override the Voice of God."
Jesus the Christ 1/16/99

Fear is the basis of so many behaviors. Fear in the extreme is paralyzing. Fear keeps us from a spiritual path because when we are fearful we are not at peace and the spiritual path is one of peacefulness, in any situation. That is why meditation is such an important factor in embarking upon and remaining on a spiritual path. Daily meditation keeps the flow open to the internal communication; communication with the Voice of God. What disrupts our peace is the idea of separateness. Believing we are separate from each other we distrust each other and our peace goes out the window. We fear for our safety and when we get behind the wheel to drive we may pray that we will not be involved in accidents. There are no accidents, unless we plan to lose our car, our health, or our lives. Some individuals are extremely fearful. They fear for their lives, their children, their neighbors, their friends. We find it difficult if not impossible to believe that God will never give us anything that is not a blessing. 'An accident' may result in a blessing. I once was in my car and it was sideswiped by a driver who then continued on. My passenger and I were treated and sent home, but my vehicle was totaled. The replacement car I purchased had fewer miles and lower payments. The 'accident' turned out to be a blessing. Fear engenders the feared experience. Job said (3:25), *For the thing which I greatly feared has come upon me.*

"We have already learned that fear and attack are inevitably associated. If only attack produces fear, and if you see attack as the call for help that it is, the unreality of fear must dawn on you. For fear is a call for love, in unconscious recognition of what has been denied." *ACIM T*-12: I: 8: 11-13

#121

"You can consciously be aware of the Voice of God. The inspiration you have is the Voice of God. The muse when creating hears the Voice of God. Inspirational speakers hear the Voice of God." Jesus the Christ 1/16/99

There is great comfort in knowing that God speaks to us constantly, to one part of the brain. It is only the other part that is easily distracted. Vigilance in listening to the Voice of God is necessary if we are to shut the door of the other part and refuse to listen to distractions. We may continue to do our task at hand, knowing that we are guided by God's Voice to accomplish the work in peace and have success with it. Distractions disturb us and defocus us from our work. Every successful person has been able to focus calmly and with vigilance on the work being done. It takes practice but it can be done. How can a task be well done if we are not concentrating on it to its completion? Mistakes we make come from a disorganized mind. Approaching a task with uncertainty usually results in making mistakes or failing to finish the job. Confidence in self and confidence in the ability to do a job guarantees success. In His constant communication with us, God directs our every thought and action. We must listen to the guidance and not allow distractions to interfere with our intentions.

"It is quite possible to listen to God's Voice all through the day without interrupting your regular activities in any way. The part of your mind in which truth abides is in constant communication with God, whether you are aware of it or not." *ACIM W*—pt1: 49: 1:1-2

CHAPTER 14

Vision above Appearances

#122

"What makes holy places holy—vortexes, shrines, healing places—is faith; the *belief* of the individual makes it holy. Bring the love of God wherever you go. Pull in holiness to fill any situation totally—not 'my way.'—to create miracles." Jesus the Christ 1/16/99

'Sin' is denying that we are God's holy children. Then we are dead to our own Identity. Then we deny God Himself. Then we seem to disconnect from our Creator. We cannot be disconnected from our Source, our essence, and the very fabric of our existence. God is, and denying God does not make Him go away, for He loves us and always provides for us. Faith in God strengthens us. Faith in ourselves strengthens our ability to live a positive, confident life. Relying on God's direction in everything we do assures us of a peaceful, loving life. Sickness never afflicts us unless we choose it. Believing in a god of sickness denies us joy. When we believe in the god of sickness we blaspheme God. His Will is perfect health for all. Personal plans based on karma, low self-esteem, victimization and self-deprecation bring sickness into our experience. This need not be. As we tell our body that we are children of God and God's Will is good health, the body must obey. Instead we believe that the body has a mind of its own and rules us with sickness or a fear of it.

"The rituals of the god of sickness are strange and very demanding. Joy is never permitted, for depression is the sign of allegiance to him. Depression means that you have foresworn God. Many are afraid of blasphemy, but they do not understand what it means. They do not realize that to deny God is to deny their own Identity, and in this sense the wages of sin *is* death." *ACIM T*-10: V: 1:1-5

#123

"Don't believe in appearances. Gabriel recently said perception is deception. I like to hear Gabriel. He teaches me much." Jesus the Christ 1/16/99

What is perceived by the five senses is what we have come to accept as reality. It is not reality, because it is temporary. What is real is eternal. Spirit is real. Spirit is eternal. We are spirit beings. We have a temporary body on earth. Everything we see is temporary. Even our bodies are temporary. The idea of eternalness of what we see perhaps persists because our lives on earth are so brief. We know that what we see will last far beyond this lifetime on earth. In the scheme of eternity one lifetime of ninety or one hundred years is but a split second. The scales of justice do not seem to operate in one lifetime, but in the scheme of eternity the scale of justice is always balanced. We make it so because we are children of God and in our unconscious mind we know this to be a fact. Perception, therefore, is deception because it is always changing. What we perceive today we perceive differently tomorrow, because our experiences and how other people treat us play a part in our perceptions. Gabriel's teachings emphasized this idea of perception being erroneous. Spirit is one and the Trinity is one. When we believed ourselves to be separate from God and each other, perception took over. We must get over it.

Ellen Wallace Douglas

"Perception did not exist until the separation introduced degrees, aspects, and intervals. Spirit has no levels, and all conflict arises from the concept of levels. Only the Levels of the Trinity are capable of unity. The levels created by the separation cannot but conflict. This is because they are meaningless to each other." *ACIM T*—3: IV: 1: 5-9

#124

"For perfect health judge less and love more. It is okay to say to a child, 'Why not just go inside of you for a minute and calm down, and see what your insides are saying?'." Jesus the Christ 1/16/99

The body does not have a mind of its own, although we have a tendency of believing so. As *The Course* explains the body's function is merely to provide a means of communication with others. Placebo drugs, placebo surgery and biofeedback applications have demonstrated the power of the mind over the body. Given the fact that the mind can heal, it is not such a leap of reasoning to accept the idea that the mind can also make it ill. Judgment affects us in negative ways. All negative attitudes affect us in negative ways, and sometimes the negative way is poor health, sickness, and dis-ease. That is why perfect health can be enjoyed when we judge less and love more. Jesus never called in sick to his followers. He loved much. He did not judge. When we believe that no one in our life is supporting us, we tend to have lower back pains. When we feel that the problems of the world are on our shoulders, we may have pains in our shoulders. When our eyesight fails it is because we lack understanding of our spiritual selves. God's Will for us is perfect health. Could the God of Love desire anything less for His children? When we see the body as a means of attack or victim of an attack, we lose sight of the fact that it is the temple of the Living God and a means of communication. And so we feel victimized or think we must attack. Attack stems from fear. Jesus feared not the crucifixion. He knew the body was temporary *and* that he could re-create it after its seeming demise.

"The body, then, is not the source of its own health. The body's condition lies solely in your interpretation of its function." *ACIM T*-8: VIII: 1:7-8

#125

"Deduction and reasoning lead to knowledge. Wisdom comes from trust in the Voice of God." Jesus the Christ 1/16/99

We acquire knowledge through reading, personal experience, formal education, experimenting in laboratories. We attain wisdom by trusting in the Voice of God. Hearing the Voice of God impels us to follow Its guidance because our Higher Self *knows* what It tells us is only truth, and Its guidance is infallible. Jesus knew the innocence of a child. He knew that a child's innocence is unaware of evil. That is why he told us to be as little children. The body of a newborn baby comes from its mother, as the product of the intercourse between two parents. The spirit of the baby comes from God. All other attributes, such as personality, soul's memory, ego, and even the body's sex, size and shape, are created by the entity. Seeming 'disabilities' come from decisions based on karma. We even decide where, when and how—and with whom—we are going to 'die' (transition to Heaven) when our work here is done. This is not predestination. We can change our minds at any moment on earth. We forget our plans at the moment of birth. When we are born we know, at some level of consciousness, what truth is. Even as adults we recognize truth when we hear it. We are not always willing to accept it. We spend a lifetime gaining knowledge, but we rarely seek a teacher who can guide us to wisdom. Even churches do not promote seeking wisdom—trusting in the Voice of God. Seeking wisdom is an individual choice, whenever we opt for it. When we do so, God shows us the way with His still, small Voice. Are we listening?

"Innocence is wisdom because it is unaware of evil, and evil does not exist. It is, however, perfectly aware of everything that is true. The resurrection demonstrated that nothing can destroy truth." *ACIM T-3*: I: 7 4-6

#126

"I am the journey." Jesus the Christ 11/20/95

These were Jesus' words that November day. It was the first time that he visited us. It was another scheduled question and answer period of Archangel Gabriel. As soon as the entity spoke through Reverend Penny we knew it was not Gabriel. Gabriel's voice sounded powerful and authoritative. This voice sounded soft and gentle. A woman approached the microphone and began asking him questions in an effort to identify him. He told us to call him The One, because he was the one to follow Gabriel. Gabriel had told us previously that there would be one to follow him to teach us. Gabriel had told us earlier that Reverend Penny was about to embark on a wondrous journey. Someone asked him if that journey was a geographic trip or the fact that he would come to channel through her. His response was 'I am the journey.' He was reminding us of his words 2,000 years ago, instructing us to follow him. What a wondrous phrase indeed! 'I am the journey.' What an exciting moment it was for me! And I believe for all the others present. The words of Scripture as given below rang in my head. Yes, I thought, he was the way then and he is the way now. He continues to prove to us that life is eternal. Deny him though we will, he continues to teach and guide us, whether in meditation, through another's words, by becoming visible, by giving words to another, or whatever means he may choose to adopt. Jesus the man was not the journey. It is the Christ Light that Jesus brought to earth. That same Christ Light is in us all, He came then, and he comes now, to remind us of our higher selves.

Jesus saith unto him, I am the way, the truth, and the life: no man cometh unto the Father, but by me. John 14:6

#127

"The intention of the first Om (Aum) is to know thyself, Child, know thyself. The intention of the second Om is to know thyself to be a part of all that is. The intention of the third Om is to know thyself as all that is without limitation or boundaries, without beginning or end, the Alpha and the Omega, the eternal circle, the ever, ever growing becoming God of you." Jesus the Christ 11/20/95, 17.

Gabriel would have us begin his seminars with sounding the Om (Aum) either once or three times, in order to harmonize the vibration of the group. If there were new people present we would sound the Om three times. He instructed us to sound the Om before meditating and upon closing a meditation. Here he explains the intention of sounding the Om. Over and over again Gabriel reminded us that we are all children of God. He also told us that over time we have forgotten that truth of us. We have forgotten because we have covered over the truth with our misperceptions that what we see, hear, and touch are real. They are nothing but illusion because they are temporal. The intention of every one of the three Oms is to *know ourselves*. To know ourselves means to know ourselves as God's beloved children, breathed forth in the beginning. Gabriel knows that repetition is the mother of learning, though he never used that phrase. He told us to remind ourselves a thousand times a day, if necessary. He gave us a mirror meditation to recite so we would learn, by repetition, the truth of the Self of us. The way, the truth, and life is us, because Jesus told us so, and he is our elder brother who came to show us the way. Two thousand years later he came again. Those who seek the truth will hear him and follow him, and know the joy, peace, and love he is, and we are.

O how I love thy law! It is my meditation all the day. Ps 119:97

#128

"Any false god will lead you from your path. Now, all truth lies within you. Great Masters come to point the way to your truth. Angels can only present to you what you have already in your consciousness, for they merely strike a resounding chord within your own mind." Jesus the Christ 11/20/95, 19

We have come to believe that angels give us ideas, but they are our own, and angels only present them to our consciousness. We believe that we must ask God for protection, but He loves us dearly and will always protect us. Nothing ever, ever befalls us that we did not ask for. We came to earth to learn lessons. We chose the lessons and we chose the experiences in order to learn the lessons. We think that God directs us from 'out there, somewhere,' yet the Higher Self of us knows exactly what we came to do and how we planned to do it. The Higher Self is part of God, and that is the part of us with which we have lost connection in our consciousness. The word 'consciousness' was not known 2,000 years ago, and so Jesus taught what he did in terms that were then familiar with his followers and the multitude that heard him. His words, however, as we have come to know, contained a symbolism that was beyond the mental powers of the Roman population. He did the best he could with the language of the time and couched his teachings, including the parables, in terms the people understood: sheep, farming, fields, family, harvest, prayer. Today, with increased awareness and intellect, we are capable of understanding the symbolism of Scripture. The symbolism enriches the lessons, brings home the truth to our modern way of thinking, and serves to awaken us to our Higher Self—when we accept it.

"Let us ask the Father in my name to keep you mindful of His Love for you and yours for Him. He has never failed to answer this request, because it asks only for what He has already willed. Those who call truly are always answered. Thou shalt have no other gods before Him because there **are** none." *ACIM T—4: III: 6:3-6*

#129

"Beloved Light, you activate centers within you that you know not of. You allow the God Self of you to bestir Itself, to stretch, to waken. My Presence allows you to become aware of that stretching and waking. It is like searching for a great and precious treasure and looking in your mirror and finding that you are it because you are." Jesus the Christ 11/20/85, 23

How wonderful it was to hear Jesus the Christ address a woman as Beloved Light! It reminded me of Jesus' word in the Gospel according to Mathew 5:14. Jesus spoke these words in response to a question about the energy that we felt in his presence. As a participant that evening, I recall very clearly that we all felt such an overcoming sense of peace in his presence that we asked if we could just sit quietly and feel it, without words. He agreed, and we probably sat for about ten minutes in silence. Jesus knew 2,000 years ago and knows still, that we must awaken to our own God Self in order to return unto the Father, as he did. Patiently he taught us, as patiently Gabriel taught us, knowing that in this lifetime or some future lifetime we would grasp and embrace the truth of our Higher Self. That leads us to the at-one-ment with God. That leads us home. That leads us to Heaven, our natural habitat. The reason we find ourselves so uncomfortable here on earth is that we are strangers here. Our soul longs to return home. Those who love it here on earth will one day come to understand the illusion that earth really is. Great masters have understood and transitioned to Heaven. They return to awaken us from the illusion we live in, to the reality of Heaven, with its joy and peace, its light and holiness.

Jesus answered them, Is it not written in your law, I said, Ye are gods? John 10:34

#130

"You think you celebrate the birth of a single individual two thousand years ago, but that was only a concentrated point at which the Christ awareness would come to earth, the love be grounded, the peace be established. Beyond that you do not understand its meaning. I will tell you of its meaning." Jesus the Christ 12/3/95, 3.

Jesus the Christ came to us that night in December to clarify for us what his birth 2,000 years earlier meant and how we should properly celebrate it. He did not mention a jolly man with a beard, in a red suit. He did not speak of fir trees or material gifts. He told us that we substituted love with fear and fear became to us a greater god. Belief in that god robbed us of our peace, the peace in which we were created. We had no idea of the ramifications of that decision because we believed that we had a mighty power that exceeded the power of God in us. He said we created death as the final proof that our creation was the only one that was real. Perceiving death as real, our perception of eternal life grew dim and we came to believe that only fear and death are real. He told us that he came at a time when the ages were changing because it was a time when vibrations around the earth could be separated, parted, rended, and caused to be broken. He came in that break and manifested the peace that we are and the love that we are. He did this not that others might worship him, but that all of us might know ourselves.

"This is the season when you would celebrate my birth into the world. Yet you know not how to do it. Let the Holy Spirit teach you, and let me

celebrate your birth through Him. The only gift I can accept of you is the gift I gave to you. Release me as I chose your own release. The time of Christ we celebrate together, for it has no meaning if we are apart."
ACIM T-15: X: 1:5-10

#131

"Christmas. If you could know, if you could open your doors and allow its truth to be where you are, you would find that there is no need to go looking anywhere except in your heart. When you choose to cast off your substitution of fear and receive in your awareness the truth of love that has never left you, then you will know how to celebrate Christmas." Jesus the Christ 12/3/95, 6

We celebrate Christmas with gifts and trees and Santa Claus. This is for the children's benefit. Some mature individuals know the deeper meaning of the birth of Christ. Some worship him, but some see him as an elder brother who came to show us the way, the truth, and the life. We base this belief on the fact that Scripture states often Jesus' words, 'follow me.' He said it many, many times. Two thousand years later, Jesus returns through a dedicated channel, to explain the true meaning of Christmas. He said that we live in the valley of shadows, believing in fear and death. We have come to believe that love must be found outside of us. What we call life on earth is death. Life is limitless. Life is love known, lived, expressed. Life is truth understood, never doubting, never far away, or faded. He told us that we can not know God and believe in evil. We cannot know God and experience hatred. We cannot know God and not call everyone our brother. For God is all of these things.

"The birth of Christ is now, without a past or future. He came to give His present blessing to the world, restoring it to timelessness and love. And love is ever-present, here and now." *ACIM W*-pt II: 308: 1:6-7

#132

"From a historical point of view, it is one of mild interest. From a spiritual point of view, it is important only in as much as you form a foundation upon which to base the Christ awareness. However, the Christ awareness is capable of standing in its own strength and doesn't need something of the past to relegate it." Jesus the Christ. 2/12/96

This response was given by Jesus, in answer to my question about the importance of knowing the Old Testament. I asked the question because I found myself more drawn to the New Testament than the Old, since there is so much violence in the Old. The New Testament is more uplifting and contains many fine words of the Master Jesus. Because Jesus often quoted the Old Testament I was impelled to ask the importance of knowing it well. He made it clear that it is a foundation upon which to base the Christ awareness. Then he said that Christ awareness does not really *need* anything for a foundation. There are many places in the Old Testament that prophesy Jesus' coming. In Luke 4:16-21 He quoted from Isaiah 61:1 and then remarked that he was fulfilling the scripture of the Old Testament. Of course every reference Jesus made to Scripture was the Old Testament, since the New Testament had not yet been written. The Old Testament made way for and predicted events of the New Testament. The New Testament made way for and predicted events of future generations. *A Course in Miracles* has now been written to clarify some of the omissions and phrases of the New Testament. All these writings make up a continuum of teachings for humanity. Each speaks to us in language we can understand. Gabriel told us that the Bible is full of symbolism. *The Course* clarifies and defines the symbolism.

I was daily with you in the temple teaching, and ye took me not: but the scripture must be fulfilled. Mark 14:49

#133

"'What is the symbolism in the Old Testament story of Joseph and his coat of many colors?' [Gabriel answered]: 'The many colors represent the many aspects of the human consciousness, the limitlessness of the human mind to take in, integrate. and use knowledge, wisdom, truth. [It] represents the various aspects of consciousness that he had passed through. Each color represented a new wisdom, a new knowledge, and a new knowingness. This is why it was only unto Joseph that it came. For Joseph is symbolic of the beginning awakening of the internal Christ within a human consciousness'." Jesus the Christ. 2/12/96, 4

Joseph's brothers were all jealous of him and his coat of many colors, made by their father. Israel favored Joseph because he was born when Israel was an old man, and he probably knew that this would be his last son. It is an interesting story about how his brothers treated Joseph, selling him into slavery and then going to him for food at the time of their famine. He forgave them for their behavior, lying to their father that Joseph was dead when he was not. Like everything else in Scripture, this story has a metaphysical meaning. The entire Bible is a book of symbolism. The Metaphysical Bible Dictionary is an excellent source of the metaphysical definitions found in the Bible. Gabriel explained to us at one time that the significance of Joseph's forgiveness of his brothers is that it was the first time on earth that forgiveness had been demonstrated by humanity. And we well know that forgiveness was one of the main lessons that Jesus taught. The word 'forgiveness' appears 495 times in *A Course in Miracles*. That number is very close to 490, the product of 'seven times seventy' times that Jesus said we ought to forgive. (Matt 18:22)

Now Israel loved Joseph more than all his children, because he was the son of his old age: and he made him a coat of many colours. Gen. 37:3

#134

"'Did the slaughter of the innocents really happen?' 'No. The slaughter of the innocents is a metaphysical term the mystery of which is in this way: The innocence represented that aspect within the human body, within the human consciousness, within the human feeling nature, within the human being in its totality. That innocence comes forth from the spirit within and radiates its light and influence in all aspects of the person, from the spirit into the mind, into the feeling nature, into the etheric and into the physical body . . . the innocence of nature was not allowed to enter into the physical form and manifest in the brain tissue as a conscious awareness of that innocence in physical form'." Jesus the Christ 2/12/96, 5.

The Bible reports that Herod commanded all children under two years of age be slaughtered. It was his way of slaying the newborn Jesus whom the wise men came from afar to worship. To be sure he killed the 'new king,' he ordered the killings. It became known as 'the slaughter of the innocents.' Here Master Jesus informs us that it did not really happen. Yet it does have a metaphysical meaning, upon which Jesus expounded. It staggers the imagination to think that a scribe would put such a story in the official canon of the church when it was pure fiction. Perhaps he was spiritually guided to write it so the deeper meaning could be explained 2,000 years later. We do not know this. Jesus told us to be as little children. The innocence that children possess holds us in awe. Children are so accepting, curious, and openly frank about their curiosity. All this makes them a joy to be around. They bring with them at birth a certain divine energy from Heaven. When we allow this innocence into our consciousness it will permeate the brain tissue and we will have that Christ awareness of which Jesus speaks.

Then Herod, when he saw that he was mocked of the wise men, was exceeding wroth, and sent forth, and slew all the children that were in Bethlehem, and in all the coasts thereof, from two years old and under, according to the time which he had diligently enquired of the wise men. Matt: 2:16

#135

"The word 'religion' actually goes back, way back to times when people dwelt in caves. Each clan had its own memory pattern. The men of the tribe would gather on certain nights, and certain vibratory rates, and they would remember from the beginning of their origin on the earth. They only knew from instinct rather than knowingness that there was a force beyond themselves. From that there came the word religio, which means to believe. Then came religion, which means a group believing in the same concept." Jesus the Christ 2/12/96, 7.

This is one of the rare times the Master Jesus referred to etymology. He told us this in response to a question about the word's origin. Gabriel had defined the word, 'hell.' He told us it originally meant 'shallow grave,' because people feared that it would be terrible to have their body dug up by beasts. 'Religion', Webster's dictionary says, comes from the Latin word meaning to 'tie back.' I think this is significant because awakening to our Christ Self means going back—in our consciousness—to our beginning, when we were one with God, and one with each other. Jesus not only did not come to start a new religion, but he certainly never taught separation. He taught us that we should love Self with all our heart and mind and soul, and love others as ourselves. Somehow we managed to distort this wondrous teaching into the compartmentalization that exists in religion. The many denominations of Christianity demonstrate these divisions. All this separation comes from judgment and judgment comes from fear. What are we all afraid of? The one God is a God of Love. Many persons still believe that God is to be feared. If fear is justified, an angry god is justified, and if God is angry with us, why are we still here?

"All religion is the recognition that the irreconcilable cannot be reconciled. Sickness and perfection are irreconcilable. If God created you perfect, you are perfect. If you believe you can be sick, you have placed other gods before Him." *ACIM T*-10: IV: 1:2-4

APPENDIX

References are to both opening and closing quotations.

Ellen Wallace Douglas

*Channeled Lessons of Archangel Gabriel and the Christ
From 1987-1999. (See Bibliography)

BIBLIOGRAPHY

BOOKS

The Christ, New Teachings for an Awakening Humanity. *Santa Clara, CA: Spiritual Education Endeavors Publishing, 1995.*

Conversation with JC, *Piermont, NY: High View Publishing, 1985.*

Donovan, P. and Lee-Civalier, M. I., Getting to Know Your Soul *(The Teachings of Archangel Gabriel). New York: iUniverse, Inc., 2004.*

Elder, D. Women of the Bible Speak to Women of Today. *Marina del Rey, CA: De Vorss & Company, 1986.*

Ferrier, J. T., The Logia or Sayings of the Master. *London: The Order of the Cross, 1991 (1916).*

Foundation for Inner Peace. A Course in Miracles. *New York: Viking Penguin Books, 1996 (1975).*

Furst, J, ed., Edgar Cayce's Story of Jesus. *New York: Berkley Books, 1976.*

Greber, J., *Communication with The Spirit World of God.* Teanek, NJ: Johannes Greber Memorial Foundation, 1974 (1932).

The Holy bible, AV.

Holmes, E.S. and Holmes, F. L. *The Voice Celestial.* New York: Dodd, Mead and Company, 1960.

King, G. R, *The "I AM" Discourses.* Schaumburg, IL: Saint Germain Press, inc., 1988 (1935).

King, G. R., *The Magic Presence.* Schaumburg, IL: Saint Germain Press, Inc., 1963 ((1935).

Levi, trans., *The Aquarian Gospel of Jesus the Christ.* Marina del Rey, CA: DeVorss & Co., 1982 (1907).

Long, M. F. *What Jesus Taught in Secret.* Marin del Rey, CA: De Vorss & Co., 1995.

The Lost Books of the Bible and the Forgotten Books of Eden. New York:: World Publishing Company,. 1971. Originally published by Alpha House, Inc. (The Lost Books of the Bible, 1926 and The Forgotten Books of Eden, 1927).

Meurois-Givaudan, A. & D., *The Way of the Essenes.* Rochester, VT: Destiny Books, 1993. Originally published as *De Memoire d'Essenien, l'autre visage de Jesus,* Arista Editions, Plazac, 1989.

Moses, J., Oneness. *New York: Fawcett Columbine, 1989.*

Prophet, E. C., The Lost Years of Jesus. *Livingston, MT: Summit University Press, 1986.*

Rodegast, P. and Staton, J. comp. *Emmanuel's Book.* New York: Bantam Books, 1987.

Sanderfur, G., ed., *Lives of the Master.* Virginia Beach, VA: A.R. E. Press, 1994.

Spalding, B. T. *Life and Teachings of the Masters of the Far East, Vol. II.* Marina del Rey: De Vorss Publications, 1972 (1927).

Tolle, E. *The Power of Now.* Novato, CA: New World Library, 1999.

(The following teachings of Archangel Gabriel and Jesus the Christ are available at SacredGardenFellowship.org)

BOOKLETS
The One: This booklet includes:
Questions and Answers, 11/20/95,
True Meaning of Christmas 12/3/95
The One: Questions and Answers 2/12/96

AUDIOGRAPHY

Internal Awareness 5/18/96

Awakening the Master Within 9/21/96

Master Jesus 1/18/97

Master Jesus II 5/17/97

Connecting to Your Source, 11/15/97

Master Jesus III, 1/17/98

The Holy Encounter 1/16/99